Praise for *Diane Stein's Guide to Goddess Craft*

"A wonderful book! [*Diane Stein's Guide to Goddess Craft*] is sacred and clear, a song of celebration in honor of the Goddess and her 20th century priestesses. Blessed be."
—Vicki Noble
Author of *Motherpeace: A Way to the Goddess*

"A must for women embarking on the various paths of spirituality. Diane provides a gentle introduction and the necessary words and tools for stepping out of the traditional patriarchal system of spirituality. Her work teaches women a way to embrace and celebrate their inherent birth-rite in the Goddess."

—Ida Shaw
Metaphysical Therapist

"Diane Stein's new book is a fascinating compendium of herstory, Goddess tradition and the newer rituals available to today's women—singly or in groups—to help empower themselves or each other. Stein shows how women can use creative visualization, imagery, music, decorative arts and various divinatory tools to gain fresh insights into both their inner feelings and their outer environment. This book will interest women who find patriarchal systems inadequate. Its underlying message to each woman is a ringing affirmation of her right to feel good about herself."

—Barbara Walker
Author of *The Woman's Encyclopedia of Myths and Secrets*

D1025847

Other Books by Diane Stein

Videos by Diane Stein

DIANE STEIN'S

Guide to

Goddess Craft

THE CROSSING PRESS
FREEDOM, CALIFORNIA

For information on bulk purchases or group discounts for this and other Crossing
Press titles, please contact our Special Sales Manager at 800/777-1048.

Visit our Web site: **www.crossingpress.com**

Library of Congress Cataloging-in-Publication Data

Stein, Diane. 1948-
       [Women's spirituality book]
       Diane Stein's Guide to goddess craft / by Diane Stein.
           p. cm.
       ISBN 1-58091-091-2 (pbk.)
       1.Witchcraft. 2. Goddess religion. 3.Women--Religious life.
I. Title.

     BF1566.S7717   2001
     291.1'4--dc21   00-064433

Contents

A witch is one who has power over her own life

one who makes her own rules
one who refuses to submit to self-denial
one who recognizes no authority with a
    greater esteem than her own, who is
    more loyal to self than to any abstraction
one who is untamed
one who says "I am a witch" aloud three times
one who transforms energy
one who can be passionate about her
    ideas/values as they are changing
one who is explosive, whose intensity is
    like volcanoes, floods, wind, fire
one who is disorderly, chaotic
one who is ecstatic
one who alters reality

Lee Lanning and Vernette Hart,
Ripening

Introduction

As long as there have been women, there has also been the Goddess. In every culture and every time period She has been known, loved, and fully appreciated as the origin of every form of life. Her image is apparent in all of Be-ing, from birth to death and everything in between, in people and animals, in sea creatures and trees, in every aspect of Creation and existence. Like Her women, the Goddess has ten thousand names and as many attributes, and all Her names and faces are One. The Goddesses are women and women are the Goddess. We are made in her image and we are She.

For two thousand years or more, Christianity and Patriarchy have tried to erase Her—both women and the Goddess. But both women and the Goddess are alive and their magick is afoot today as never before. The Goddess was just beginning Her awakening when this book was written in 1985, a necessary outgrowth of women's awakening through the Women's Movement. In 1985 we had an idea of what the Goddess meant, but only a beginning one. We had an idea of what it might mean if divinity were female again as our foremothers knew her, but were only starting to understand how to bring her back to Be-ing. The Goddess and Her women are wide awake now, and instead of being erased, the vitality of both is strong and bright. The Goddess is fully alive and has fully returned to Earth in the year 2000.

We have come a long way in fifteen years. In 1985 everything we did was new and rudimentary. No one knew exactly what the Goddess religion consisted of in the ancient times; we had to start from scratch and create it all fresh for current times and modern cultures. Much or most of the older knowledge and skills was lost to us and had to be rediscovered or newly developed. Psychic ability, central to the Goddess Craft, was only an elusive rumor and we had to learn what it meant and how to use it. No one knew how to do a ritual or a healing, how to read the tarot or use herbs. If everything seemed harder then, and much more elementary, it was also quite exciting. Everything we tried and succeeded at was a triumph and another step forward, another piece of knowledge regained.

This is a beginning book in women's spirituality and in discovering the Goddess. While we have grown in skills and sophistication in fifteen years, everyone still starts at the beginning and needs a guide to point the way. This is where to start. This is where the Goddess awakens in each woman who finds Her. She changes everything She touches and everything She touches changes. This book is the Goddess' first touch.

Diane Stein
April 23, 2000

1

What Is Women's Spirituality?

Women's spirituality is a return to the goddess, to the female principle of creation that is uniquely women's own. It's the joyous group bonding of national women's festivals and conferences, the local small groups and covens,[1a] and the single self-blessings and rituals done in bedrooms. Women's spirituality is a celebration of the lives, lifestyles and values of women, women's participation in the cycles of the earth and universe, and women's working toward making a better world. It's Sabbat rituals by the sea and full moons under the stars, the power and beauty of energy raised by groups of caring sister-friends, the affirming activisms of Diablo Canyon, Greenham Common and the Seneca Women's Peace Camp. Women's spirituality is the creativity of individual women, the writers, artists and musicians who make beautiful forms with their bodies, hands and minds. It's women healing themselves and each other by crystals, massages, colors and herbs, learning the tarot and I Ching together, re-claiming and dis-covering women's herstory and skills. It's the midwife delivering a child, the struggle to birth a new women's publication, and the effort to build safe havens on woman-run land.

Women's spirituality is a growing re-cognition of the goddess as planet, as the earth herself, and of women as part of the earth and her divine Be-ing. The goddess is everything creative, everything that exists in nature and in women's lives, including every woman in her Be-ing,

---

[1a]Coven, from the root word *covenir*, is a gathering of like minded individuals to celebrate the goddess, the moon and the Wheel of the Year. The word is related to *covenant* and has the same root.

growth, self and power. She is the shared circle of birth, maturing, death and regeneration in all life, the changing of the seasons, the waxing, full and waning moon, the daily tides, and the rising-setting sun. She is childhood joy, first periods, falling in love and giving birth, motherhood and menopause, aging, and death until being reborn. She is circles unending and created in choice—movement, growth and change celebrated by women, and reflected in communal and individual transformations in women's lives.

The goddess is the all-giver and all-taker, the inter-connectedness of life, the earth and cosmic forces. What affects the earth, the goddess, affects all who live there, and all who live on her affect the earth and each other. Clean water and unpolluted forests benefit all, while Love Canal and mountains of burning strip-mine slag do harm to the goddess who is everyone. Likewise, women's harmony inwardly and together, women's power, benefit all, while conflict, separation and noncaring, indeterminism, do universal harm to men and women both.

The goddess is not an out-there force among the far stars or beyond death, but is here and now and living. In philosopher Mary Daly's concept of active creation, she is verb rather than noun and is women's Be-ing.[1] Since the goddess is everyone within and all around us, the powers of divinity and creation are both individual and shared by all. She is the power to make of women's lives what women will. With the tenet, "Thou art goddess"[2], freedom of choice is a central issue; women take charge of who they are and what they do, not with blame or guilt, but with responsibility for their actions and choices. What benefits one does not deprive another, and in goddess philosophy there is enough for everyone. Given a society that contains the potential for nuclear destruction in totality, women who are the goddess see changing things as part of their ethics and responsibility, see caring about each other and the world as a law of the universe. Actions made in this light achieve balance, and responsibility begins with the self. From disharmony and abuse of resources come the change to peace and empowerment, and women see their own happiness and self-determination as part of the plan.

In this system, natural law *is* the universal plan, a movement to achieve harmony in oneself and the world, a working in accord with other women, with the goddess and her cycles. Since nuclear leakage

---

[1] Mary Daly, *Beyond God the Father: Toward a Philosophy of Women's Liberation*, (Boston, Beachon Press reprint, 1985), p. 33-34. The hyphenated word concepts of Be-ing, re-claiming, dis-covering, etc. are also Daly constructs.

[2] Principle wiccan saying.

at Three Mile Island, for example, is harmful to the earth and her inhabitants, it violates natural law and is something to change. Women who choose activism are changing it, delaying or halting the plant's reopening, educating about its dangers, working to clean up the environment. Since likewise, the inner stresses of technological patriarchy have caused poverty, isolation, depression and physical disease in women, women who choose reflective healing turn their work that way. Choosing communal living, crystals and aura balancing, herbs, meditation skills, tarot and massage to achieve harmony, they learn to break the hold of stress that harms women's lives. Through outward action made by inward learning and sharing of skills, women are taking control of their destinies and their world. Those involved with women's spirituality are recognizing disharmony and returning to natural balance, to the universal law of the goddess, and finding success and inner peace. Women who do so achieve their own good and the good of the earth.

As participants in goddess, women's individual and collective potential and power are valued as natural law. The individual woman is important in women's spirituality as in no other form of theology, and communities of women working together are nurtured and affirmed. What she does and who she is matter, and women's spirituality encourages women, for the first time in patriarchy's thousands of years, to actively be all they can be, to participate in active Be-ing and the goddess, to re-learn themselves, and then to join together to change the wrongs of the world.

With an emphasis on individual creativity and universal worth and respect, and also on pooling skills and sharing trust, no one class, age, race, sexual preference or physical status is considered more or less valuable than any other. Every woman in women's spirituality is uniquely herself and her combination of learnings, choices and heritages. Each is her own strength and has something to offer for the good of all. Morality is not judgmental but is responsible to oneself and others: "Harming none, do what you will".[3] Sexuality is a natural and positive force, a sharing in the goddess to be used with mutual respect and joy. Given the tenet that "What's sent out returns threefold,"[4] ethics become active choices, positive choices, and are ruled by cause and effect in natural law.

Women's spirituality has much to do with re-newed and re-membered forms of witchcraft, the Old Religion or wicca, and nothing at all to do

---

[3-4]Principle wiccan sayings.

with Satanism or the repressions of Judeo-Christian and Islamic patriarchy. A religion of poetry and creative beauty, of celebrated seasons and candlelit rituals, women's spirituality is an inward and external lifestyle, a positive path to the sisterhood of woman-sharing, a connection to the goddess in all. An outgrowth of international feminism, it is multiracial, cross-cultural and worldwide, a re-claiming of lost lives, of women's lost and nearly lost artistry, learning, autonomy, literature and herstory. It's a healing and re-claiming affirmation of religion and women, a healing of the planet and of all who live there, a healing that extends to Be-ing for women in every sense, and a healing that is here and now.

The women's spirituality movement of today, though rising from the second wave of feminism since 1969, did not begin with it. The goddess religion goes back to the beginning, not only of feminism but of time. Before the institutional Protestant or Catholic churches, before Judaism, before Islam or classical Greece, before there was God or gods, there was the goddess, the great mother. In every culture and civilization on every part of the earth, she was worshipped as the source of life, and women were reverenced as her birth-giving image. Every culture had its creation and power stories involving her, and had one or many aspects and names for her Be-ing. In her thousand names and herstories, she is universal, and is the undeniable root of all religions and of the concept of religion itself.

In addition, evidence of anthropologists and archeologists indicates that pre-God (goddess) civilizations were both matriarchal and peaceful, and structured far differently from today's world.

> No evidence of human strife or violence has been found in any of the ancient cities of the Near East until late in the third millenium, when patriarchal nomads first invaded.[5]

Not restricted to the Near East, the so-called "cradle of civilization", the Golden Age triad of goddess worship, matriarchy and peace extended to Egypt, the Greco-Roman world, Crete, Persia, Britain and Ireland,[6] and to Africa.

In these cultures and dozens of others, the goddess and women ruled. Families were composed of mothers and daughters in communal groups that remained close to home for agriculture and child-care, and

---

[5]Elizabeth Gould Davis, *The First Sex*, (New York, Penguin Books, 1971), p. 66.
[6]Ibid., p. 65-66.

participated in the cycles of the moon and the seasons. Sons were excluded from those mysteries that were considered women's-only, and after puberty moved in freer-ranging all-male groups. The male role in reproduction was probably known by later women but held secret from men, and inheritance and family recognition were by birth through the mother's clan or family. There was no fatherhood in these societies, since even when conception was understood, women were non-monogamous. A child belonged to its mother or to the community as a whole. In cultures where the goddess as planet was reverenced, where all life was seen as having a shared source and as a gift of the female, the taking of human or animal life was beyond thought. Where the supreme deity was the earth herself in the form of a female being giving birth to all, women who held the mystery and knowledge of birth within their own bodies were the mothers and rulers of civilization. There was among women a maiden-mother-crone progression of learning and social roles.

Birth, until the Genesis version, is always a female act, and the creation stories of pre-God cultures universally are acts of goddesses giving birth. Merlin Stone, in her book *Ancient Mirrors of Womanhood: A Treasury of Goddess and Heroine Lore from Around the World,*[7] records at least two dozen of these stories of goddesses birthing the universe. From Kwan Yin and Nu Kwa of China to Aido Hwedo and Mawu of Africa, from Isis (or Au Sept) of Egypt to Gaia of Greece and Spider Woman of the Hopi, the creator of the world and of people is female. Though her name changes from culture to culture, she is still the great mother, the all-giver, bringing forth life and nourishing it from her body. And like the goddess above in the universe, women below on earth continue the mystery of giving and nourishing life, of menstruation, birth and breast-feeding. Archeological artifacts worldwide portray birthing goddess/woman figurines, big of breast and belly and their legs spread wide in labor. Reverence for the life force was carried over into reverence for women.

To women, too are attributed the beginnings of agriculture, tools, and the survival skills collectively known as civilization. Beings seen as holders of the mystery of life, as images of the goddess, are likely to be active in exploring their world and expected to use choice and initiative. Early women are recognized as the originators and dis-coverers of weaving, sewing, cooking, basketry and pottery, as well as planting and the

---

[7]Merlin Stone, *Ancient Mirrors of Womanhood: A Treasury of Goddess and Heroine Lore from Around the World,* (New Sibylline Books, 1979 and Beacon Press, 1984).

15

domestication of animals. Both functional and artistic, these women's crafts and the tools they developed for them, made survival possible. They changed society from gathering to farming, the place where civilization starts. With farmers' awareness, too, of the seasons and cycles, of the procession from birth through growth, ripening, decay and death, the Great Sabbats of the first religion—of goddess worship and women's spirituality—began.

To men, the children and beneficiaries of women's work, tools and inventions, are attributed the arts of hunting. In perhaps a time of drought, when women's agriculture or gathering failed to feed the people, their contributions also meant survival. Not bound by children, pregnancy or care of the fields, men had more mobility than women, more energy, time and aggressiveness to channel. Considering the difficulty of hunting on foot, of bringing down game with the crudest of weapons, their efforts increased the food supply, but could not have entirely fed their tribes. Through hunting, however, men developed communal bondings and groups that mirrored women's. They came together in shared efforts to kill game, and in an increasing envy of women's power.

With the change-over to hunting, life for the first time was taken by other than the goddess herself, and the hierarchy of "who is better" began with the hunter's rationalization of lesser and greater lives. From the beginnings of this hierarchy, with dominance first over food animals, then in competition over hunting skills, and finally in aggression over other humans, killing began to escalate. Men's respect for the oneness of life, for natural law and the goddess as planet and birth-giver, was strained and refocused on the aspect of death, on the goddess as all-taker that men could participate in and somewhat control. Not able to give birth, to begin life, a few men as hunters discovered the power of ending it, a power to rival the women's mysteries they were excluded from. Increasingly challenged to prove this ability and individual power in the group, willing and unwilling men were forced by peer pressure into aggressive dominance, forced by the hierarchies men had created and had let get out of hand.

By this time the goddess that men could not image, the female who gives and takes all in equal abundance, was no longer enough. Reflecting this change, the concept of a hunter god began, first as consort to the goddess but increasingly superceding her, and

Slowly the powers of the gods underwent a transition. At first, the male appeared only as an adjunct to the Great Mother.

Later he became the lord of storms and the moon.[8]

Later still, and no one knows how long it took to happen, the male god supplanted the female aspect entirely—women, birth and the goddess—in the universal order and on earth. The split between the dualities of male and female, death and birth, earth and universe, the change from the goddess to patriarchy, was a world revolution. In the quest for taking and holding power, for male dominance, men joined against the ruling order they were not enough a part of, joined against women and the goddess, and even against the feminine in themselves. The peaceful matriarchies and peaceful men in them could not withstand the use of force, and slowly and eventually fell.

Men's part in reproduction by now known, the new patriarchy's way to hold power and dominate the life force was to both deny its value and control it through women. Ending the rulership of the female, the old regime of the goddess, was politically crucial. To do this the new patriarchy separated and subjugated women and children into possessions without communities, each bound to a single male. Slavery, incest and rape began, the ownership oppressions used by an unstable order to suppress a colonized people. Unable to give birth themselves and needing women to do it for them, patriarchy chose to own women's power by owning women. In place of the goddess, it instituted male-only gods of strength and battle, gods not born of the female. The hunter god-consort became God, and worship of the great mother and her female life values was harshly repressed. The goddess as planet and birth-giver, as the immanent beauty of natural law and planetary cycles, as the peaceful interconnectedness of life, and as the reverence of women and the feminine in men—was sacrificed to the struggles of patriarchal power. The goddess became Yahweh, the jealous male God of the desert Jews, and even his own female aspect was eventually laundered out.

But long before the Jewish morning prayer that says, "Blessed art thou, O Lord our God, who has not made me a woman," the Hebrew God *was* a woman, traced as Iahu-Anat by Davis[9] and as Ashtoreth by Merlin Stone and others. In the process of patriarchal takeover, the Jewish Yahweh was also once the hunter god-consort of Anat or Ashtoreth, and known as Tammuz or Baal.[10] The progression began with the

---

[8]Helen Diner, *Mothers and Amazons: The First Female History of Culture,* (Garden City, NY, Anchor Books Reprint, 1973), p. 12.
[9]Elizabeth Gould Davis, *The First Sex,* p. 67.
[10]Merlin Stone, *When God Was A Woman,* (New York, Harvest/HBJ Books, 1976), p. 109.

17

goddess, with Ashtoreth or Anat the great mother. She gained a later male consort that as patriarchy grew in strength was merged with and superceded her. As the goddess was diminished and erased, her consort was elevated and was himself still being suppressed as late as the writing of the Old Testament. The worship of Ashtoreth, Tammuz or Baal is attacked again and again in the Bible as the enemy to be destroyed. Hosea 2 says:

> And I will put an end to all her mirth,
>   her feasts, her new moons, her sabbaths . . .

> And I will punish her for the feast days of the Ba'als
>   when she burned incense to them . . .[11]

The references to feasts, new moons and sabbaths are obviously references to women and goddess worship, with or without Baal, that Judaism sought to end and sought to end particularly in women.

Jewish creation also shows remnants of the progression to patriarchy. Lilith, the first woman, was made of earth, as was Adam, the first man. When Lilith refused to be subordinated to Adam, she left Eden as a monster to frighten children with. Her meeker replacement, Eve was then made from Adam's rib and given the burden of world sin to carry. Eve's sinning took the form of eating of the tree of knowledge, the tree of life symbol of Ashtoreth.[14] Adam, Eve and Lilith were not created by any form of female birth, and the concept of Eve's sin or anyone's does not exist in goddess theology. God in the Old Testament is always male, but has a little-emphasized female aspect still unerased. Shekinah, the Bride of Sabbath, is a figure of great ritual beauty and power, a goddess aspect of Yahweh that women of today are reclaiming, and that women embraced in the past.

Maintaining the male power of the early Hebrew God required holding women and life in total submission and uprooting the goddess completely. Women became slaves, their only value in bearing male children and in the work of caring for men's homes and possessions. As patriarchy took over, women were refused education, as well as any form of leadership or authority. The few active heroines that appear in the early parts of the Old Testament, Deborah, Jael, Miriam, Judith, Ruth and Rachel, are seen as working for God against the hated Baals. Orthodox Judaism later said that women had no souls; by the time of

---

[11]As quoted by Rosemary Radford Ruether, in *Womanguides: Readings Toward a Feminist Theology,* (Boston, Beacon Press, 1985), p. 164-165.
[12]Merlin Stone, *When God Was A Woman,* p. 217.

Christianity they legally owned nothing, including their bodies and destinies. Property of the father before marriage, women were then owned by their husbands, whom they may not have met before the wedding day. They were veiled and dragged to the altar, symbolically or not. If a woman's husband died, she became the chattel of his brother or her own oldest son. Women were segregated in worship and excluded—as men had once been in matriarchy—from participation in religion, but the strict religious observance of the family was the wife's responsibility. Yet the goddess was not eradicated, and Judaic writings continually warn men to be watchful of her abominating influence. Even far into written history, when women had internalized the patriarchal values forced upon them, the goddess still appeared among Jews as the joyously welcomed Shekinah, and was only thinly hidden in the remaining women's rites and customs.

By the beginning of Christianity, the Eastern world and Judaism were under Roman Empire rule. The classical matriarchies of Greece and Rome had been diluted to a patriarchal pantheon of all-too-human gods and stereotyped goddesses. From the single great mother, Gaia or Hera, came a fragmented Olympian family headed by god-consort Father Zeus. Hera was devalued to a nagging wife, Venus-Aphrodite to a sex object, and Athena reduced to supporting the patriarchy over her mother's and sisters' interests. The political system was thoroughly male, with women kept publicly silent and bound to the home, despite their former and remembered positions of rule and authority. Women were held monogamous in arranged marriages, with marriage and heterosexuality only for the uses of procreation and legal lineage. According to the men of the time, women were not worthy of male love; true love was only between noble men, and love between women was considered of no value. It was a somewhat different patriarchy from that of the Jews, but patriarchy indeed, with women reduced from goddesses to property.

Early Christianity was seen by a few of both Romans and Jews as what Rosemary Radford Ruether calls a redemptive or exodus community. As in the Hebrews' earlier exodus from Egypt, however, the "definition of a liberation from bondage does not include the bondage of women under patriarchy."[13] At first it seemed otherwise, but the very early active participation of women in Christianity was quickly reconsidered and stopped. The majority of Near East cultures were still pagan, with a goddess and hunter god, and many were still matriarchal.

---

[13]Rosemary Radford Ruether, *Womanguides*, p.158.

As Christianity grew from a small cult of Jewish heretics to a world institution, it grew in its anti-goddess/anti-woman misogyny. Reflecting the Judaic position, women were to be silent and subservient, to own nothing in the law, and to be ruled by their husbands or fathers in all things. They were the vessels of original sin, since Eve had partaken first of Ashtoreth's tree of life, the goddess, and were to be punished eternally for her error. Men were the new images of God and his son, a God not of life and birth, but of the all-taker, of sacrifice on the cross. The roles were not positive for men, either, and Christianity's cross is a reversal of Ashtoreth's tree of life.

Jesus at least was woman-born, with whatever equivocations as to how that came about. It is here, in the aspect of Mary, great goddess and mother, that the female and goddess worship shines through, only barely changed and veiled from women's times. In the later matriarchal cultures, where the addition of a god-consort exists, the great moon mother of various names gives birth at Yule,[14] (December 22, Winter Solstice) to a male child of the sun. She then enters a trance of winter sleep and self-renewal. The child in this version of the year cycle, the Wheel of the Year, is called variously Adonis, Tammuz, Damuzi or Baal, and grows up with the reawakened goddess, who emerges as daughter at Candlemas (February 1). They play and grow together through the spring rebirthing of the world, and at the Summer Solstice (June 21) they consummate their now grown love in the fertility of the earth. At Lammas (August 1), the mature god dies and goes into the grain that is harvested as his body at the Fall Equinox (September 22). The goddess of the moon mourns his sacrifice and she ages, but she is pregnant with him again. He is reborn from her, the infant sun/son at Yule.

The parallels of this cycle with Christianity are unmistakable. Christ is born at Yule, or three days after it in the current Western calendar, following a series of miraculous (psychic?) occurrences to Mary, the dates of which follow the goddess' Sabbats. Christ's Easter (the word comes from 'egg', and Eostar or Oestar are goddess names of the Spring Equinox Sabbat), is on the first Sunday after the first full moon of the equinox. His sacrifice and rising from death, symboled violently and in a reversal of female birth and life, assures salvation only after life on earth is ended. The god-consort's death assures the harvest, the seed's continuation of life and nourishment here and now on earth. As in the goddess cycle, the Christian calendar celebrates the stages of Christ's life and death, and less-so the occurrences to Mary, in a cycle of yearly

---

[14]Celtic-Christian sabbat names are used intentionally here.

holy days.

Mary, to the still matriarchal peoples that Christianity conquered, first with messengers of good will and then with the sword and genocide, was obviously the great mother and Christ her god-consort son. It was often just a matter of changing the god's and goddess' names. She made Christianity seem logical and acceptable during the off and on times when the Church recognized her existence, and she went underground as the beginnings of witchcraft or wicca when it didn't. The early Church, when its misogyny allowed it to look the other way about Mary, made conversions in her name everywhere. When it refused to accept a female whose power equaled or exceeded the Son of God's, it took escalating violence and warring crusades to press Christianity on the world.

Queen of Heaven, Mother of God, Mary represented mercy and caring, birth, the life force and the sanity of natural law to both women and men. The oppressions of patriarchy, by now institutionalized as the Church and sanctioned and enforced by governments and armies, were lessened and made bearable by Mary as the feminine goddess aspect of the Christian regime. As slaughter spread through the East and into Europe, it was

> only when Mary, against the stern decrees of the Church, was dug out of oblivion . . . and became identified with the Great Goddess (that Christianity was) finally tolerated by the people.[15]

Her worship within the Church was an emergence of the tip of an iceberg, the sanctioned or at least ignored women's religion that appeared once again in full view. Art, from towering churches to great oils to the affectations of portraitists, sang Mary's praises and worshipped her far beyond the male Christ or God. Mary appeared in prayer, poetry and drama, was seen in early Byzantium and Germany as part of the holy trinity, and appealed to for mercy by all. Positive witchcraft was her other side, the hidden and carefully preserved rites of the goddess and god, or of the goddess alone, among women and men everywhere. When in the Middle Ages, the Church became too threatened by her, by the power of Mariolatry and goddess worship as witchcraft and healing, the power of women and women's skills, it forcefully sought to end their existence. The Inquisition that burned a guessed-at nine million people to death,

---

[15]Elizabeth Gould Davis, *The First Sex*, p. 243-44.

most of them women, was one of its solutions.

An all out war on the female, on Mary as goddess and the goddess herself, on women who were pagans and witches and women and men who weren't, the Inquisition spread a reign of death and terror over Europe from the fourteenth to seventeenth centuries. Woman's crime at this time in history was the fact and power of her existence, of the existence of goddess worship despite all repressions, and of the survival among women of ancient knowledge and healing skills that were the state of the art science of the time.

Witchcraft was a woman's sin. In Sprenger and Kramer's *Hammer of Witches,* the Inquisition Bible, it is stated that the very word for female, *femina,* was said to mean lack of faith, and that women were viewed as the source of world evil. There was the popular saying, "one wizard to 10,000 witches,"[16] and the Inquisition meant a female genocide that virtually depopulated much of Medieval and Renaissance Europe.

It was mainly women past child-bearing age who died, but also girls before puberty; it was poor women, and women whose physical beauty or intelligence and skills were a threat to patriarchal supremacy. Any woman who healed—who alleviated pain in childbirth or poulticed a wound, who quieted a colicky child or eased a grandmother's dying— was risking her own death and the total impoverishment or death of her family. Men at this time were taking medicine and midwifery away from the hands of women, and the Inquisition removed their rivals.

Any woman who attended a Sabbat or did the self-blessing, or even kept a pet that might be her familiar or a broom or tool in her kitchen that might be pagan, could be accused by anyone at all of witchcraft. There were no civil rights, and once accused there was no innocence, only torture, death and the confiscation of property by the Church. Much of the real wealth of institutional religion today is land once stolen from accused witches by the Catholic and Protestant Inquisition courts.

The church's obsession with witchcraft and the evils of women was based on a jealous distortion of its own fears. Witches and women held power, the power of birth and life, of knowledge, healing and universal worship that patriarchy wanted for its own. Goddess worship refuted the church's negativities and reversals: it said there was enough for all right here on earth; it took joy in living, honored sexuality, and reverenced the life force, natural law and women. Its stances were gentle and popular, and could not be tolerated by an order that was their opposite, that held

---

[16]Sprenger and Kramer in Matilda Joslyn Gage, *Woman, Church and State,* (Watertown, MA, Persephone Press reprint, 1980. Original Edition, 1893), p. 97.

and misheld power from without instead of empowerment from within.

Through the conquering of matriarchy, through centuries of Judaism and the rise of Christianity, through the agony of the Inquisition, the goddess and women's power still survived. She could not be erased despite every method and attempt to disenfranchize her or to control her worshippers. The Inquisition devastated much of Europe for three hundred years and spread to the New World. The persecutions continued into Protestantism, and it was the Calvanist Parliament of Scotland that finally declared an end to witch burnings in 1784, a bare two hundred years ago. The goddess and women still survived, and do today.

Just sixty-three years after 1784, the first wave of feminism, whose beginning is marked by the 1848 women's rights convention at Seneca Falls, New York addressed the issues of women's rights, of patriarchy and religion. With an awakening in women of who they are and always have been in society, a re-cognition of what had gone wrong and why, came the forerunner of the re-emergence of the goddess. Elizabeth Cady Stanton's *Women's Bible* (1895) and Matilda Joslyn Gage's *Woman, Church and State* (1893) focused on spirituality and raised questions that rejected women's exclusion from patriarchal religion. The major energies of this period went into gaining the vote for women (1920), however, and the first wave's momentum was eventually diffused by the long vote struggle and by the World Wars that expanded women's roles and job opportunities.

After World War II, women were coerced back into the home, into motherhood and silence to the exclusion of all else, away from the real world and the factories they had run without men. Unable to accept this after seeing the other side, an increasing aura of malaise and discontent arose among questioning women in and out of suburbia. In 1953 Simone de Beauvoir's *The Second Sex* was first published in France, but did not reach widespread American notice for twenty more years. When in 1963, Betty Friedan's *The Feminine Mystique* (New York, W.W. Norton) wrote about "the problem that has no name", women were ready to do something about its message.

As the first wave of feminism began with the Abolition of Slavery movement of the 1820's, so did the second and current wave emerge in the 1950's and 60's from the influence of the Ban the Bomb and Civil Rights movements. As Mary Daly has pointed out in *Beyond God the Father* and *Gyn/ecology* (Boston, Beacon Press, 1974 and 1978), feminism and peace and feminism and civil rights are inextricable results of the same patriarchal mindset and excess situations.

The bomb movement was too early, and Civil Rights was another exodus community that failed women, but women were awakened fully now. As Civil Rights merged into the Vietnam Peace movement, activist women began discussing issues of their own spirituality and self-determination across racial lines. What they were looking for went beyond Civil Rights and Vietnam and did not lie in the sixties' sexual revolution, which simply made women more available to men, but in a revolution of their own.

The writings of mid-to-late sixties women were tentative, exciting, and increasingly radical in perspective. In politics, law and civil rights women made demands that they no longer permitted to be ignored. The process included an examination and rejection of patriarchal religious attitudes, begun in the first wave, a reclaiming and going beyond. Helen Diner's *Mothers and Amazons,* (New York, Julian Press, 1965), Mary Daly's *The Church and the Second Sex* (Boston, Beacon Press, 1968), and Elizabeth Gould Davis' *The First Sex* (New York, Penguin Books, 1971), brought religion and matriarchy to women's attention. Through these early books and others, women analyzed institutional religion and society, and learned what had been before it. By doing so, they rediscovered witchcraft, women's spirituality and the goddess.

A group of New York radical women, at Hallowmas, 1968, named themselves WITCH and began a new branch of the women's movement. More involved with political action than actual spirituality, they were nevertheless a link, a catalyst idea whose time had come, and a breath of free fresh air. In their paper titled "New York Covens," the unnamed women stated that witches have always been women activists and "the living remnants of the oldest culture of all—one in which men and women were equal . . ."[17]. Every woman is a witch if she dares to be:

> You are a Witch by saying aloud, 'I am a Witch' three times, and *thinking about that.* You are a Witch by being female, untamed, angry, joyous and immortal.[18]

Many women thought about it, the time was right, and they wanted to know more. Early spirituality activists like Z. Budapest began leading rituals, writing about and publicising the goddess.

Resisted at first by the majority of the women's movement, women's spirituality has grown quietly and surely into powerful importance. The

---

[17]WITCH, "The New York Covens", in Robin Morgan, ed., *Sisterhood is Powerful: An Anthology of Writings from the Women's Liberation Movement,* (New York, Vintage Books, 1970), p. 605.
[18]*Ibid.,* p. 606.

attitudes it presents of positive choice, free will, joy in living, activism and self-determined responsibility produce in individual women the movement's ideals for all. Much of the presenting of these attitudes and the growth of the women's spirituality movement has come through the women's small press, important politically and in literature as well. As articles on spirituality and the goddess began to appear in women's newspapers and journals, interest grew. A newspaper named *Wicce,* begun in Philadelphia in 1973, began as a spirituality publication, then changed its focus to radical politics. When *Country Women* in 1974 produced its special Issue Ten on women's spirituality, the response was so great that two of the women who worked on it decided to begin *WomanSpirit,* a periodical devoted to the goddess.

WomanSpirit, begun by Jean and Ruth Mountaingrove on women's land in Wolf Creek, Oregon was perhaps the greatest single medium that brought women's spirituality to the front of the women's movement. Published quarterly from Autumn Equinox, 1974 to Summer Solstice, 1984, *WomanSpirit* became an international forum for reclaiming and redeveloping goddess worship among women. It was a work of love for ten years by the women who worked on and contributed to the magazine. In explaining the publication's goals, Volume One, Issue One states:

> What women are doing by exploring the spiritual sides of their lives is essential for the building of a new women's culture . . . The sharing and comparing in that process is the reason for this magazine.[19]

WomanSpirit contained poetry, rituals, articles, stories and essays on every facet of women's spirituality and the goddess, from herstory and myth to herbalism and activism. Its effect was profound and gentle, and under its influence women everywhere felt safe to begin searching for the goddess in themselves.

Other periodicals began and continue. There was *Lady-Unique-Inclination-of-the-Night* (begun in 1976), special issues in *Chrysalis* and *Quest, Heresies'* Number Five *Great Goddess Issue* in 1978 and more. *Telewoman* began in 1978, *Harvest* and *Thesmophoria* began in 1981, and *The Wise Woman in 1980.* With the announcement in 1983 that *WomanSpirit* would stop with Issue Forty (Summer, 1984), a group of new magazines was started to fill the impending gap: *Of A Like Mind* in 1983, *The Beltane Papers, Goddess Rising,* and *Woman of*

---

[19] Jean and Ruth Mountaingrove, "Why WomanSpirit?", in *WomanSpirit,* Vol. 1, Issue 1, Autumn Equinox, 1974, p. 1.

Power (1984), *Sage Woman* in 1986. Nancy Passmore's *Lunar Calendar* has been published yearly since 1976.

Books and articles on women's spirituality continue to be published increasingly as well, with the continuing work of Mary Daly, the tarot and anthropology expertise of Vicki Noble and Barbara Walker, the archeology and goddess stories of Merlin Stone and Charlene Spretnak, the meditation skills of Diane Mariechild and Hallie Iglehart, Z. Budapest's and Starhawk's rituals. There are too many more to name. In art is Judy Chicago's work with the 1969 *Dinner Party* and current *Birth Project* involving hundreds of women. Women's music too, in every genre, from Kay Gardner and Musica Femina in classical work to Alive!'s joyous jazz, Betsy Rose and Kathy Winter's, Ruth Barrett and Cyntia Smith's folk, and Sweet Honey In the Rock's gospel, include the goddess.

Women's spirituality skills and rituals are shared in addition at several music festivals, yearly summer events that are wellsprings of women's culture of all sorts. Held for women only, these camping weekends bring women from all over North America and the world to share women's music and crafts, and participate in workshops on every topic. Practitioners, authors and speakers on women's skills, on tarot and I Ching, meditation, healing and ritual come together to informally learn and teach. Goddess jewelry, crystals and gemstones, books, ceramics and fabric arts of wiccan design are sold. Some of these are the Michigan Womyn's Music Festival, the Southern, National and West Coast Women's Music Festivals, Campfest, and the New England Women's Music Retreat. A new one in 1985 is the Women's Alliance Summer Solstice Camp, two weeks devoted entirely to women's spirituality. The National Women's Music Festival in Bloomington, Indiana presented its first Women's Spirituality Conference in 1985. The festivals draw attendances of two to ten thousand women, and are unforgettably joyous events.

Everywhere women have awakened themselves and the goddess, the great mother, sources of all life. They reject the rule of patriarchy that says women are silent, passive and dependent to embrace and affirm the natural law of the goddess that says just the opposite. Women in women's spirituality are increasingly taking charge—of their own lives, of their communities and of their world. Where patriarchal religions have separated and divided women, the goddess and women's spirituality brings women together. On every full moon and sabbat worldwide, women of all cultures and races meet. They join in groups from a few to hundreds to celebrate the cycles and beauty of the earth, or work alone knowing that uncounted thousands of other women are doing the same. Women who worship the goddess alone know they are not alone, but are part of a heritage that began before time and will continue beyond time's end.

The goddess is here and now, and no longer sleeping or lost in patriarchy's winter trance. The process of re-claiming her, re-learning, re-membering and re-visioning her skills, knowledge and rituals is a dis-covering of women as well, a healing of humanity and the earth. This re-claiming, re-visioning, dis-covering and healing are what women's spirituality is.

2

Creation and Creation Goddesses

_____

Creation is the beginning of Be-ing—in the universe, the earth and the individual. It's the start of a solar system from nothingness, the flaming into life of a galaxy, the making of the sun and moon. It's the forming of the earth, of primal seas and volcanic mountains, of people, animals, fishes and plants, of the phases of the solar years, lunar months and human lives. Creation is the springtime, the returning cycle of birth to the planet. It's the awakening of sprouting seeds, new bear cubs, the hatching of eggs that follows life's returning to the mother at winter's death. Creation is individual and personal, too. It's the birth of a child, the lighting of a mind's idea, the joining together of many women to organize a march or a ritual. It's hands creating—shaping clay, cloth and paint, building buildings and businesses, bringing music from a piano, making a home. It's the writing of a book and the deep breath that starts a song, the labor that climaxes in new thought forms, new inventions, new ways.

Creation is the moment of starting action from which all life and accomplishment proceeds. In the universe or on earth it is potential, the limitless possibility and mystery of uncharted paths. It is The Fool in the tarot, the child and self who walks with innocence and trust into her own unknown and makes of it what she wills. The arising of form from nothingness and chaos, of order from disorder is creation, the beginning that becomes fulfillment. And creation in every ancient culture is a female act.

Before the patriarchal era, people everywhere described the beginnings of the universe in terms of the goddess and her symbols, the female giving birth and life. From pre-Hellenic Greece, to the Native American Hopi, to Africa, the Near East and South America the stories are tides of one sea, a sea as deep as birth herself. First there was the nothingness that becomes chaos—all things in infinite potential but without form or order, the watery abyss of the universe. Chaos is a female fertility concept associated with the moon, and the evolving sea on earth or woman's gestating womb are her parallels. The creator of this teeming abyss is Gaia, Yemaya, Spider Woman, Ishtar or Ashtoreth, and Demeter, and has a thousand other names. She rises from chaos and orders it into form, puts things in their places and births planets, people and all of life as companions for her loneliness.

> The Goddess of All Things rose naked from Chaos and found nowhere to place her foot. Separating the sea from the sky, she brooded over the waters until she gave birth to life: Herself.[1]

She is always the moon, and her body is also the earth that she creates, the land and seas, with all that live there emerging and nourished from her womb and breasts, and returning to her at death. She shines in the universe above, waxing and waning in her cycles, and is the planet and life below. In later ages she is given a consort, male or female, but born from the goddess parthenogenetically as her daughter, companion or mate. The stories of Ashtoreth and Baal, Ishtar and Tammuz, or Demeter and Persephone are examples, and they mirror the process of creation in the changing cycles of the year. The phases of the moon are her cycles in the universe beyond.

Symbols of the all-creative goddess are universals that surround human consciousness. The sea and sea creatures, eggs, woven mazes or labyrinth spirals, circles and triangles, the self-renewing serpent, and a myriad of goddess fertility figures from cultures worldwide evidence the unsuppressible importance and awareness of female and goddess creation.

Life came from the sea and all that is of oceans are the lunar goddess. Many cultures depict the great mother as a mermaid, including the Yoruban Yemaya, Tiamat of Babylonia, Atargatis of Syria, and the Sumerian goddesses Nina and Nidaba, Nu Kwa of China and the Japanese Kwannon.[2] Fish are associated with many sea goddesses, a symbol

---

[1]Vicki Noble, *Motherpeace: A Way to the Goddess Through Myth, Art and Tarot*, (San Francisco, Harper and Row Publishers, 1983), p. 23.
[2]See Merlin Stone, *Ancient Mirrors of Womanhood: A Treasury of Goddess Lore from Around the World*, (Boston, Beacon Press Reprint, 1984, original 1979), for a wealth of mermaid, serpent and other goddess legends.

adapted into Christianity, along with a wonderful variety of snakes and sea serpents. These range from as far diverse as Coatlique of South America, the Egyptian Ua Zit, Haitian and African Aido Wedo, Bachue of Columbia, the Cretan Snake Goddess, and Australia's Rainbow Serpent.

Their similarities as creators of all life and their form combined with their widespread geographies are interesting and indicative. Interesting too, is their transformation under patriarchy from benevolent life symbols to the downfall of Eve and the embattled sea monsters and dragons of Western literature and film. Robert Bly, in his article "I Came Out of the Mother Naked," describes the British epic poem *Beowulf* in terms of patriarchy's defeat of the creator goddess:

> The dragon in inner life is man's fear of women, and in public life it is the matriarchy's conservative energy.[3]

The goddess of the moon and sea who birthed all life became a monster to be slain by men, an idea historically consistent. Snakes, long known as goddess symbols for their self-renewing shedding of old skin, are loathed and feared. They—goddess worship—tempted Eve. Saint George slew the dragon, the forces of matriarchy and goddess religion in Christianizing Europe. There is fear of the Loch Ness Monster and the Saturday movie matinee, and fear of the lunar night and sea.

Yet scientists agree that evolution is marine, and that human gestation in the sea of the womb reflects the symbols and changes of evolving life. The sea is the universal female abyss, the lunar chaos from which life began, and that was sorted out and brought to land by the goddess. Seashells from this abyss are female symbols, symbols of wombs and birth, fertility and emergence from the sea. The cowrie, used as currency and worth by island cultures and Native American peoples, as well as in Egypt and Asia, is a clitoral female birth symbol—all life emerges from the ocean of the female womb. Aphrodite, a powerful fertility aspect of the great goddess in pre-patriarchal Greece, is described as sea-born, and often pictured standing on a flat shell. Teteu Innan, an Aztec goddess, wears a seashell skirt, and the Navaho White Shell Woman is a savior of her people.[4] Shells, pearls and fishes are associated with the Chinese Kwan Yin, and the conch that sounds of the sea is in India the sound that made the universe.[5] Many shells are rounded and hollowed womb or

[3]Robert Bly, "I Came Out of the Mother Naked", in *Sleepers Joining Hands,* (San Francisco, Harper and Row Publishers, 1973), p. 30.
[4]Merlin Stone, *Ancient Mirrors of Womanhood,* p. 87 and 293.
[5]J.C. Cooper, *Symbolism, The Universal Language,* (Great Britain, The Aquarian Press, 1982), p. 76.

moon symbols and some are spirals—the shape of DNA and the labyrinth mystery symbol of the unfolding universe, the birth canal and the creative goddess.

Eggs are also universal symbols of creation, birth, rebirth, the moon and the goddess. They are often seen in conjunction with the serpent or snake, and egg imagery is still accepted positively in the West where the serpent is not. Judy Chicago in her *Birth Project* art depicts the story of the snake and the egg. The goddess birthed both from her body and they floated on the waters of chaos. By wrapping herself around the egg, the snake broke it open, and from it hatched all the forms of the universe. In the Hindu, the cosmic egg is laid by a golden bird, and the halves of its cracking form the earth and sky. Egg and bird symbols are goddess symbols as well, with several cultures depicting goddesses in bird form.

In Egypt, the cosmic egg from which the sun hatched was either formed in the serpent's mouth or laid by the goose of the Nile.[6] The goddess Maat is portrayed with an ostrich feather in her hair, and the ostrich hieroglyph closely resembles the hieroglyph for *Ba,* the soul. Both figures, Maat and Amunet, and dozens of other names given her as the great goddess, the Lady of the Amenta, are associated with the egg and bird-or-serpent concept of creation.[7]

Eggs in their elliptical shapes and pearlized colors are symbols of the earth and shining moon, and the dark and brooding inside of the egg corresponds to the waning/gestating year and to the moon's dark gestating phases. The goddess is seen as the moon herself in every culture, and as the moon's dual opposite, the earth. Eggs are a symbol, too, of the "twice born," in their double birth of laying and hatching,[8] as the moon and earth in their cycles are also continually reborn and renewed. Initiation into women's mysteries is seen as a rebirth and participation in the "natural process of transformation that is analogous to the 'work' of a brooding hen,"[9] to the creation and phases of the moon and planet. The cracked halves of the hatched cosmic egg create the earth and moon in some cultures, the goddess herself, and in most form the duality opposites on which goddess philosophy rests. The Chinese yin and yang are an example of this system of dualities, in their original meaning not only of male and female, but of earth and moon, receptive

---

[6]*Ibid.,* p. 17-18.
[7]Merlin Stone, *Ancient Mirrors of Womanhood,* p. 259-265.
[8]J.C. Cooper, *Symbolism, The Universal Language,* p. 17.
[9]Nor Hall, *The Moon and the Virgin: Reflections on the Archetypal Feminine,* (San Francisco, Harper and Row Publishers, 1980), p. 49.

and creative, light and dark, land and sea, beginning and ending, winter and summer, birth and death. These dualities and others like them are complementary opposites; one cannot exist without the other, and both are positive poles of one wholeness in the universe and individual. These opposites and the law of changes within them are all birthed from the cosmic egg, from the all-creating goddess who is earth and moon.

The circle and ellipse, as shapes of the egg and moon, are major goddess creation symbols, too. Moon, egg and womb are all round and contain the darkness of creative gestation within their fertile walls. A circle is an infinite form; it has no beginning or end, but simply continues in perfection and completeness, as does the universe, earth and the life force. The endless cycles of the universe, moon, the year on earth and all of life begin with creation, proceed through growth into maturity, age into death, then begin again. The moon has her circle of phases and the year awakens with spring, waxes into fertile summer, matures at harvest, and wanes into winter. A woman is born, grows into childhood, adolescence, maturing, aging and death. She is Maiden, Mother and Crone in reflection of the moon and the year. In all of these is the infinite circle. The dark moon becomes new again, and winter is the gestation of spring; women who celebrate the goddess' circle believe in life's continuation after death. The moon becomes new, the earth goes on, the circle turns, and the soul is reborn. Time loses its terror where the wheel has no end, where birth and death are natural law and the dualities of creation's wholeness.

As symbol of continuation, the circle is seen in all aspects of goddess and matriarchal religion. The center of a circle is protected space, the inside of the moon, womb or egg, and casting a circle is the beginning of all wiccan rituals. Native American, African and Eastern desert peoples build circular houses or tents, and the Hopi's underground religious space, the womblike kiva, is always round. Goddess temples of India, Egypt, Crete, Greece and South America, temples worldwide including Stonehenge, are based on the shape of the circle of creation.[10] Circles with dotted centers are some of the oldest discovered Neolithic art, and goddesses and priestesses from Egypt to Europe, to the Near East and South America are pictured holding the egg-round moon in their hands or on their heads.

Down-pointing triangles are similar creation symbols that represent goddess and female fertility and sexuality, the womb and vagina. They

---

[10]Mimi Lobell, "Temples of the Great Goddess," in *Heresies*, Issue Five, *The Great Goddess Issue*, 1978, pp. 32-39.

are the delta or mound of Venus, the most fertile land in agriculture, and the passage through which creation and all life emerges. Goddess figures from dozens of cultures emphasize the female triangle, but much of this symbolism is also represented in the circle and carried over into the spiral, maze or labyrinth that with the seashell and moon-egg are the infinite womb of the great mother.

Spirals begin at the center, the point of beginning and creation at center that is the dot of Neolithic circle paintings. They radiate outward in ever increasing and infinite moving coils, the coils of the snake and the continuing of circles. They are the process of creation and birth, of the passage from the hidden to the seen, from the dark inner egg or dark moon to the light of hatching, birth and fullness. They are the emergence from marine chaos to the created earth and mcon, from the sea to the land, from the womb to the manifest world. Like the egg-circle-moon or seashell, snake and sea creatures, spirals are found universally as symbols of goddess creation. They are representations of the inner, hidden lunar life and the underground, undersea or womb world. Spirals are the transformations of birth and death, and the process of moving changes in between; they are also rebirth and reincarnation when seen reversed, as moving from the outside to within.

The spiral is in evidence in many goddess temples—Stonehenge in England, the Egyptian Temple of Dendara, the Ziggurats of Erech, and even the later European Mary chapels of Christianity.[11] The Oracle of Delphi in Greece is a cleft in the earth, the creation, vulva and emergence place of birth or the spiral. The *sipapu* in the Hopi religion, present in the kiva, is a hole in the earth, the place of birth and emergence into the world. Where made into a physical path or building, the spiral becomes the labyrinth, a journey inward into dark, as in Theseus' invasion of the minotaur at matriarchal Crete. Movement from the center of the spiral outward is goddess creation and birth through the vagina, the triangle delta, but the labyrinth enters from the light, from outside, and moves toward the mystery of the center and the darkness. In mythologist Joseph Campbell's analysis:

> the labyrinth, maze and spiral were associated in ancient Crete and Babylon with the internal organs of the human anatomy as well as with the underworld.[12]

---

[11]*Ibid.*, p. 34-37.
[12]Joseph Campbell, *The Masks of God: Primitive Mythology*, (New York, Penguin Books, 1959), p. 69.

The purpose was to recreate the womb of the mother through which to be reborn, a spiral continuing of goddess creation in the universe and individual. The spiral dance of women's spirituality and wicca, probably of Greek origin, is a celebration of birth, rebirth and the life force of the goddess, a re-creation and re-cognition of the spiral. DNA, the molecular structure of biologic life was discovered in the 1950's by Rosalind Franklin (before Watson and Crick) to be shaped in spiral form.

Close variations of the spiral are the encircled maze, swastika or equal armed cross, the spiral as the tree of life. This has appeared, a positive creation symbol of the goddess until Christianity's and Nazism's use of it, in Egypt, Greece, Crete, Native America, South America, India, China, Africa, Scandinavia and Europe.[13] The Hopi maze, Greek key, Chinese tau and Celtic cross patterns are examples. The equal armed cross is a life and rebirth symbol originating for some cultures with the Egyptian ankh of Maat. It is also the Road of Life of the Hopi, the origin of the wiccan pentacle as the four directions and the center, and the tree of life of Ashtoreth. The figure suggests dynamic movement, a simplified spiral galaxy, and may have been derived from the moving constellation of the Great Bear.[14] It is the tree on which Eve's forbidden fruit grew, the tree of knowledge of birth, the life force and creation—of the female.

Spirals, labyrinths and mazes have been found in artwork worldwide, spanning the ages of human existence. They appear in conjunction with other creation symbols and goddess figures—female images with emphasized deltas or pregnant bellies and breasts, women wearing snakes as clothing or holding the moon in their hair, women as mermaids, women holding the ankh or sometimes holding a child, women often naked and often sexually suggestive or giving birth. The images and symbols remain today as powerful reminders of the force of female creation, of the goddess in her full recognition as mother of all, as the great goddess who birthed the universe, earth and people. The symbols of the goddess are symbols of women's mystery, of the bringing forth and nourishment of life; they are reminders of the creation and beginnings of the universe and earth, and are everywhere.

Goddess creation stories are varied and similar, but all answer the question of how the world came to be in female terms, in the natural order terms and symbols of the birthing of life. Some goddesses create alone, and some birth their mates as other gods or parthenogenetic

---

[13]J.C. Cooper, *Symbolism, The Universal Language*, p. 26-27.
[14]*Ibid.*, p.26.

daughters and sons. They create people as acts of birth or acts of making and shaping, and are in themselves the universe, earth and moon.

The oldest pre-Hellenic goddess is Gaia,[15] though by no means the oldest of goddess creation stories. Like the Babylonian Tiamat, the sea, Gaia the earth arose from her self, from chaos. Whirling in darkness, she became a galaxy of fiery light and created the sun and the moon, the mirror of heaven. Merging with heaven, herself in the mirror, she gave birth to seas and after cooling became the planet.

Gaia's body is the mother, the female, fertile earth. Her deep breasts are mountains and her watery dark openings are oceans, her skin the soil from which all plants and nourishment grow. Her interior is birth, death and the underworld of rebirth, the place where crystals and volcanoes form, where life begins and ends. From the sea of her womb came the egg and serpent of all life, the fishes and shellfish, snakes and sea creatures that later evolved to dry land. From her womb came the birds and the animals, the insects that fly and walk and that crawl upon her body. She is Gaia the all-giver, all mother, and Pandora is another of her names. She gave birth to six women and six men,[16] to the goddesses and gods.

The omphalos or navel of Gaia is the Delphic Oracle—the word "Delphi" means womb—watched over by the goddess' serpent daughter Delphyna or Phythia and her priestesses.[17] Her caves and shrines are the places of inner wisdom throughout her lands, connections of the born to the unborn, the surface to the underworlds, the places of goddess where all time is now. All come to hear Gaia's wisdom through her priestesses, and she grants the gift of prophecy to those who ask.

The takeover of patriarchal gods, the family of Zeus by the time of Classical Greece, is seen in the progression of Gaia's later stories where her sons become rulers, and she is increasingly written out of the action. From reigning creator of a universe born of herself, Gaia is first seen as birthing by parthenogenesis a son, Uranus. Uranus is heaven to her earth, and their sexual union releases both Gaia's creativity and her son's male jealousy.

Fearing for her other children, Gaia holds them in her womb unborn, while arming Chronos (Time), another son, with a sickle. The blood of Uranus' emasculation by Chronos birthed the Furies, upholders

---

[15]These stories are drawn from mixed sources. They are eclectic and poetic creations, footnoted where appropriate.
[16]Charlene Spretnak, *Lost Goddesses of Early Greece: A Collection of Pre-Hellenic Myths,* (Boston, Beacon Press Reprint, 1984, original 1978), p. 45-53.
[17]Merlin Stone, *When God Was A Woman,* (New York, Harvest/HBJ Books, 1976), p. 203.

of matriarchal law, and also the race of giant Titans from which Zeus descended.[18] Zeus later overthrew Chronos to mount the throne of Olympus, once known as Gaia Olympus and the seat of the mother, and his son Apollo took over the Delphic Oracle. There are no stories of takeovers, wars or blood other than menstrual or birth-blood, before patriarchal times.

Zeus' wife is Hera, who is either Gaia herself or daughter of Gaia's child Rhea.[19] She is a constant matriarchal thorn in Zeus' side, a great goddess whose power is increasingly coopted and belittled under patriarchy's gains. From the great mother, queen creator of all the universe and birthing source of all life, Hera/Gaia by the time of Classical Greece is seen as no more than a nagging wife. Yet the stories of Gaia are not lost, the stories of the female beginnings of the universe, the all-giving mother and the Oracle.

Another story of goddess creation is that of the Yoruban mermaid goddess Yemaya. She is known in West Africa and throughout South and Central America by several names, including Umoja, Ymoja, Yemanza and Iamanza. A great goddess of the wiccan-Christian Santeria religion in Cuba and Brazil, she was brought from Africa by people enslaved.

Yemaya is a moon goddess of waters and oceans, and mother of the fertile river spirits. Women come to her asking for children,[20] since Yemaya birthed the children who began the world. Often portrayed with the tail of a fish, she is described in Santeria as beautiful, wearing white clothing and blue beads, and having yellowish skin.[21] Offerings are made to her of chickens and yams.

Merlin Stone relates Yemaya to the Summer Solstice, with a lovely ritual of flowers, boats and wishes on a moonlit sea:

> as our boats of prayers are set afloat
> upon the edges of your being,
> your gently caressing waves
> washing about our bared legs,
> cleansing away our sadness and our troubles

> we know that you are waiting
> for the messages we sent
> Iamanja, Holy Queen Sea.[22]

[18]Patricia Monaghan, *The Book of Goddesses and Heroines,* (New York, E.P. Dutton, 1981), p. 114.
[19]Merlin Stone, *Ancient Mirrors of Womanhood,* p. 373.
[20]Patricia Monaghan, *The Book of Goddesses and Heroines,* p. 309.
[21]Migene Gonzales-Wippler, *Santeria: African Magic in Latin America,* (New York, Original Products, Inc., 1981), p. 26. Much of the reference for this goddess comes from Gonzalez-Wippler.
[22]Merlin Stone, *Ancient Mirrors of Womanhood,* p. 97.

The women's jazz ensemble Alive! perform a chant to Yemaya on their first album titled *Alive!* In their lyric the goddess is:

> Yemaya,
> Ocean Mother,
> In the beginning
> You gave birth to the heavens
> And to all the gods and goddesses,
> Sister of the Fishes.

> Take me home again,
> Take me home again,
> Yemaya.[23]

In the Yoruban Genesis story, when the immortal first man's conceit caused the gods to destroy all life, Olodumare (creation), felt sorry and created a new but mortal god-human, Obatala. Earliest sources call Obatala she, later sources, he. Obatala was given a wife, Oddudua, who is portrayed as a young Black woman breastfeeding a child. This madonna image is a familiar one in Christianity in Mary, and also is the image of the Egyptian great goddess Isis. The children of Obatala and Oddudua were Aganyu and Yemaya, who together bore a son, Orungan. As Orungan grew in male aggressiveness, he began to challenge Aganyu and the natural order, and finally raped his mother, Yemaya. The lunar goddess of oceans cursed her son till he died, then choosing her own end, she herself died of sorrow at the top of the earth's highest mountain. At her death her womb opened, and she gave birth to the fourteen Yoruban gods and goddesses. These are Chango, Oba, Oya, Oshun, Ochosi, Olokun, Olosa, Chankpana, Dada, Aye-Shaluga, Orisha-Oko, Oke, Orun, and Ocha. The deluge of her birth waters caused the great flood, an event described universally in ancient legends from the Hopi to Sumeria, and filled the seas. From the goddess' bones were born Obafulom and Lyaa, the first human man and woman, parents of the people.[24]

Yemaya is an image of fertile birth and creativity of all sorts, of the life-giving, life-emerging waters. Her symbols are boats, seashells, flowers and fans, and her colors are the blue and white of calm waves.[25] She is imaged as the moon and is a women's deity, a goddess of mercy

[23]Alive!, lyric to "Yemaya, Sister of the Fishes," recorded on *Alive!*, (Urana Records, WWE 84, 1979). Available through Ladyslipper, Inc., POB 3130, Durham, NC 27705.
[24]Migene Gonzalez-Whippler, *Santeria: African Magic in Latin America*, p. 24-27.
[25]*Ibid.*, p. 16.

reminiscent in many ways of the Chinese Nu Kwa or Kwan Yin. In the eclectic South American Santeria, Yemaya is merged with a saint's aspect of Mary as Our Lady of Regla. She is one of the Seven African Powers, a goddess of great popular appeal, whose syncretization with Mary helped make Catholicism acceptable among African-descended Cubans and South Americans. Associated with sea waves, seashells and sea creatures, Yemaya is a goddess of ocean creation, of women and the female moon.

Her counterpart in southwest North America is Spider Woman, the weaver of life, great mother of the Hopi Indians. In Merlin Stone's version from Sia Pueblo,[26] Spider Woman arose from nothingness at the time of the dark purple light before dawn. The goddess spun a silver strand from her Spider's body and cast it out to connect the east and west of the horizon. Then she spun another strand from north to south. By doing this, Spider Woman created the four directions, with herself as the center: she created the Hopi Road of Life in the shape of the equal-armed cross. The great mother sang the Creation Song from her place at the center of the web of the universe, and her daughters Ut Set and Nau Ut Set were born from the sound. The twin goddesses made the sun and the moon from seashells and colored stones on earth, and put them into the sky in their places. They created the Star People to light the night way when the moon went too far to see. In Hopi anthropologist Frank Waters' version of Taos Pueblo,[27] Spider Woman made twin sons called Poqanghoya and Palongawhoya, the north and south poles. They created harmony and balanced the earth, made it rotate safely and in tune.

Spider Woman

> then created from the earth trees, bushes, plants and flowers,
> all kinds of seed-bearers and nut-bearers to clothe the earth,
> giving to each a life and a name. In the same manner she
> created all kinds of birds and animals—molding them out of
> earth, covering them with her white-substance cape, and
> singing over them.[28]

She took the four colors of clay and made them into the four colors of people, red, yellow, black and white. She spun life from her body, wove it into a white cape of creative wisdom, and covered the four people with her magic. As they each awoke, they discovered that a thin strand of

---

[26]Merlin Stone, *Ancient Mirrors of Womanhood*, p. 289-90.
[27]Frank Waters, *Book of the Hopi*, (New York, Ballantine Books, 1963), p. 4-5.
[28]*Ibid.*, p. 5-6.

spider filament connected them to the goddess' body at the *kopavi*, the purple light chakra at the crowns of their heads. The mother instructed them to always keep this door open to her, to creation, spirituality and the life force.[29]

The Hopi have a system of colors of light that match the colors of the steps of creation. These in turn match parts of the body, are a system of chakras and chakra colors very close to that of India and Tibet, and are used in psychic healing and the Craft in the West. The axis of the earth mirrors the spinal column of the body, and radiates out to these light centers or chakras. Through the *kopavi*, the human spirit connects and speaks to Spider Woman and the universe.[30]

Spider Woman sent the four people to live on the earth, to find joy and the Beauty Way, to populate the world. They emerged through the *sipapu*, the center of the earth and the womb. She taught women the secrets of weaving, how to spin wool and flax into yarn and weave the yarn into blankets and clothing. Ut Set gave the people corn, the milk of the mother's breasts, and Nau Ut Set showed them how to use the corn for food and for prayer.[31] Spider Woman taught the Hopi of the Road of Life, gave them eagle feathers to protect them, and told them again of the *kopavi*, the door that kept open connects them to her wisdom. Among Spider Woman's many names in the southwest United States are Spider Grandmother, Hatai Wugti, Awitelin Tsita, Huruing Wuuti, Sussistanako (Thought Woman), Kokyangwuti, and Tsitsicinako.

The goddess Ishtar or Ashtoreth, like Spider Woman, Yemaya and Gaia, is another creation figure and great mother. She is also a goddess whose far-reaching influence has shaped world culture, world religions and civilizations. Her origins are Babylonian, but her worship extended throughout the Near East, and she became the prototype for Isis, the Egyptian great mother goddess, as well as for the Greek Aphrodite or Venus. Her Canaanite forms as Ashtoreth, Asherah, Astarte or Anat were the matriarchal origins of the Hebrew Yahweh. Her story also relates closely to that of Inanna, the Sumerian goddess whose "Descent to the Underworld" is an exciting epic poem still read and appreciated. The descent to the underworld of Ishtar/Ashtoreth/Inanna explains why there are seasons, and along with the Greek story of Demeter and Persephone, establishes the Wheel of the Year in women's spirituality and wicca. The Hopi Road of Life is a similar ritual wheel.

Legends in the fertile crescent and on Cyprus associate Ishtar with

---

[29]Merlin Stone, *Ancient Mirrors of Womanhood*, p. 290.
[30]Frank Waters', *Book of the Hopi*, p. 11-12.
[31]Merlin Stone, *Ancient Mirrors of Womanhood*, p. 290.

Venus and say she descended in fire from the stars, landing in the sea with her holy women at Aphaca.[32]

She is depicted as a serpent goddess, her body entwined with snakes or carrying a snake-encircled staff, and bearing the lunar disc and crescent horns upon her head. Serpents, lionesses and sphinxes are among her symbols. Among her names are Serpent Lady and Ashtoreth of the Horns, but always she is the Queen of Heaven. She is linked with the sea and the sea goddess Atargatis,[33] in the original ocean birth of Aphrodite.

Named as creator of the universe and seen as the moon, the earth and the morning star, Ishtar/Ashtoreth/Inanna is a goddess of fertility and affirming sexuality, and is seen primarily in those terms. All life—plant, animal and human—are children of Ishtar's womb, but the moon has four phases and the goddess who is life is also death and rebirth.

Ishtar/Ashtoreth/Inanna created the universe from chaos, but was lonely. By parthenogenesis, she gave birth to a son, Tammuz, Baal, Adonis or Damuzi, who grew to manhood first as her playmate and then as her lover. In the Western wiccan calendar, which dates slightly differently from the original desert seasons, Tammuz is born at the Winter Solstice, and emerges with the awakening goddess at Candlemas, February 1. They grow and play together through the spring, and consummate their sexuality and love at Beltane's Sacred Marriage in May. Summer Solstice is their time of fertility and fulfillment, the fertility and fulfillment of all the earth. At Lammas' first August fruits, however, the goddess must sacrifice her consort to assure the harvest and the continuation of life on earth. Tammuz in the underworld becomes the Fall Equinox grain, the seed that sustains life and is planted again for new births after winter's death. While he is dead, Ishtar mourns him bitterly, and all sexuality and birth on the planet are halted. This time of Tammuz was a major ceremonial period in the Near East and is also the time of Persephone's death in the Greek Eleusinian Mysteries, and remnants of Ishtar/Ashtoreth/ Inanna's mourning remain in the Fall Equinox ceremonies of Ramadan of Islam and the Jewish Day of Atonement, Yom Kippur.[34] At Hallows, the goddess descends to the underworld to rescue Tammuz, and October 31 connects the living to the dead in cultures and the wiccan Craft worldwide. Securing her son-lover's rebirth, Ishtar/Ashtoreth/Inanna returns from the underworld pregnant with him once more, and life and the earth's

---

[32]*Ibid.*, p. 103 and several references following.
[33]*Ibid.*, p.115.
[34]M. Esther Harding, *Woman's Mysteries, Ancient and Modern*, (San Francisco, Harper and Row Publishers, 1971), p. 157-8.

fertility are allowed to return.

The cycle reflects the eight sabbats celebrated in women's spirituality: Winter Solstice, December 22; Candlemas, February 1; Spring Equinox, March 22; Beltane, May 1; Summer Solstice, June 21; Lammas, August 1; Fall Equinox, September 22; and Hallows, October 31. These are the wiccan Wheel of the Year. The Hopi have a similar ritual cycle, and the cycle is reflected in the Hebrew, Chinese and Christian calendars of the past and present.

Fragments of "Inanna's Descent to the Underworld", the Sumerian epic poem, in part describe the goddess' efforts to rescue the lover she herself has sacrificed. Inanna had condemmed Tammuz (or Damuzi or Baal) to take her place in the underworld when in her previous absence there her lover had set himself up as a god. The story of Inanna's own entry and rescue from death, from the underworld goddess Erishkegal, is the main body of the epic, a major women's adventure, and is the first great story of resurrection. Someone had to take Inanna's place below, or there would be no mating or birth, no human, plant or animal life in the world above again, and in her anger at his conceit, Inanna condemned Tammuz. But once it was done, and Tammuz had died and gone to the underworld, the goddess of life and sexuality missed her lover-son and mourned his loss inconsolably.[35]

Inanna bargained with Erishkegal, and won from her goddess sister her lover's life for half of each year, for the time of growth and blooming. In some versions, it is Tammuz' sister, Gestinanna, who rescues the god-consort, Inanna's daughter rather than Inanna herself.[36] Tammuz lives from Winter Solstice to Lammas by the Western wiccan calendar (from Winter Solstice to Summer Solstice in the east), and goes to death and the underworld for the waning of the year. The cycle of birth, growth, sexuality and death are established in the seasons and in all of life by the story of Inanna and Tammuz. The story is a circle with no ending, and rebirth comes after death, as the year begins again and Tammuz is reborn. Sexuality is stated intrinsically as the vehicle of the life force, and sexual pleasure is a gift of Ishtar/Ashtoreth/Inanna, of the great goddess herself. When the change-over came that made the creator male and the Jewish patriarchy had to control and own this life force of women, sexuality was repressed along with the goddess, and creation, rebirth and the life cycle became a male-only event. Strong vestiges of the Ishtar and Tammuz story and cycle are present in Christianity, in Mary, Christ

---

[35]Patricia Monaghan, *The Book of Goddesses and Heroines*, p. 149-150.
[36]*Ibid.*

and the resurrection. Jesus' arising from death was long pre-dated by a woman, by the goddess Inanna.

Another version of this theme, a woman-only year cycle representing a mother and daughter as the three-form goddess, is the Cretan-Greek story of Demeter and Persephone. The original pre-Hellenic story contains no mention of Hades' or Pluto's rape of Persephone,[37] her abduction from the earth her mother, but rape's later inclusion by Homer can also be read as a metaphor of patriarchal change. The sacrifice of Demeter's daughter to the underworld was voluntary, and as in the Sumerian Inanna story, Hades was once female, the Hecate-Crone aspect of Demeter herself. As the three-form triple goddess, Persephone is Maiden or daughter, Demeter is Mother, and Hecate of the underworld is the Crone.

Demeter as the great goddess, the being who created the universe, is associated with Gaia, and along with Hera was a daughter of Rhea and Chronos. Rhea and Gaia are often seen as one goddess, and Hera, Rhea and Demeter may all be aspects of Gaia. The earth is Demeter's body, made by her from chaos, and all who live on it are born of Demeter's womb. At death all return to the mother, to the underworld, to Demeter-Hecate as all-giver and all-taker, to the womb of birth and rebirth. The body of the earth, like the breasts of the female everywhere, provide nourishment for the human, animal and plant life that live on it and Demeter is also this nourishment. She is the basis of life, the plants and grain—wheat in Greece, corn in Native America, and Eve's Near Eastern fruit—what the Hopi call the milk of the mother's breasts. Demeter's denial of life while Persephone is dead in the underworld consists of the barrenness of winter, the denial of the growth of life's plants. Ishtar/Ashtoreth/Inanna's denial is that of sexuality and birth, but the stories are very parallel.

In addition to being the earth, Demeter as a creation goddess is also the moon. The moon in her cycles has four quarters, but is more often personified as the three female ages of Maiden, Mother and Crone. In the pre-Hellenic creation story, these ages are Persephone, Demeter and Hecate—spring, summer and winter, or the waxing, full and waning moon. The three aspects are one goddess, the triple or three-form goddess of women's spirituality. They are both separate and one. All three are aspects of Demeter, but are also present in the great mother as Gaia, Ishtar, Spider Woman or Yemaya, and are all present in the times and lives of every woman, the creative, fertile and death-goddess

---

[37]Charlene Spretnak, *Lost Goddesses of Early Greece*, p. 105-6.

aspects of all life.

Demeter created herself, the earth and moon, from the chaos of galaxies that was also her existence.[38] She birthed birds, fish, animals and insects to inhabit the earth, her mountains, valleys, plains and seas. She created grasses and grains, herbs, fruit, nuts and seaweeds to nourish the children of her body. The time was ever spring, and all were well-fed and satisfied, and Demeter was pleased with her work.

But Demeter was lonely for female companionship, and a mother needs a daughter. The goddess conceived parthenogenetically, swelled with the fullness of pregnancy, and Persephone was born. Demeter's happiness while nursing and then teaching her growing daughter, an intelligent and independent child, knew no bounds.

One day while walking, the adolescent Persephone followed a deer trail and happened upon a cavern. It was a dark and awesome place, calm and beautiful, and the daughter went in. The further she walked, the deeper into a labyrinth the girl was drawn. Wondering about this place that was new to her, but knowing she should turn back, Persephone followed the cool passages deep into the earth.

She walked a long time, spiraling downward, and at the bottom of the path found an underground room. Crystals glittered from the walls, stalagmites and stalactites, and a fireplace and iron cauldron burned at the center of the chill round cavern. A woman was there, the room obviously her household. She was old and grey-haired, and left her work to welcome Persephone.

"I am Hecate," the woman said. "All begin and end here, and are welcome, but this is not your time."

Persephone explored the room, not feeling timid about touching things or asking the woman of her life. She sat down to the bowl of pomegranates Hecate offered.

"Your mother misses you," the old woman told her. "You cannot stay here. Time on earth passes rapidly, though here nothing changes."

"I want to learn from you," Persephone said. "You have much to teach me. If I go now, may I come again?"

"While you are gone, the earth dies," Hecate said. "Your mother suffers without you. If you and she agree, I will teach you all I know, but now you must go back to her. Go quickly."

Persephone saw Demeter appear in the doorway, and the mother was distraught but did not speak. The daughter knew her image for a

---

[38]This version of the Demeter-Persephone story is influenced by Spretnak, but also by a lifetime of Greek mythology and years of goddess reading. The story is a favorite, and I've made it my own.

vision, and followed it from Hecate's room. When she reached the top of the labyrinth and stepped into sunlight alone, she was amazed to see the world covered with snow, to feel its damp and coldness. Demeter found Persephone, held her close and kissed her, and the two of them talked and cried. The snow melted and a carpet of white and purple crocuses bloomed at the women's feet. Persephone told Demeter of Hecate and the underworld, and of her wish to go back and learn the teachings of the old woman. So great was her wish that Demeter agreed that Persephone must go, but only for a portion of each year.

Persephone is born at the Winter Solstice and her childhood is the spring. She discovers the labyrinth at the time of her menarche, Summer Solstice, and enters it. She reaches Hecate at Lammas, and the time of Demeter's grief climaxes with the Fall Equinox. The year wanes and plant life dies. Demeter finds Persephone in the underworld at Hallows and the daughter returns with her, enters the world newborn again at Winter. Life returns with rebirth in the spring, with the blooming of Persephone's coming home.

By the time of Classical Greece, the Demeter-Persephone story became one of rape. Hades sees Demeter's beautiful daughter and abducts her, holding her captive as queen of his underworld, death. Demeter in her rage halts the grain, and drought and famine threaten to destroy the earth. At the intercession of Zeus, Persephone is released, but because she has eaten four pomegranate seeds, she must return to Hades four months of each year.

Both versions of the story mirror that of Ishtar and Tammuz, but in the Eleusinian Mysteries, the women's mysteries of ancient Greece, the all-female version of Demeter and Persephone remained unchanged through classical times and into the advent of Christianity. This is the version adopted in Dianic wicca and in much of women's spirituality today that attempts to reconstruct and reclaim it. The Demeter and Peresphone story establishes a Wheel of the Year cycle on which the eight great Sabbat rituals and the moon phase rituals are based. Other versions, involving the goddess alone or with the god-consort are also used.

Each of these creation goddesses and others—Gaia, Yemaya, Spider Woman, Ishtar and Demeter—create the earth by birth or by shaping, create all life. They are the earth and moon at once. Their symbols and legends are examples of stories worldwide and throughout time that establish a goddess as the creative force of the universe. They are the basis of women's spirituality and wicca, and since in goddess worship every woman is a part of the creative mother, every woman participates in creation by her own acts of birthing and shaping. While the woman who chooses motherhood is seen in this light, the woman who creates in other ways is the creative aspect of goddess Be-ing just as strongly. A woman whose writing births a book brings life into the world, or who performs a ritual or a piece of music, weaves a cloth, creates a painting, makes a home for herself and others. The woman who actively takes control of the power of her own life participates in the Be-ing and creation of goddess that exists in all women. This Be-ing is symboled and made manifest in many ways, is present and seen in all of life, but is first found within. The goddess was there in the beginning and has been there always; she will be there always to come. The great goddess, mother of the universe, is creator of the world, of all Be-ing, and is part of the Be-ing of all women's lives.

3

The Wheel of the Year – I Group Rituals

Hear the words of the Great Goddess, the Great Mother of the universe—
Gaia, Yemaya, Spider Woman, Ishtar, Ashtoreth, Mary, Inanna, Demeter—
known by a thousand names across geography and time:

> Whenever you need anything, once a month and best when
> the moon is full, and eight times more in the year, you shall
> meet in some safe place to celebrate my spirit, who am queen
> of all women. You shall meet in freedom, and as a sign of trust
> you shall be naked in your rites. Sing, feast, dance, make
> music and love, all in my presence, for mine is the ecstasy of
> the spirit and joy on earth. My only law is love unto all. Mine is
> the secret that opens on the door of birth, and mine is the mys-
> tery of life that is the Cauldron of Hecate, the womb of immor-
> tality. I give knowledge of the all-creative spirit, and beyond
> death I give peace and reunion with those gone before. Nor do
> I ask any sacrifice, for I am the mother of all things and my love
> is the breast milk that nourishes the earth.

The Charge of the Goddess[1]

The rituals of women's spirituality are wiccan-based and celebrate the
full and new moons, plus the eight Great Sabbats of the Wheel of the
Year. The rites are traditional and woman-created, and are unique in their
emphasis on the female, exclusively in most covens, but only primarily
in others. Some groups include the god-consort as the male principle
within women, the male as the duality to the female life force. Other

---

[1]Adapted from Starhawk, *The Spiral Dance: A Rebirth of the Ancient Religion of the Great Goddess,* (San Francisco, Harper and Row Publishers, 1979), p. 76.

groups are Dianic and honor only the goddess, seeing all of life's elements in her totality. The two choices reflect Ishtar and Tammuz or Demeter, Persephone and Hecate, but both celebrate the changing year, the turn-ing Wheel of the seasons and of birth and death, the phases of the moon. While the rituals in this and Chapter Four are group-oriented, a great many women work in the Craft alone, adapting group rituals and researching, writing and developing individual ones to fill their needs. Chapter Five of this book deals more fully with individual work.

Research is on-going in the women's community to understand and reclaim the goddess rituals of the past and of other than European cultures. Much has been lost beyond reclaiming, deliberately destroyed or distorted beyond meaning. Women are sifting the evidence of the past and finding the present there, learning and filling in the many gaps. Where the past fails reconstruction, women are creating their own rituals, establishing new traditions for the present and future, working in poetry, music, literature and dance.

This aspect of women's spirituality and Craft is an exciting one. Patriarchy has written women out of religion, and patriarchal rituals have little place for creativity or improvising. Women's spirituality has no Bible or cast-in-concrete ways of doing anything at all. Often only outlined beforehand, each ritual takes its own flavor, influenced by the women who together create it and the inspiration of the goddess attending. With a majority of covens and circles run by consensus, rituals are often eclectic in the traditions they draw upon, and the blend of cultures is something totally new in religion. While some group rituals are done with a chosen high priestess, other groups prefer to have everyone participate, and several women lead the several sections of a ritual. A coven of six women becomes a coven of six high priestesses, six leaders, when developed this way, and the leadership skills gained from that reflect in the women's everyday lives. Each priestess becomes the god-dess in the course of the ritual, and remains the goddess when she goes home. Each of her sisters does the same. The women of a ritual sit down together to decide what to do in a ritual, and each participates in a creativity that extends beyond the group. Circles and covens in women's spirituality are composed of women only, women and female children.

All of these things are very different from traditional wicca, where there is a goddess and a god, and the role of high priestess and priest are taken by the same people at all times. The covens are composed of men, women and children, and in many covens, the high priestess writes the full ritual or draws it from her own handed-down tradition.

48

Consensus and improvisation are less in use, though the rituals run more smoothly and raise more directed energy. The consensus governing of women's spirituality is less coordinated than in groups with one leader, and until a circle has become fully bonded the momentum between sections in a ritual is delicate. Where in a traditional wiccan coven the high priestess and priest are the mother and father of the group, the goddess and the god, in a women's circle the members are direct equals. Love and joy are major forces in both ways of working, with sisterhood and woman-bonding primary in women's spirituality. Everyone in the circle is the goddess.

If the consensus organization of women's groups sounds structure-less, it is not. Consensus simply means that everyone agrees and that no one in the coven disagrees on a particular issue. Consensus is not always reached quickly, but once it is, everyone participating is happy with the decisions. Where no one has had to give in to a majority, everyone is willing and the group operates in peaceful balance.

Esbat or Sabbat rituals in this framework are structured on a basic outline that remains the same, but the content varies from ritual to ritual and season to season, varies with the way individual women create each part. The philosophy of groups on how formal or informal their rituals are, what tools to use, and how traditional or open, constructed or improvised they choose to be are things that vary. Some covens delight in theatricality and performance for their rituals, while others do not. Some emphasize sacredness and women's mysteries, while others prefer poetry or to party. Each circle is composed of women who are unique individuals, whose individuality is encouraged, and each woman's creative influence has equal weight in consensus group process. A circle whose membership contains a poet does different things from one influenced by a member that's a dancer: no two groups or two rituals in women's spirituality, within the structure, are alike.

A circle in sunny California celebrates Winter Solstice skyclad on a private beach; a similar women's coven in New England meets in someone's city living room dressed in jeans and heavy sweaters. The size of a given group is an aspect also in the choices and elaboration of their workings. A group of thirteen women, top size limit for most covens, has more resources to draw upon than a group of three, the lower limit in size, but the group of three is much more intimate. The outline remains the same, but its working out does not. Structure, though fluid, exists and is important.

The basic outline of a women's Sabbat or full moon ritual is as follows. First there is a process of checking in, of meeting and greeting among the members, and this may or may not be done formally. When the ritual starts, there is an easing into meditative moods and sacred space by a purification and a mood-attuning meditation. The circle is cast, the four directions and the center are invoked, and the main purpose of the ritual is begun. There is a raising of group energy, the cone of power, by chanting, music, invocation, visualization or further directed meditation, and a channeling and directing of the power raised. The energy is grounded, the circle opened, and a time of sharing and relaxation, of feasting and partying, ends the evening. While seriousness, grace and mystery are present, there is also lightness and joy—the joy of being together, of sharing and creating, the joy of celebrating the goddess and the season or moon.

Checking in is simply waiting for everyone to get there. Women talk informally, catching up on what everyone has done since they were last together. It can also be a formal process, with the group sitting in a circle and each in turn making a statement of what's happening in her life, what's affecting her in being there. For groups that meet infrequently and women with busy lives, checking in can be extremely important as an aspect of group bonding.

Purification is next, as an entry into the mood of ritual. It's a separation of the self from daily life, from traffic and jobs and general worries. The women sit on the floor in a circle, each wearing a necklace that pleases her, and each has added her chosen object to an altar in the center. Candles are lit, white or with colors that fit the season. Sometimes each woman brings her own candle, and always the electric lights are turned off. Nothing creates the mood of a ritual more than candle light.

The women pass a chalice or bowl of salt water clockwise around the circle. Each sprinkles herself or the woman to her left with a few drops of water. Salt is a purifier and water is the source of all life, the salty water a reminder of creation, oceans and birth origins. The sprinkling is done quietly, in silence or with a few words of opening, of why the ritual is being done. Sometimes there is the self-blessing.[2]

Stroking each other's auras with a large feather or stalk of wheat is another method of purification. Doing the same with a burning incense stick or smoking cedar branch are other ways. The stroking, which is done a few inches away from the body, starting at the head and moving to the feet, is soothing, balancing and calming. It removes negativity, and is a letting go. Incense smoke, along with being extremely pleasant

[2]See Chapter Five.

to most women, is a strong purifier and psychic opener. Stroking the aura with a live flower is a good purification, too. Use a daffodil for Spring Equinox, a white rose for Candlemas, and a stalk of wheat for Fall. Gear each aspect of the ritual to its season.

A guided meditation is next. This is led by one member of the coven, as the purification was led by another, or by the high priestess of the evening. It is written by the woman leading it, improvised, or taken from any of the books on the subject that are available. A major source-book for women's guided meditations is Diane Mariechild's *Mother Wit: A Feminist Guide to Psychic Development* (Trumansburg, NY, The Crossing Press, 1981).

Meditations are visualized journeys. They begin with a process of deep relaxation, of letting go of daily reality to enter the deeper realities of the inner mind. The group is directed to close their eyes and breathe deeply and slowly in rhythm, then to relax each part of the body, step-by-step, from the feet to the head. Once this relaxation takes place, the mind is receptive to follow the journey, to travel into new realms. These realms are inward, and again are geared to the Sabbat or to the purpose of the ritual. A guided meditation at Winter Solstice might involve birth, and at Candlemas a journey of emergence. Spring Equinox is growth and inner blooming, while a Beltane journey is loving and sexual. The Summer Solstice is fulfillment and Lammas anticipates harvest, personal harvests and ripening. The Fall Equinox is gathering in, the witches' Thanksgiving, and a meditation journey at Hallows could explore past lives.

Returning from the meditation, women are in a receptive state, psychically open and ready to cast a circle. The circle can also be cast after the purification, before the guided meditation begins. The act of casting a circle, creating protected sacred space and inviting the god-dess' presence from the four directions, is a central one in wiccan ritual. It is done in women's groups as poetry, as formal magick, or as a simple invitation to the directions and goddess. The four directions themselves (or eight in some traditions), and the series of things they correspond with, are visualized as spirit watchers, guides, guardians or goddess names. Along with each direction, some quality of the ritual can be invited—the goddess of beginnings for the east, of sisterhood for the south, flowing for the west, of caring for the north. These can be any aspects the women choose to bring into the ritual.

A formal circle casting is a thing of great beauty that invokes the protection of the goddess universe, and creates that universe below and within. One woman casts the entire circle, or different women call to each of the directions and the center. Choosing her athame—which in most women's covens is not the traditional sword—the priestess traces the outline of the circle behind the seated or standing women. She can also trace the circle by passing a stick of lit incense or a candle around it to her left (clockwise, deosil), or using a long feather or live daffodil, or whatever her choice of athame or wand. When the tool returns to her, she uses it with upraised arm to salute the earth and the sky.

The priestess invokes each direction, tracing an invoking pentacle in the air as she begins, and at the end of each, sprinkles a few drops of

Invoking

salt water toward it, saying, "By salt I purify the east." Then she holds a candle up to the direction, saying, "By fire I charge the east," (or west, or whichever direction she has invoked). She begins with the direction nearest to her left, begins with the east, or begins with the direction that corresponds closest to the season—the east for Candlemas and Spring Equinox, south for Beltane and Summer Solstice, west for Lammas and Fall Equinox, and north for Hallows and Yule. In traditions that use eight directions, there is one direction for each Sabbat.

Below are given sample invocations to each direction and the center, and a list of directional correspondences. A source of great beauty for more traditional circle casting material is Starhawk's *The Spiral Dance: A Rebirth of the Ancient Religion of the Great Goddess,* (San Francisco, Harper and Row Publishers, 1979).

While the steps are the same for casting a circle in most women's covens, the invocation is the group's creation. It invites the goddess' presence and protection at the ritual, and this is done in a variety of ways. Casting the circle is separate from invoking the directions in traditional wicca, but is often combined with it in women's spirituality rituals. Creating a sensual and visualized picture of the seasons and directions is an object of the invocations, and the full beauty and magick of wiccan ritual is embodied in them.

The center is the last direction cast and invoked; the culmination of the other four. In Spider Woman's creation story, her webs were cast to the four directions, and the strands bisected the circle at the center that

Invocation to the East[3]

blue flame
and the five pointed star
blue flaming star
pulsing door of the winds
tower of air of the east
raise the silver glint athame
to powers of the sky
raise the rose glint athame
to dawn and to spring
raise the violet glint athame
to knowledge
and mind

windhover falcon
eagle and lark
raise the silver lady's breath
through sky current wings
bright the rose of dawning
through all that is born
blow the violet of awakening
through the crocus pale stems
young eaglets young squirrels
new daughters
hail kore hail persephone hail
gaia
renewing rebirthing the air

---

[3]The Invocations to the East, West, North and South were first published by *Harvest,* (POB 228, S. Framingham, MA 01701), Vol. III, No. 4, Spring, 1983. Written by Diane Stein.

Invocation to the South

blue flame
and the five pointed star
blue flaming star
blue pulsing door of the sun
tower of fire the south
raise the wand alloyed
of metal heat
raise the sparkling wand
electric as the shocks
that raise a mind
raise the cone
of will

lioness
bright orange and gold
burning summer of the veld
candle flame
lightning rod
desert whirling wind
volcano flow and hearthside
combustion molten stars
the noonday glare
of solstice singing cells
hail goddess lady ishtar
star of tower south

Invocation to the West

blue flame
and the five pointed star
blue flaming star
pulsing star of the sea
tower of ocean the west
raise the shell curved chalice
of the brine of all that lives
of the wine of salty blood
warm milk of yemaya
the courage to raise
her seashell cup
and to dare

dolphin and mermaid
dragon and whale
anemone and coral cliff
surf sounding breaker sands
small fishes swim
inside the blue star door
sea green sea grey
sea twilight
smell of moon or autumn tides
hail lady hail cybele
hail inanna tiamat
star of the blue serpent flame

Invocation to the North

blue flame
and the five pointed star
blue flaming star
pulsing star of the planet
tower of mysteries the north
raise the pentacle
the unrevealed new moon
darkness and becoming
the maiden wakes alone
strength of body
of the mountain
and of all that comes from earth

cow with curved horns
night frozen under snow
brown of tree trunks sheathed in ice
hibernations of the bear
black of deepest wombs
unknown of unknowings
and of weight and hidden bone
from silence comes listening
from midnight comes morning
from winter the springtime
great demeter of dark caverns
of all birth

Invocation to the Center

mother of galaxies
cauldron of hecate
rainbows end
three legged cooking pot
oatmeal bowl
stew
sipapu
black hole
the goddess womb
stars rising
moons phasing
brew of ending to begin

enter in fragments
to be made whole
enter to be reborn
gestation
creation
dissolving
candle flame
bonfire
incense char
the wheel

who centers emerges
transformed

Correspondences[4]

East	South	West	North
air	fire	water	earth
athame	wand	chalice	crystal
morning	noon	evening	night
spring	summer	fall	winter
Candlemas Spring Equinox	Beltane Summer Solstice	Lammas Fall Equinox	Hallows Yule
birth	growth	aging	death
egg circle	triangle delta	seashell serpent	spiral labyrinth
Gaia Persephone	Ishtar Ashtoreth	Yemaya Inanna	Spider Woman Demeter
Persephone	Demeter	Demeter	Hecate
intellect	will	emotions	body
beginnings	fulfillments	flowings	endings
Gemini Libra Aquarius	Aries Leo Sagittarius	Cancer Scorpio Pisces	Taurus Virgo Capricorn
Crown Chakra & transpersonal point	root & belly chakras	throat & third eye	solar plexus & heart chakras
violet white	red orange	blue indigo	yellow green
topaz	ruby	aquamarine	quartz crystal
plains	valleys volcanoes	seas, rivers lakes	mountains
birds	animals	plants	minerals

---

[4]Various sources. Also see Starhawk, *The Spiral Dance: A Rebirth of the Ancient Religion of the Great Goddess*, p. 201 ff.

was herself. The center rerpesents birth and rebirth, creation, destruction, spirit and change. It's the *sipapu* of the kiva, and the Cauldron of Hecate in the story of Demeter and Persephone. It's the overflowing womb of Gaia or Demeter or Yemaya, the source of life. The wiccan chant, "She changes everything she touches, and everything she touches changes"[5] is symbolized in the center of the circle. It's the point of transformation, the mother's womb, where beginnings end and endings rebegin, and where time as we know it does not exist. The altar in most women's rituals is placed in the center, with objects on it to represent all four directions, the full moon or the Sabbat being celebrated, and a bowl or other open vessel symbolizing the cauldron. Where each woman brings a candle, her candle is there, representing herself as a part of the center.

When the circle is cast and the four directions and the center are invoked, the priestess again salutes the earth and sky and seals the circle. She does this by declaring the circle cast and the ritual begun, by passing a kiss to the woman on her left that travels clockwise around the group. The candles at the center are lit now, if they were not lit before. The coven has entered the protected space that is known as "between the worlds." The women are at the center of the universe, held securely in the goddess' womb, inside the egg, a place beyond time and mortality. The air crackles with energy, with excitement and heightened awareness, with power and peace. Once the circle is sealed, no one leaves it until its opening at the end of the ritual. If a woman *must* leave it, she symbolically traces a doorway in the circumference, and takes a portion of the circle with her until she returns. Leaving is not encouraged. It disturbs the delicate mood that has been achieved and interrupts the ritual.

With the circle cast and the directions and center invoked, the stage is set for the raising of power and the main working of the ritual. This is the celebration of a new moon, full moon or Sabbat, and could also be a healing. The object of ritual, done in many ways, is to raise group energy, the cone of power, and direct it for some purpose. It may be directed outwardly, to heal the earth or someone not present, inwardly to give healing, blessings or energy to women there, or channeled to make something visualized happen and manifest.

Power raised in women's spirituality covens is not the power of big businesses and patriarchy's oppressive governments. It is rather the inner power available to everyone, the ability to create, to make choices,

---

[5]Starhawk, *The Spiral Dance: A Rebirth of the Ancient Religion of the Great Goddess*, p. 67.

to direct one's own life. The cone of power is the energy of Be-ing, of active living, of validating and affirming the group and individual self, of joy, and of the goddess as part of everyone. This is never a power directed at others, even for healing, without their permission. It is not used to manipulate or influence anyone, only to direct and self-determine one's own goals, or a goal agreed upon by the women of the group. The power of women's spirituality and the goddess is power within, it is not externalized as power over others.

The cone of power is raised in a women's ritual in several ways, all of them based on the joining of women together, the merging of their auras and minds in a state of heightened psychic awareness. This merging and awareness have been carefully created in the ritual so far, in the purification, meditation and circle casting and invoking, in the candle lit room, the altar and in being together. Power is raised by chanting and singing, repeating a chant over and over until tension rises and mounts. It may be done in dance, or with musical or percussion instruments, by further invocations such as the Charge of the Goddess, or by directed visualization, theater or deeper meditation. This part of the ritual is more vital than quiet, and movement, sound and activity are involved.

While partaking of mystery, raising power is done with group excitement and joy. The women feel the power grow, feel it rise from each of them to merge into a fountain of light that surrounds them and leaps above. They add themselves to the rising cone, to the growth of energy that is almost visible and is certainly heard and felt. When the power reaches its fullest pitch, the women simultaneously or by a priestess halt it, hold it for a moment to feel its strength, then direct it where they wish it to go.

"We direct this power to the stopping of nuclear weapons."

"We direct this power to our prosperity for the year."

"We direct this power to helping Rebecca recover."

"We direct this power to the goddess, she who births and protects us all."

With raised arms, the women visualize the cone flying to its goals, or falling in a sparkling fireworks of blessings and joy on the members of the circle. Everyone is vitalized, glowing with the power raised, with the directed cone of energy. They breathe this vitality for a moment, this portion of the life force, take joy and pleasure in it, see it do its work, then ground it.

Grounding is done to release the excess of built up power. The energy raised by six or eight women together is more than each can receive or channel comfortably for long. Ungrounded energy causes emotional upsets, sleep disturbances and nervousness that are unwanted and unneeded. The women bend to the ground or sit on it, touching the earth with their palms or foreheads, and indoors reaching for the ground beneath floors. They visualize and feel excess energy flowing through their hands or third eye and into the earth, feel the power leaving them in moving waves. When they have released enough, and each woman knows by feeling what enough is, they lift their hands but remain sitting. The ritual is ended, the cone of power winging through the universe. The women are energized, aware and returned from psychic states. The circle is opened.

Opening the circle is simpler than casting it, and is a process of releasing the goddesses and spirits invoked, of thanking them for their presence and protection. Moving counterclockwise, the direction of unbinding, the priestess at each direction traces a banishing pentacle in

Banishing

the air with her athame. She begins at the direction invoked last, and says something like:

> Lady of the north,
> Spider Woman,
> Great Mother,
> Thank you for being with us.
> We ask your blessing
> As you leave our circle.
> Go in peace.

This is done at each direction. The priestess than releases the center, and raises her athame to salute the earth and sky once more. The traditional unsealing of the circle reads:

> The circle is open but unbroken.
> May the goddess' peace go with you.
>
> Merry meet and merry part,
> And merry meet again.
>
> Blessed be.[6]

---

[6]See also Starhawk, *The Spiral Dance: A Rebirth of the Ancient Religion of the Great Goddess*, p. 157-158.

The women are released from the ritual and the circle is open. Now is the time for feasting, for a sharing of cakes and ale (or coffee, herb tea, wine or fruit juice), for relaxing, partying, talk and fun. The group bonding that arose in the ritual makes the party all the more special. The women end the evening peaceful and fulfilled.

Often feasting is comprised of food that each woman contributes, a potluck dinner or snacks, or only fruit. Women who worship the goddess become very aware of what they eat, of what enters their goddess bodies and affects their mind states. Many women are vegetarians, refusing to kill things, and learn that non-meat diets enhance their psychic skills. Some covens use alcohol in their chalices for rituals and feasting, but many do not, preferring water, herb teas or white grape juice. Some herbs and herb combinations are psychic openers, that besides their good taste enhance rituals. Often the food brought to a potluck reflects the Sabbat, with mooncakes for lunar Esbats, breads and grains for Fall Equinox, eggs for Spring, or pomegranates for Hallows. The continuation of the ritual's theme into its afterward is another source of group bonding.

Using a sharing circle to end a ritual evening is another way to continue the ritual's mood and celebration. Each woman brings things to give away, and if there are five women in the coven, each brings five objects. The objects are small ones: copies of a poem, bits of gemstone, feathers, whole nutmegs, pieces of costume jewelry discarded in a drawer cleaning, seashells or things handmade. A blanket is set up somewhere in the room or ritual area and the contributions are placed on it. After the women have eaten, or while waiting for food to be set out, each goes to the blanket and chooses five objects for her own, any five that attract her. One woman's castoffs are her sister's treasures, and the delight of finding and taking starts discussions that affirm friendships.

Once the circle is opened, the happenings of the ritual are discussed too, and the work of preparing the feast and cleaning up is done together. Coven business meetings or the planning of the next ritual are not usually held the same night, but the setting of the next meeting is. Before leavetaking, there can be a group hug.

Women leave the ritual with a sense of continuity—they have participated in an event that is mirrored by individual women and women's circles around the world. If the night is a full moon, women everywhere are celebrating it with them, meeting in covens like their own, sharing altars and circle casting, feasting and sharing the group hugs, watching the goddess rise over the treetops, over the ocean, or through apartment windows as the moon herself. If the night is a Sabbat, then the goddess earth celebrates it with them, along with thousands of other women from Florida to Asia. The woman who celebrates the Sabbat solitary in her bedroom is likewise not alone.

The cycle of moon and the seasons celebrates the process of life from beginnings to endings to beginnings again. Symbolized in women's rituals, women who are themselves part of the cycles remember their own connectedness to them, remember they are part of the goddess and of all that lives. Ritual is a reenactment of the mysteries of the earth and universe, of birth, death, and the life force—of the goddess as creative deity and the goddess within each other and the self. Women together in covens and circles, and women alone, celebrate the goddess' rituals everywhere.

4

The Wheel of the Year – II
The Sabbats

Hear the words of the Great Goddess, Mother of the universe, she who is galaxies, the earth and moon, she who exists in all:

> I who am the beauty of the green earth and the white moon among the stars and the mysteries of the waters, I call upon your soul to arise and come unto me. For I am the soul of nature that gives life to the universe. From me all things proceed and unto me they must return. Let my worship be in the heart that rejoices, for behold—all acts of love and pleasure are my rituals. Let there be beauty and strength, power and compassion, honor and humility, mirth and reverence within you. And you who seek to know me, know that your seeking and yearning will avail you not, unless you know the mystery: for if that which you seek, you find not within yourself, you will never find it without. For behold, I have been with you from the beginning, and I am that which is attained at the end of desire.
>
> The Charge of the Goddess[1]

The Wheel of the Year consists of eight Sabbats that mark the seasons and are spaced approximately six weeks apart. These Sabbats, along with the full moons that occur every twenty-nine and a half days, are the formal rituals of women's spirituality. In them women connect their own lives to the life of the earth and the universe, realizing that all lives are one. They celebrate the goddess, the earth and the life force,

---

[1]Starhawk, *The Spiral Dance: A Rebirth of the Ancient Religion of the Great Goddess,* (San Francisco, Harper and Row Publishers, 1979, p. 76-77.

and see themselves as part of the beauty of the whole. While the rituals in this chapter are designed for groups, all of them are adaptable for solitary work. The details are deliberately left open, since the grace of a women's ritual comes from women's creativity in making it. These rituals are also only suggestions, with the possibilities as endless as the universe herself.

Covens and rituals in women's spirituality are very different from traditional wicca since they are composed of women only. The traditional Craft bases Sabbats on a male-female equal duality, Ishtar and Tammuz, where women's spirituality focuses on the completeness of the feminine, Persephone-Demeter-Hecate. The rituals in this book are designed for groups accepting either cycle, but that contain only women members. Women find that the dynamics of all female covens are very different from male-female groups. With their focus on feminine wholeness, they validate and release a sense of pride and Be-ing in women that patri-archy has long suppressed. The women's spirituality movement, while not denying the dualities of men's place in the universe and Craft, is committed to this reclaiming.

Winter Solstice (Usually December 22)

Winter Solstice is the night of longest dark, the point of deepest night and winter before the returning of new life. It's the last moment of gestation, the time in the womb that's about to end in birth, the nothing-ness that becomes the universe. The Hopi call this time Soyal, the time of turning the sun. This is the moment when Inanna begins her return from the underworld, and the moment again of her rescue of Tammuz in her second descent. The goddess returns from death to life, from winter to spring. Hecate releases Persephone to her mother Demeter; Tammuz and Persephone are reborn. It is no coincidence that Christianity's god-dess Mary birthed Jesus at the time of Yule. Winter Solstice is the moment of the goddess' birth herself, the point of creation to come at the next moment after. This is the first passage, into awareness, from nothingness to the chaos of all hope and potential. It's the total stillness of winter, the furthest descent before winter cold gives way. Rituals for Winter Solstice reflect the passage, the turning back, the birthing and awakening of death into life.

The circle area is decorated in winter white, with evergreens, holly and mistletoe, and the ritual uses white and red candles. A Christmas tree in the room is not out of keeping, as long as its light does not distract, and bells used in invoking the directions are an added touch. The altar is at the north quarter of the circle, the direction of winter and earth. It is made with a white cloth and decorated with gold, snowflakes, a goddess image draped in white, pine and holly boughs and objects for the four wintery directions.[2] A red candle for each woman present is placed on the altar, but not yet lit.

From the Hopi Soyal ceremony comes the rite of the Hawk Maidens.[3] The women begin the ritual by purification with cedar smoke or pine incense, and cast the circle and invoke the directions in their winter attributes, lighting white candles at the quarters. There is no other light in the room. At the center of the circle is a large nest, made with pine boughs or straw. In it are seeds of all kinds, and objects to symbolize life, people and animals—objects brought to it by the women of the coven who build it as part of the ritual. Feathers represent birds; small figures, toys or pictures are animals, insects and humans; seashells are marine life; the seeds are for plants and all nourishment.

The high priestess of the evening says,

> We are gathered here tonight to give birth, not only the births of our bodies, but the births of the universe and our minds' Being. The longest dark is the ending of the death from which all life is born. Tonight we turn back the sun, and our efforts birth the goddess, Persephone and Tammuz, all of life and ourselves.

Each woman of the coven takes her turn at sitting on the Hawk Maiden's nest, which tonight is the cauldron of transformations, and they brood the return of life. As each takes her place there, she talks of her own life's creations, of her hopes for the year, of her projects underway or beginning. When each has experienced this brooding before birth, this gestating of her life, she goes to the circle and lies down, curling herself into a fetal position, waiting for hatching and the birth of her hopes.

The women curled as fetuses meditate on darkness and non-being, dreaming in the state between life and death, listening to her sisters' dreams from the safety of the womb. The room is almost dark, and as the women finish on the nest and lie down, the room grows quiet with their meditation, nothing heard now but their breathing. One begins a

[2]Ed Fitch and Janine Renee, *Magical Rites from the Crystal Well,* (St. Paul, Llewellyn Publications, 1984), p. 46.
[3]Adapted from Frank Waters, *Book of the Hopi,* (New York, Ballantine Books, 1963), p. 196.

humming sound, a wordless chant, and the others take it up.[4] They are led in the process of birth by a woman of the circle, a priestess who massages each of them lovingly to life, or they experience birth simultaneously and themselves. As one woman is awakened, she helps to birth the next, or one curls in the circle alone for the others to birth her, and then another takes her place. The chanting continues throughout.

As the energy rises, the time within the womb, the time of sleep, waiting and non-being comes to an end. The women let go, choose life, are propelled into the world, into Be-ing and creation. They uncurl slowly, open their eyes and stretch, and are led and welcomed to the earth by their sisters. Each woman as she rises lights a red candle and places it on the altar. Born, she savors newness, savors feeling loved and cherished, savors the knowledge that all she hopes for is possible and beginning. She is the newborn goddess about to create the universe of her life, and she helps her sisters to be born as well.

As each woman lights her candle she remains standing in the circle. When all are standing and the altar glows with the women's light, they begin to chant and hum again or sing in an increasing tempo of emerging and Be-ing.

> Isis, Astarte,
> Diana, Hecate,
> Demeter, Kali—
> Inanna.

The cone of power forms, and the women channel it to nourish their creations and projects, to nourish the newborn goddess, Persephone, Tammuz and the earth. They direct it to creativity, to beginnings, to Being, to turning the sun, to spring. The women ground the energy by placing their hands on the floor, and open the circle. They keep the seeds from the nest for spring planting in their gardens to come.

Candlemas (February 1)

Candlemas is the feast of returning light, a festival of purification and dedication sacred to the moon in her three aspects. The equal armed cross or spiral are symbols of this Sabbat,[5] and it's a time of nurturing the fragile life flame born at Winter Solstice, the magick of new

---

[4]Adapted from Hallie Iglehart, *Womanspirit: A Guide to Women's Wisdom* (San Francisco, Harper and Row Publishers, 1983), p. 25-27.
[5]Janet and Stewart Farrar, *Eight Sabbats for Witches*, (London, Robert Hale, Ltd., 1981), p. 64.

fire and the life force. Candlemas is the day on which winter turns upward to the spring. Persephone, Tammuz and Inanna return from the underworld, and the sun child (maiden) born at Solstice nurses at her mother's breasts. Hecate, crone of winter, retreats from her reign.

Winter and death are cleansed away at Candlemas, the original spring cleaning, and as the days lengthen, hope grows for the warmth of new life. Candlemas is nurtured beginnings, a sweeping away of the past and an affirmation of things to come. The Hopi name this Sabbat Powamu, and symbolize it by the growth of hundreds of green bean sprouts—symbols of spring and the life force—in the kivas.[6]

Candlemas rituals in women's spirituality, reflecting traditional wicca and the Hopi Road of Life, nurture inspiration, creativity and healing. This is the feast of poets, the nine muses. It is also the time when women choose their ritual names, are initiated into the Craft and dedicate (or rededicate) themselves to the goddess. These are sacred acts not entered lightly, acts both powerful and empowering, and very personal things.

A Candlemas initiation ritual begins with purification, a cleansing away of winter by salt water, cedar smoke or incense of myrrh, rosemary or frankincense. Negativity and the past, the dead of winter, are dispelled. More incense burns in a cauldron at the center during the meditation and ritual, and one white candle is placed there—the rest of the room dark—when casting and invoking the circle.

The high priestess says,

> This is the feast of Candlemas,
> The time of returning light.
> Behold the three-form goddess,
> The maiden mother and crone.
>
> Without light there comes no darkness,
> Without darkness no light.
>
> Without spring there comes no summer,
> Without summer, no winter,
> Without winter, no spring.
>
> Blessed be the great mother—
> Persephone, Demeter, Hecate.
> Blessed be the moon in all her forms.[7]

---

[6]Frank Waters, *Book of the Hopi*, p. 214-215.
[7]Adapted from Janet and Stewart Farrar, *Eight Sabbats for Witches*, p. 70.

A woman asks to join the coven in perfect love and trust. She has been sponsored by everyone in the circle. The women prepare a candle-lit ritual bath for her, the water filled with lavender blossoms and rose petals.[8] They bathe and dry her lovingly, with laughter and quiet play. The women of the coven lead the initiate from the bath and return to the cast circle and altar.

The initiate's sponsor hands her the white lit candle from the center and escorts her to the east, presents the new maiden to Persephone and Gaia, the new moon. The initiate dedicates herself, in her own words, to beginnings and the goddess, and lights the white candle of the east. They move clockwise to the south, and she dedicates herself to Demeter and Ishtar, the full moon mother, to the growth of free will and the life force, and lights a white candle at the south. In the west, the new member and her sponsor invoke Demeter and Yemaya; the initiate dedicates her inner growth to the goddess of oceans, the waning moon. In the north she accepts endings, dark Hecate, darkest moon, and Spider Woman of the turning Wheel. She dedicates herself to the Road of Life, to accept-ing natural law, to creating and making positive her place in it.

When the four candles at the directions are lit, the initiate goes to the cauldron, still holding her central candle, and dedicates herself to spirit and transformation, to the connection of beginnings and endings. The women of the coven embrace and kiss her and begin a circle dance, the new member at the center, to raise power. The cone is directed at blessing, empowering and welcoming her, at blessing the new begin-nings in them all. Energy is grounded, the circle opened, and a feast is held in the new member's honor, for the maiden and the spring.

Candlemas is a time of great mystery and beauty. The mood is of untouched newness, of delicacy with great inward strength, the potential of awakenings. Rituals are not somber, but are not raucous either. Initiation is a passage into new realms, treated seriously, lovingly and with joy. Light returns with white candles, the birth of spring on the earth.

Spring Equinox (Usually March 22)

Spring is the time of bursting forth, of realizing the potentials of Winter Solstice and Candlemas. The eggs of the Solstice nest hatch into new springtime robins, new bear cubs, new flowers, new children, new joy. The fragile infants of Candlemas run on sturdy legs, inquisitive

---

[8]Vicki Noble, *Motherpeace: A Way to the Goddess Through Myth, Art and Tarot,* (San Francisco, Harper and Row Publishers, 1983), p. 123.

with rainbow brightness. Persephone returns to earth, playing with Demeter in fields of purple crocuses. Ishtar and Tammuz, the goddess and god, dance together, growing up together wild as the spring. The goddess is young, is the daughter—Gaia, Persephone, the Maiden—T'ui in the I Ching, the Ace of Cups or Fool in the tarot, a being filled with wonder and bursting with growth.

On the equinoxes, light and dark are equal in a moment's balance. At the Spring Equinox, light is ascending, and at the Fall Equinox the dark is. Spring is represented by the Wheel of Light, many green candles, and painted eggs. The Easter egg (Easter being a name from Oestar or perhaps Ishtar), was the cosmic egg of pre-Christianity, the goddess' egg opened by the serpent. Spring rituals in women's spirituality are bright with candles and blooming with fresh flowers. There are eggs to share on the altar, and color and abundance in the circle and the world. The Sabbat above all is for children, for one's daughter or the daughter in oneself.

The women of the coven meet. They choose flat ground out of doors or a room without rugs indoors. There are spring flowers everywhere, daffodils, daisies, heather, lilies and hyacinth. Flowers are planted to 'grow' from the ground, tied with bright ribbons to tree branches, piled in baskets or vases at the four directions. The altar is made with a circle of green candles, one for each woman present, a bowl of hard-boiled eggs, one for each, and a vase of daffodils, a stalk for each woman. The cauldron at center is filled with clear water; a piece of dry ice makes it boil for effect.[9] Purification is done with salt water, and the meditation travels to childhood, to childhood's favorite things.

Using a daffodil for an athame, the circle is cast and the directions invoked using flower names. There are white flowers in baskets at the east (daisies, lilies); yellow, orange or red ones at the south (daffodils, heather, daylilies); blue ones at the west (hyacinth, or water plants and ferns may be easier to find); and greens (ivy, herbs, fruit branches) at the north. Each woman comes to the altar to light her candle on it.

When the circle is cast, the women clear a space in its center to play childhood games. A hopscotch court is chalked or scratched on the floor or ground. In smaller space, try jacks, marbles, cat's cradle or Old Maid. The women of the coven are daughters again, letting their child selves come out to play. Awkward at first, their laughter fills the air, charging the circle with joy. Everyone is Persephone and Tammuz, the daughter goddess and the god. Power is raised by Round and Round the

---

[9]Ed Fitch and Janine Renee, *Magical Rites from the Crystal Well*, p. 20.

Mulberry Bush or London Bridge. Each woman takes a flower from the altar to carry in the dance as she sings.

The cone of power is directed to healing a laughter-starved world, to affirming the child in children and adults. After grounding, each woman receives an egg, symbol of blooming emergence, of the hatching of her winter hopes, of self-fulfilling birth. The circle is opened, and Oestar eggs are featured at the feast, green salads and fruit juices. "When I was little" stories keep the laughter flowing, and everyone leaves the ritual as refreshed as the springtime earth. The mood is right for a sharing blanket, a group hug. The women carry the flowers of the ritual home with them to remind them of their childhoods and child selves for many days.

Beltane (May 1)

The mood of delight continues at Beltane, the adolescence of the goddess year. The Equinox small child is almost grown, and is discovering her budding sexuality. In the Hopi Road of Life, there are no spring ceremonials. Planting time is too busy for them and is ceremonial enough. May—Uimuya—is the planting moon.[10] In the Ishtar-Tammuz cycle, the time is one of courtship and pursuit, frankly sexual and full of play and fun. The god chases the goddess in a green scarf dance, and she eludes and tantalizes him, allowing him finally to catch her.[11] Persephone and Demeter play a similar game, and lovers play it everywhere, portraying the fire and fertility of the earth's joy.

Beltane or Summer Solstice is the time of the Sacred Marriage in the Craft, and this is enacted symbolically or truly in some covens' rituals. Also are the customs of dancing skyclad in the growing fields on Beltane night for the fertility of the grain,[12] and of jumping over the Beltane fire. For Shekhinah Mountainwater, Beltane is first menstruation, the celebration of women's blood. The object of all of these is honoring Ishtar's (or Inanna's or Demeter's) sexuality, the life-giving fertility of the blooming planet. Sexuality at Beltane is an affirmation between woman and woman, between woman and man, between each and the goddess.

The women of the coven dance the weaving of life as a Beltane ritual. Each brings a roll of colored ribbon, and before the ceremony begins, they build a Maypole outdoors. Using a wooden laundry pole, they attach a one- to two-inch wide ribbon at the top for each member present, the ribbons half again longer than the pole. They dig a hole

---

[10] Frank Waters, *Book of the Hopi*, p. 235
[11] Janet and Stewart Farrar, *Eight Sabbats for Witches*, p. 88-92.
[12] *Ibid.*, p. 86.

deep enough to support the pole at the bottom, bracing it with large rocks. A Beltane fire is in readiness to one side of the Maypole, far enough away from the dancing but within the circle to be cast. This can be an actual bonfire, a small charcoal grill placed close to the ground, or a cauldron with a candle inside. It is not lit before the ceremony. As at Spring Equinox, there are flowers everywhere.

The women purify with feathers or cedar, and the meditation directs them to think of love, what love is in the fertility of their lives. The circle is cast, invoking the spring and blooming aspects of each goddess and direction, and using a green branch for an athame. The candle in the cauldron or the bonfire is lit, and the Maypole is the center of the circle. In the spirit of weaving, of Spider Woman's creation of the universe, each woman wears a garland of fresh flowers in her hair, and the weaving of these can be made a part of the ritual.

Each woman carries a percussion instrument in one hand, something that takes only one hand to play. Bells, rattles, shakers, tambourines and castanets work very well. Each selects her ribbon from the pole and they stand inside the cast circle.

The high priestess of the evening says,

> This is the time when sweet desire weds wild delight, the greening of the year. We weave this web of Spider Woman and of Ishtar to affirm life, to honor desire, to rejoice in the spiral. We meet in the time of flowering to renew the earth with our dance.[13]

The women begin the May dance, twirling and weaving the Maypole by their movement, singing and making music. Alternate women move clockwise, the others counterclockwise: they become two circles moving in opposite directions. As she passes her sisters in the dance, each woman goes under and then over her sisters' ribbons. When the pole is twined from tip to ground, they stop, and go to the Beltane fire, still singing,

> Weave, weave, weave, weave,
> Women weave the web of life.
>
> Weave, weave, weave, weave,
> Women weave the web.

The fire is stoked, and women jump over the burning flames, moving

---

[13]Adapted from Starhawk, *The Spiral Dance: A Rebirth of the Ancient Religion of the Great Goddess*, p. 176-177.

in circular clockwise procession for luck. As each leaps, she gives to the Beltane fire something she wants banished by love: any form of loneliness, discord, or disharmony. On her second turn, each woman draws a love wish from the fire's energy. They jump and wish several times, direct the rising cone of power, and sit on the earth to ground the energy they've raised.

After opening the circle, the women share cakes and wine, honey and grain cakes for the fertile season. They toast marshmallows in the fire and admire the Maypole, a woven work of rainbow art that stands in the circle all summer long.

Summer Solstice (Usually June 21)

Summer Solstice again turns the Wheel. Where at Winter, the light of spring returns and the sun is turned back, at Summer waxing ends and Winter is reaffirmed. This is the shortest night of the year, Midsummer's Night, and from here the circle wanes toward darkness and winter's mystery, though winter is still far away. In the Hopi Road of Life, the time is Niman Kachina, the Home Dance, when Kachina spirits leave the earth for the underworld until Winter Solstice's Soyal.[14] Summer Solstice is also the beginning descent of Inanna to the underworld in her jewels, and the sacrifice of Tammuz to death in her place. In the Persephone-Demeter story, it's the maiden Persephone's coming of age at menarche (Beltane) and her entrance to Hecate's realm. The earth at her greatest fulfillment consummates and embraces the other side, the death and ending that approaches but is not yet real. In this time of the year's greatest bounty, the opposite polarity to winter, birth and death are linked again as one.

Women design rituals that reflect fulfillment, abundance, consummation, the turning Wheel of love and fortune, and women's and the goddess' mature reign. This is a season of magickal mystery, of the aspect of the Mother, of entrances into the unknown. The fulfillment of wishes is the theme of a Brazilian Summer Solstice ritual for Iamanja (Yemaya), based on Merlin Stone's poetry [15] and adapted for coven work.

The coven meets near water on the night of Summer Solstice, by the sea, a pool or flowing stream. They make a bonfire at the circle's center. Where women meet for this Sabbat inland, a large water-filled cauldron

[14]Frank Waters, Book of the Hopi, p. 242.
[15]Merlin Stone, Ancient Mirrors of Womanhood: A Treasury of Goddess and Heroine Lore from Around the World, (Boston, Beacon Press Reprint, 1984), p. 96-97.

is used to represent the ocean, placed in the center of the circle and banked with flowers. Red and green are the colors of the ritual. A basket of red roses waits near the cauldron or by the shore, and there are seashells on the altar.

Purification is done with water from the sea or center cauldron, sprinkled from a rose. A similar rose, but not the same one, can be used for an athame. A red candle for each woman of the coven is placed to surround the cauldron or line the shore of the water. These are lit after casting and invoking the circle. The meditation and theme of the ritual are on fullness and abundance, the height of the earth's bounty, on love, and on the goddess as Yemaya, the Mother. The circle is cast and directions invoked, thanking each direction for her many prosperities and gifts.

Women meeting at the seashore or stream bank bring wishing boats, the boats of Yemaya, and float them in the water. These are made of bark, driftwood or large leaves, woven straw, tied sticks or flat shells; any buoyant, organic, non-polluting material. Logs from the center fire, their upward surfaces kept dry, are set upon the waters and lit as torches to illuminate the drifting boats. The women of the circle, each carrying a red candle and several roses, wade out to the fragile rafts before they move too far to reach. Their cares are washed away in the moving waters, given to the goddess' waves and shifting sands. Each woman wishes on a rose, one rose for each of her wishes, and sets the flowers on a raft to float to sea. When each woman has placed her wishes, she returns to shore, to the cauldron fire on the beach.

Women doing this ritual on land first dip their hands in the water-filled cauldron at the circle's center to wash away their cares. They visualize their worries leaving them, floating away and dissolving. Then they place their wishing roses, stems removed and without rafts, to float in the cauldron's water. The women's wishes, dreams, desires travel to the goddess of oceans, to Yemaya, gentle mother of birth and the Solstice. An aura of magickal beauty accompanies the flame-lit, candle-lit ritual, the flowers, wishes and dreams.

> Yemaya, ocean mother,
> We give you our wishes,
> Our dreams and our hearts.
> Protect us and comfort us,
> Wash away our cares.
> See our desires fulfilled,
> Our lives accomplished,
> With your love.

Chanting is used to raise power, "She shines for all, She burns in all,"[16] or the women move silently in a spiral dance. The energy of Solstice Night is vital and very strong. The cone is directed to the fulfill-ment of the wishes, and women at the beach ground by going into the water, on land by sitting and placing their hands on the earth. The women leave the Sabbat refreshed and renewed, knowing their wishes are fullfilled, even as Yemaya's boats float to sea.

Lammas (August 1)

Lammas is the Sabbat of first fruits and green corn, the ending of summer. The fertile, prosperous harvest that assures life's survival is nearly ready but not yet certain, is vulnerable to weather and change. Rituals in the Hopi to assure the harvest are the alternating Flute and Snake-Antelope ceremonies, rituals where women are prominent. The Sacred Marriage of the Hopi Road of Life occurs in this season, with the Snake Maiden that symbolized mother earth. In the Eastern and Pre-Hellenic cycles, Tammuz lies dead in the underworld and his body becomes the grain, the renewing nourishment that is the reason for his sacrifice. Persephone has entered the labyrinth, and Demeter the all-giver stops life's blooming. The goddess as reaper and all-taker, winter and Hecate, begins to claim the earth, though summer still reigns and days are longer than the nights. The time is one of waiting and changing, and focus is on things to come.

The women's ritual and altar are decorated with fruit, corn and grain—grapes, colored Indian corn, stalks and sheaves of wheat, oats or rice. The women make corn dolls as part of or outside the ritual, placing them on or near the altar, and taking them afterwards to decorate and bless their homes. A bowl of cornmeal is also on the altar. There is a fire at the center of the outdoor circle, or a cauldron with a candle indoors. At the edge of the fire or inside the cauldron is a loaf of cornbread or whole grain bread or a basket of poppy seed cakes. Green, orange and yellow are the candle colors, summer changing into fall, with green represent-ing prosperity.[17] A candle for each woman is lit after casting the circle and invoking the directions.

Purification is done by stroking the aura with a straw handbroom or using the leaf end of a shucked ear of corn. A different type of grain can be placed to mark each of the directions in a basket or sheaf, the

[16]Starhawk, *The Spiral Dance: A Rebirth of the Ancient Religion of the Great Goddess*, p. 174.
[17]Z. Budapest, *The Holy Book of Women's Mysteries, Part I*, (Oakland, CA, Susan B. Anthony Coven, No. 1, 1979), p. 44.

bread of transformation in the cauldron center, and the circle is cast with a wheat stalk athame. "What do you ask of the harvest?" is the theme of the ritual, and the women meditate on gaining prosperity, on accomplishing their needs and goals for the good of all.

The high priestess of the Sabbat says,

wheat ripens
apple reddens
time of waiting in the fields
time between the grain and bread
celebration of green corn
light shortens
year passes
aging enters on the earth
reapers ready for the scything
for the sacrifice of ending
harvest yet uncertain
as we join to turn the wheel

may her hope
be with us always
may her gathering grow sweet
may her hope
be with us always
may her gathering grow full
may her hope
be with us always
in the sheaf and in the seed
may her hope
be with us always

as We fade
and are reborn

A woman of the coven passes a chalice of wine or white grape juice clockwise around the cast and invoked circle. As each member receives it, she drinks a toast to the coming harvest, giving thanks, and stating the harvest's meaning in her own personal terms. Wine is the fruit of the season, symbol of the earth's abundance, and earth, sun and water are elements of summer and fall, the elements that mature the grapes and grain. This is a time of turning inward toward the darkness, of inner and individual work, a time of maturing and aging, of experience, growing wisdom, fulfillments past and to come. Lammas is change, the transformation of grapes into wine, of grain into baked bread, of summer into winter, the Mother into Crone, of life into death and back again. "She changes everything she touches, and everything she touches changes."[18]

Each woman takes a handful of cornmeal from the bowl on the altar. She goes to a corner of the room indoors, or outdoors to a private distance with the cornmeal in her hand. Indoors, she touches the cornmeal to her third eye, holding the rest in her left hand, and meditates privately on what harvests in her life she waits for and what she can do to achieve them. Outdoors, she digs a small hole in the earth, a *sipapu* or womb, and places her cornmeal in the hole. She tells the mother what harvests she needs from the earth, resolving how to achieve the goals in herself, and asking for blessings, prosperity and strength in making her goals real. Completing this, she thanks the goddess, and covering the cornmeal and hole with earth again, returns to the circle.

When all of the women return, the high priestess says,

> The harvest comes, harvest of foods of our labors. Good fortune and the goddess' blessings touch us all. May her bounty keep us strong in will and gentleness, in body, mind and spirit. May she bring us prosperity and peace.[19]

Power is raised by dance, the women moving clockwise to charge and affirm their harvests, then counterclockwise, inward in the direction of the year and the inner self, the labyrinth. They can chant or not while doing this. The cone of power is directed toward reaping the plenty of food on earth and achieving the women's needs, to prosperity for all. After grounding, but before the circle is opened, the women take the bread or cakes that have been near the fire or cauldron. They break them in pieces to share with each other, symbols of the transformed grain, of changing and aging seasons and the cauldron of Hecate, and eat them to end the ritual. The circle is opened, with thanks for harvests now and to come.

Fall Equinox (Usually September 22)

Fall is the witches' Thanksgiving, a time of gifts and blessings worldwide. The crops are harvested, the means to nourish life through the death of winter, and winter is not far away. Day and night are equal,

---

[18]Starhawk, *The Spiral Dance: A Rebirth of the Ancient Religion of the Great Goddess*, p. 67.
[19]Adapted from Z. Budapest, *The Holy Book of Women's Mysteries, Part I*, p. 45.

and the balance of giving and taking, of light and dark, summer and winter, life and death are the focus of the Sabbat. In the Hopi, the women's healing rituals of Lakon, Marawu and Owaqlt are held, emphasizing harvest, reproduction and the female life force.[20] In the Ishtar and Tammuz cycle, and Persephone and Demeter, Fall Equinox is the mourning of the goddess for her consort or child. The Eleusinian Mysteries and Thesmophoria of Demeter, Persephone and Hecate were held in the Fall Equinox and after it.[21] Though the year is waning and winter approaches, the emphasis is less on death than on the message of rebirth in the harvest seeds and the plenty of the season.

The women of the coven build an altar to the goddess. On it are objects to represent the four directions, a crystal cluster or largish rock for north, a conch shell for the west, a thick orange candle for the south, and a large feather for the east. There is an image of the goddess, a chalice of wine, cider or grape juice, another of salt water, and a vase or basket of fall flowers. A bowl of unshelled nuts becomes the cauldron and center when the circle is cast. The circle area is decorated with gourds, nuts and acorns, apples, pine cones, sheaves of corn and grain, chrysanthemums and turning leaves.

Purification is done with salt water, for this is the season of the west, or with corn straw or red leaves. The circle is cast and invoked, thanking each direction for the harvest and remembering her gifts. The priestess passes a kiss around the circle clockwise, and then the cup of wine. As each woman receives the chalice, she offers thanks for something in her life, something she has reaped. A libation to the earth is made, and a toast.

> Great goddess of life and good fortune, accept our thanks for
> our growth, insights, and accomplishments, and the sustain-
> ing food you have given us.[22]

The high priestess of the evening passes the crystal cluster or rock around the circle saying, "You are goddess. You hold the earth in your hands. What will you do to heal her?"[23] The women of the circle meditate on earth and reply,

"Demonstrate against nuclear armament."

"Clean up the field behind my yard."

[20]Frank Waters, *Book of the Hopi*, p. 283-291.
[21]Merlin Stone, *Ancient Mirrors of Womanhood*, p. 416.
[22]Z. Budapest, *The Holy Book of Women's Mysteries, Part I*, p. 45.
[23]Forever Forests, "Welcome to the Land of the Faeries!", in *Circle Network News*, Spring, 1984, p. 18. Ritual is adapted, and designed to be handicapped accessible.

"Respect my body."

The priestess next passes the conch shell, saying, "You are goddess. You hold the sea in your hands, the life source. What will you do to protect her?" The women of the coven reply,

"Save the seals and whales."

"Work for women's rights."

"Help clean up Lake Superior."

The process continues with the candle, "You hold fire in your hands, the spark of life. What will you do to rouse her?" And the feather, "You hold breath in your hands, creativity. What will you do to nurture her?" Finally the bowl of nuts is passed, and the high priestess says, "You are goddess. You hold immortality in your hands, the earth and universe. What will you do to love yourself?" The meditation lasts a longer time as each woman accepts the bowl. Replies may be aloud or silent and private.

When the objects are returned to the altar, a woman of the circle says, "We are given much in this season, and also must give. I ask a gift for the goddess from each of you." The women begin a sharing circle, each offering a small object to her sisters, or better yet sharing a skill or something creative. A poem, song, karate kata, piece of learning about the season, the use of a fall herb, a composition on the flute are all possibilities.

After this is done, the women sing to raise power and use harmonies and rounds:

> We all come from the goddess,
> And to her we shall return,
> Like a drop of rain,
> Flowing to the ocean.

They direct the cone of energy to healing themselves and the earth of negativity and damage, imagine the planet beautiful in an aura of glowing light. They ground by placing their hands on the earth and sitting down if they are standing. The circle is opened, and fall foods such as apples, nuts and cider are served in the Sabbat feast.

Hallows Eve (October 31)

She who would understand light must understand darkness, and honoring darkness is the theme of Hallows Eve. Hallows is the labyrinth of the underworld, the path of Persephone to Hecate and of Tammuz and Inanna to Erishkegal. It is the underground cavern of the land of death, the Isle of Apples and the womb, from which also comes rebirth and new life. On this night and from death, Persephone and Tammuz are conceived again in the womb of Demeter and Ishtar who come to seek them. In the Hopi cycle, the ceremony is Wuwuchim, when the plan of life and creation for the year is established in the universe and on earth.[24] It is the Hopi new year and the new year of wicca and women's spirituality, the time when the separation between life and death, between the born and unborn, the veil between the worlds, is at its thinnest.

Hallows is the dark moon and Hecate's rule, the descent into barren winter, the time of the white-haired Snow Queen. Yet it is the dark sky and dark night that make the new moon and new year possible, the intrinsic duality of new beginnings. A starclad, white-robed figure enters the Hopi Kiva and says, "I am the Beginning and the End,"[25] and this is the mystery and message of the Sabbat. That beginnings and endings meet is the great law and mystery, the circle and spiral of women's spirituality and the goddess.

Apples, pomegranates and mirrors decorate the women's altar, and objects of late fall—nuts, dried corn ears, pine cones and pumpkins— are used in the ritual area. A cauldron burns incense at the center of the circle, rosemary, frankincense and sandlewood,[26] and the pot is one that holds fire safely. A fireplace or outdoors fire, with glowing coals but little flame, is ideal. A dark-sided bowl filled with water, a hand mirror or crystal placed at the bottom, can also be used for the scrying portion of the ritual. Hallows is the time of contact with the dead and unborn, and this is the year's best night for scrying.[27]

A row of candles, alternating black and white ones, circle the altar unlit. The candles at the directions are white, and the black candles are lit after closing the circle. Purification is done with incense, breathing and circling the aura with smoke. Do not omit the purification on this night. The meditation is held until the main portion of the ritual, not done as usual in the beginning.

After the circle is closed, the high priestess of the evening says, "Tonight we celebrate Persephone and the pomegranate seeds of her death:

love apple
moon blood

[24]Frank Waters, *Book of the Hopi*, p. 168-187.
[25]*Ibid.*, p. 178.
[26]Scott Cunningham, *Magical Herbalism*, (St. Paul, Llewellyn Publications, 1983), p. 119.
[27]Themes for this ritual were suggested by Janet and Stewart Farrar, *Eight Sabbats for Witches*, p. 121-136.

woman's flesh and tears
tears that stain the hands
tears that fill the heart
the womb with fruit
seeds that stain and bleed
Persephone ate four tear drops
from inside the ruby globe
tasted blood from beneath
the poppy flower
beneath the clitoris' crown
she ate pomegranate
woman seeds
chose flesh and blood and tears
chose mortality the spiral
gained summer/winter/spring
gained giving living birth
chose to change sweet stasis
for the sweeter tasting wheel
for monthly blood
for sensuality
for woman's seed and fruit
gained blood
gained milk
gained salt and honey
and she tasted/gained the dark

The women of the coven begin a spiral dance, winding inward through the labyrinth, Persephone's path. This is done in silence, and a cone of power is immediately evident. They move counterclockwise (widdershins) into the darkness and winter, into the land of death. When the moment is right, the spiral changes to a counterclockwise circle, the women still moving slowly and solemnly around the cauldron or fire. Each woman in turn or at random casts something she would banish into the incense-smoking fire. This can be done verbally, or the women can write their negativities on pieces of paper to give to the flames.

"I banish rape," one woman says.

"I banish hunger in Africa and America," says another.

"I banish my unemployment."

"I banish the leak in my bedroom roof."

"I banish depression."

The things banished are the problems of everyday life, major and minor, and the list continues until the women run out of banishings to add. Thrown in the fire on paper, they flash and pop and are gone; verbally, imagine them doing the same.

When this is done, the women sit down in the circle, still lit only by the black candles at the altar and the white ones at the directions, and do a guided meditation. The meditation journey first relaxes them, then directs the women to remember one or more past lives. Several tapes are available for this journey, and there are past life meditations in books. Diane Mariechild's *Mother Wit: A Feminist Guide to Psychic Development* (Trumansburg, NY, The Crossing Press, 1981) has some good ones.

Returning from the meditation, the women are ready to scry. This is done by staring into the fire, incense smoke, a crystal or the mirror-bottomed dark bowl of water. The high priestess begins this by inviting positive spirits who wish to communicate to do so, and welcoming them. No woman forces the presence of any being or forces herself into realms she does not choose to go. When all have completed this, the women share their experiences quietly, telling what each has seen if she wishes to share it.

"This is the night that connects the dead to the living," a woman of the coven says. "We have journeyed into death." She blows out all of the black candles, leaving the room in near darkness. After a moment's meditation on the dark, she strikes a match and lights the white candles that surround the altar between the black ones. "Life is the other half of the Wheel."

The women rise and repeat the spiral dance, this time moving toward the light, clockwise from death into rebirth. The cone of power is raised once more, directed toward affirming the life force, then grounded by sitting down and allowing the excess to flow into the earth. The circle is opened, with recognition that the trip into the labyrinth is ended. The new year is begun, and past the coming winter waits the spring.

Sabbat Correspondences

Date	Sabbat	Other Names	Hopi Ceremonial
December 22	Winter Solstice	Yule	Soyal
February 2	Candlemas	Brigid Imbolc	Powamu
March 22	Spring Equinox	Eostar	[Isumuya–March Whispering Noises of Breezes
			Kwiyamuya–April Windbreaker
May 1	Beltane	May Eve	Uimuya—May Planting Moon][28]
June 22	Summer Solstice	Litha Mid- summer's Night	Niman Kachina Home Dance
August 1	Lammas	Lughnasadh First Fruits Green Corn	Flute Ceremony Snake-Antelope Ceremony
September 22	Fall Equinox	Mabon	Lakon Marawu Owaqlt
October 31	Hallows Eve	Samhain Hallows Halloween Witches New Year	Wuwuchim

[28]Frank Waters, *Book of the Hopi*, p. 235. Bracketed items are names of lunar months.

5

Self-Blessing

Women who celebrate the goddess celebrate and are part of the Wheel of the Year, and are also tuned on a daily basis to the cycles of the moon. The year is comprised of thirteen lunar months of twenty-nine and a half days each, as measured from the night of the new. Within the lunar month are four phases or quarters, climaxed by the full moon at the center. The moon waxes, increases in light, from the new to the full, and wanes or decreases in light from the full to the next beginning. The phases take approximately a week each to transit, and the time of the full includes three days before and after the actual full moon date.[1]

The moon is the goddess, visible and luminous, beautiful, shining and serene in all her forms. Modern patriarchy's attempts to conquer her in spacecraft have essentially failed, just as ancient patriarchy's attempts to conquer the goddess have not lessened her power or her mystery. She is the Maiden and daughter in her waxing—Persephone, Diana and Gaia newborn, Astarte newly risen from the sea, the Aces, Fool and Daughters in the tarot deck (Motherpeace), and all of the youthful aspects of women's lives. At full the moon is the mother goddess, the Empress and High Priestess—Demeter, Yemaya, Spider Woman, Ishtar and Ashtoreth—maturity, peace, power and abundance. The waning moon is dedicated to the goddess as Hecate or Inanna, the Shaman, Crone and Wisewoman, the dark aspect and grandmother. She is women's wisdom and experience of aging, of turning inward to validate the self at any life stage, and of the endings that change to rebegin.

---

[1]Marion Weinstein, *Earth Magic: A Dianic Book of Shadows,* (Custer, WA, Phoenix Publications, 1980), p. 35.

The phases of the moon affect all life, from the ocean tides to plant growth. If the moon in her distance rules the sea, it's not illogical that she rules women's bodies, since the physical human is 97% salt water. Women who celebrate the moon, living by lunar cycles instead of resisting them as solar-oriented patriarchy has taught men and women both, become in tune with the goddess, the moon and themselves. They become increasingly aware of the moon's influence in their physical and emotional lives.

The female menstrual cycle is an obvious correlation. Women who live together, particularly country women whose cycles are less disturbed by artificial lighting at night, discover that they menstruate together at the end of the moon's last quarter, the waning or new moon. They also ovulate together at the full.[2] Women's emotional tides and dream and creativity cycles are lunar influenced. Evidence indicates, too, that women who resist or repress these cycles are more likely to suffer menstrual pain and dysfunctions than women who recognize, utilize and flow with them.[3] The physical and nonphysical implications of these facts are obvious and profound. They are keys to women's power, and were likely the roots of power in the goddess-centered, pre-god, peaceful matriarchies. Power comes from within, almost literally, in a way that women's spirituality of today is only beginning to dis-cover and re-claim.

Women's moods and minds are as connected to the moon as their bodies are. The new moon is a time of beginnings, of ideas that are increasingly outward-directed as the moon waxes. This is a time of creativity, of words and actions, of making ideas manifest and real, putting them on paper, into clay or paint or everyday life. The full moon culminates this waxing cycle. She is an intense time of fulfilling the potentials and beginnings gained in the new and waxing periods. Her power is intense, too intense and nervous for some women, needing to be channeled; creativity at its manifesting peak. The waning moon is inward, a time of disintegration on some levels and the laying of new roots on others. Ideas are formed here, not yet gestated enough to express. This is the premenstrual time for some women, and may be marked by depression when the full moon intensity is not channeled or grounded enough. For many women who flow with the moon, the waning phases are their most productive times. The days at or preceding the new moon, menstruation, are days of gathering things together, of

---

[2]Helen G. Farias, "The College of Hera: The Beginning Lesson of the Pool", in *The Beltane Papers,* (POB 8, Clear Lake, WA 98235), Vol. 1, No. 8, Eostre, 1985, p. 20.
[3]*Ibid.*

preparations for beginning again,[4] of validating and honoring endings.

Stated simply, the waxing moon is outward and increasing, the full moon is power to channel for fulfillments, and the waning moon is the inward ending of one cycle by the laying of foundations for the next. Women who don't menstruate at the dark moon, or who don't menstruate at all, still find these observations valid, and some who work with lunar cycles find their bodies changing gradually and comfortably to fit them.

The rituals of women's spirituality and this chapter reflect the phases of the goddess moon. Because the moon is central in all women's lives, these are individual rituals, rituals done alone or shared with an intimate friend by women who flow with the goddess and the moon. As in the group rituals, these are adaptable to either group or solitary work, and are only suggestions, brief beginnings of the many possibilities to find and create from within. If something feels right to do in a ritual, then do it; its meaning becomes evident in the action. Likewise, and this is true in any ritual or act of women's spirituality, if something feels wrong to do for an individual or at a particular time, it shouldn't be done. Women's power is within, and a primary purpose of women's spirituality is the dis-covery of that. The answers and knowledge are within the goddess self.

Information on moon phase dates is printed on most calendars, but specific information and deeper working or astrology correlations require a lunar calendar. Nancy Passmore's *Lunar Calendar: Dedicated to the Goddess in Her Many Guises* comes immediately to mind. It is published yearly and available from Luna Press, POB 511, Kenmore Station, Boston, MA 02215. Llewellyn's yearly *Astrological Calendar, Daily Planetary Guide* datebook and *Moon Sign Book* offer lunar as well as astrological transits and information, and detailed material on planting and planning by the moon. These are available from Llewellyn Publications, POB 64383, St. Paul, MN 55164-0383. Susan Baylies' Snake and Snake Productions publishes a lovely and inexpensive single-page lunar calendar at POB 128, Copper Hill, VA 24979, and Sandra Pastorius' *Laughing Giraffe's Lunar Monthly Digest* is at POB 2344, Santa Cruz, CA 95062. The rituals and workings of this chapter require only the phase dates, though the phase times are desirable, and should be easy information to find.

---

[4]Ibid. Also, Penelope Shuttle and Peter Redgrove, *The Wise Wound: Eve's Curse and Everywoman*, (New York, Richard Marek Publishers, 1978), p. 113-114. Very highly recommended.

The New Moon

The new moon is an invitation to enter the labyrinth mystery, the mystery of initiation. Women enter the darkness, the unknown, without fear and experience their personal depths with joy and wonder.[5] The new moon is the beginning of the process, an entrance into the spiral of the goddess, the center of the self. Change begins on the new moon; the old is ended with the start of new cycles, leaving the positive to build on and the negative gone. The woman who menstruates at the end of the waning moon has completed a cycle of her body at this time, and like Diana, emerges unpregnant and Maiden. On the night of the new, time is poised between ends and beginnings, and as at the birth of anything, all things are possible in potential.

Women who honor the goddess also honor the goddess in themselves. They build or renew their altars at the new moon, and dedicate or rededicate themselves. A dedication of the self to the goddess is a blessing of the self to growth and women's Be-ing. It's an affirmation of choice and free will, of taking charge and responsibility for one's body and life, and also a willingness to enter the depths, the internal unknown, the dark lunar side of subconscious wisdom and personal self-knowledge and self-love.

A woman creates an altar to the goddess on the night of the new moon. She builds it in her bedroom on a dresser top in front of her mirror, on the floor, the top of a stool or a table anywhere in her home. An altar is as small or large, simple or complex as the woman wishes it. She covers the place with a scarf or brocaded cloth, and puts on her altar a white candle and objects for each of the four directions. She uses a favorite glass filled with salt water for the west, her candle in a holder for the south, incense or a pheasant's feather for the east, and a good-feeling crystal for the north. She places a small mirror at the center (if her altar isn't backed by a mirror), or a small bowl as her cauldron, a reminder of the self as goddess. The woman adds other things of nature, art or the season that please her—a seashell, pine cone, flower, a string of silver beads, sprig of yarrow, more candles, a poem. A small Kwan Yin statue is her goddess image. A less formal altar might have only the candle on it, or the candle and a flower, a photograph of any woman for the image, or whatever she wants to be there.

Formal craft tools for the directions are a chalice for the west, for

---

[5]Vicki Noble, *Motherpeace: A Way to the Goddess Through Myth, Art and Tarot*, (San Francisco, Harper and Row Publishers, 1983), p. 129.

water; a wand or candle for the south, for fire; an athame for the east, for air; and a pentacle of clay for the north, for earth. The center of the formal altar includes an iron pot or ceramic bowl, the cauldron of transformation and spirit. These objects and correspondences are flexible in women's spirituality and women's altars. Objects that have personal meaning, and especially that are natural or hand made are the most often used. Building an altar is a creative act, a gathering together of symbols that are beautiful and that invoke feeling in the woman who uses it. The goddess is everywhere and in all things of pleasure and beauty; anything that feels right belongs there.

In traditional witchcraft, the oldest and most sacred of goddess altars is the living and vibrant female body,[6] and honoring that body is a ritual of the new moon. When a woman consecrates her altar, she consecrates symbolically the earth, the goddess' body, and her own, and does so again in the self-blessing ritual. These are particularly powerful acts on the night of the new moon, acts that validate, honor and empower the woman who performs them. They are acts that connect an individual woman with all women and with the Be-ing of the goddess as the moon and earth. The rituals are an entrance into the labyrinth, the mystery and depths of the connections between the self and divinity, between body and mind, between physical and spiritual essence, between all life and immortality. The lack of this connectedness is one of the imbalances of patriarchy and modern religions and governments. "Thou art goddess," is a principle wiccan rule.

On the night of the new moon, the woman prepares a ritual bath, candlelit and strewn with herbs,[7] as preparation and purification for ritual. Wearing a necklace that pleases her, symbol of the circle of life, she enters the warm bath and allows it to relax her completely, taking her time to wash away the day's cares and remove her from the daily world. The room is silent or backed by soothing, nonvocal music, such as that of Kay Gardner or Georgia Kelly. Emerging from the bath as Persephone, as Diana renewed by the sacred pool, she dries herself slowly, paying attention to the beauty of every part of her body in turn. If her hair is long, she loosens it to flow freely, and she does not dress.

The woman stands or sits before her altar and lights the white candle; there is no other light in the room and the room is now silent. To dedicate or rededicate her altar, she lights incense of vervain, frankincense,

[6]Janet and Stewart Farrar, *What Witches Do,* (Custer, WA, Phoenix Publishing Co, 1983), p. 79.
  "For in the old time, Woman was the altar, . . . / the origin of all things, / Therefore should we adore it."
[7]Z. Budapest suggests vervain in *The Holy Book of Women's Mysteries, Part I,* (Oakland, CA, Susan B. Anthony Coven, No. 1, 1979), p. 70.

rosemary,[8] or rose, but changes to rose for her self-dedication, as rose is a love-drawing scent. (These herbs are inexpensive, and they and the charcoal blocks to burn them on are available at food co-ops or herb stores in most cities, and also by mail through many catalogs. Flat thick seashells make good burners and are attractive.) The priestess sprinkles salt water from her chalice on each object and says,

> I bless this altar and dedicate it to the goddess, to Demeter, Yemaya, Spider Woman, Gaia. Let it have power for goodness and to do my will, tonight on the new moon and in all the nights to come.

Once the altar is consecrated, the woman uses its objects to cast a circle and invoke the directions, either formally or informally, as in rituals for groups. She uses goddess names and attributes in her workings that have personal meaning for her, and invites the goddess' presence and protection in her circle. She then begins the self-blessing.

Standing on salt sprinkled on the floor or onto a sheet of white paper, the woman wets her fingers with a few drops of water (wine or oil can also be used) from her altar chalice and touches them to the top of her head, the crown chakra, *kopavi* of Spider Woman. Visualizing the chakra's clear violet color, she says,

"Bless me mother, who is your child."[9]

She dips her fingers into the water again and touches her third eye, the indigo chakra between and just above the eyes, and visualizing the color says,[9a]

"Bless my mind's eye that I may think of you and see you clearly."

She wets her fingers again and touches her throat chakra, visualizing its healing sky blue color, saying,

"Bless my throat that I may speak well, and speak of you."

She touches her breastbone, the green colored heart chakra, and says,

"Bless my heart that it be open to your essence."

She touches drops of water to her solar plexus, the navel chakra, imagining its bright yellow color, and says,

"Bless the center of my energy, that I am centered in your earth."

She touches her lower abdomen, the orange belly chakra of her womb and ovaries, and says,

---

[8]Scott Cunningham, *Magical Herbalism*, (St. Paul, MN, Llewellyn Publications, 1983), p. 25.
[9]References for this traditional ritual come from: Migene Gonzalez-Wippler, *The Complete Book of Spells, Ceremonies and Magic*, (NY, Crown Publishing Co., 1978), p. 266-267, and Helen G. Farias, "The College of Hera: The Beginning Lesson of the Pool," in *The Beltane Papers*, Eostre, 1985, p. 23. Ritual is adapted to chakras.
[9a]The color and chakra designations given in this book are the ones most personally familiar, but there are several other systems and correspondence sets. Choose what works and feels right for the individual using it.

"Bless my womb that creates new children, new ideas in your name."

She touches her genitals with the chalice water, visualizing the clear red root chakra spiraling with energy, and says,

"Bless my vagina, gateway of life and pleasure, *sipapu* of emergence, the labyrinth."

Finishing the chakras, the woman can stop and complete the ritual, go on to her hands and feet, or go to the senses. She blesses her eyes, "That I may see you"; her ears, "That I may hear your names"; her nose, "That I may breathe your fragrance"; her lips, "That I may speak of you". She blesses her breasts, "That I may nurture, as you have nurtured me."

She touches the water to the palm of each hand, saying, "Bless my hands that I may do your work and healing," and touches the sole of each foot saying,

"Bless my feet, that I may walk in your paths."

To complete the ritual, the priestess says,

"Bless me mother, who is a part of you,"

and she takes a sip of water from the chalice. She meditates on the chakras and senses as she does the ritual, on herself as a part of the goddess and interconnected with all of life. Looking in the mirror at the center of her altar, she sees goddess and herself.

When she has meditated enough and feels calm, renewed, relaxed and generally very clean and good, she opens the circle, thanking the directions and goddess for her presence. She blows out the candle, saying, "So mote it be" to seal the ritual, and allows the incense to burn itself out. Placing her hands on the floor, she earths the excess energy, saying, "Thank you" to the goddess, and ends the ritual with, "Blessed be."

The Full Moon

The full moon is the matron, the Mother and Lover, accepting or rejecting the beginnings of new life.[10] She is woman at the height of her choices, strength, and power, the High Priestess and Empress of the tarot, the goddess-creator of her own paths, and the lunar labyrinth source of life and birth. She is Demeter and Gaia, the mature all-giver, Selene and Venus-Aphrodite, Spider Woman of the creative cape, Hera, and Yemaya, mother of oceans. The full moon is Ishtar/Ashtoreth/

[10]Helen G. Farias, "The College of Hera: The Lesson of the Cave of the Moon", in *The Beltane Papers*, (POB 8, Clear Lake, WA 98235), Vol. 2, No. 1, Beltane, 1985, p. 19.

Inanna and Astarte, the goddess of sexuality extending her favors in the fire and ecstasy of pleasuring her body.

The full moon is fertility, birth and abundance in traditional wicca and in women's spirituality, but fertility for women is far more than literal pregnancy and birth. The Mother aspect means taking self-decision of women's lives, and includes both mind and body actions. Women are the source of birth, the source of life for others and themselves. Be-ing is creative and women's creativity is also her fertility, her artistry and grace in producing beauty in her life and sharing it with others, in creating her own environments and survival.

Fertility includes the full moon conception of children, as well as of books, music, photography and paintings, the creation of films and stage plays, pottery and poems, the making of businesses, homes and rituals. Whether or not to become pregnant or continue a pregnancy is each woman's personal decision, separate from her sexuality and other creativity, and subject to nothing but herself. The full moon radiates power, the energy of free will and empowerment from within, and all acts of love, pleasure and creation are the goddess' full moon rituals.

Women who menstruate on the dark moon ovulate on the full, and some are aware of the moment that they do so. It is also true that many moon-celebrating women are in life stages before or after their years of ovulating and menstruating, that women who are pregnant do not menstruate, and that many menstruating women experience irregular cycles. Pollution, artificial lighting, and nutrition loaded with chemical additives affect and disturb women's cycles and change the nature of women's life stages; but the phases, emotions and dream wheels of the lunar month are still valid. On the full moon or at ovulation, women dream of babies and breasts, of eggs and round pearls or moons.[11] Gonzalez-Wippler lists the full moon week as a time of precognitive dreams, dreams that come true.[12] It's a time when women experience a surge of energy that if unchanneled becomes nervousness. Channeled and directed, this surge of women's full moon power initiates actions that make wishes and dreams happen, brings gestations to births, interconnects women everywhere, and moves the new moon's beginning ideas into manifest realities. At the full, women reach the peak of their will and creative Be-ing, and drawing down the moon become goddess.

In women's spirituality, full moon rituals are "The Infinity of Solu-

[11]Helen G. Farias, "The College of Hera: The Beginning Lesson of the Pool", in *The Beltane Papers*, Eostre, 1985, p. 21.
[12]Migene Gonzalez-Wippler, *The Complete Book of Spells, Ceremonies and Magic*, p. 228.

tion,"[13] and are done as powerfully alone as with a group. The solitary woman at her altar who draws down the moon empowers herself in ways that no other ritual can duplicate. The act is universal; a woman who takes the full moon into her body, who ritually becomes the creative goddess, shares the act with thousands of women everywhere who are doing the same and are doing it at the same time. Attempting on the full moon to connect with these like-minded women through scrying or meditation is a vital and wondrous experience.

Affirmations, the thanks and wishes ritual done on the waxing and full moon, inspirits the goddess into the woman's subconscious. By stating her wishes aloud as already fulfilled and visualizing them as obtained, the woman as goddess makes them happen. She creates a thought form in the universe that filters down to the material earth, and by her own real actions makes her dreams come true. Drawing down the moon, affirmations, and connecting with women and the earth are the skills and power of a woman's full moon ritual.

On the night of the full moon, and at the astrological full moon time if possible, the woman who is priestess prepares her ritual to the goddess. Indoors she bathes and comes to her altar skyclad, her hair free and she wears only a necklace. Outdoors in a private place she makes her altar on the earth and purifies herself with incense or salt water, skyclad or wearing what she will. She lights a white candle, breathes or meditates to a reflective state, casts a circle and invokes the four directions and the center. Then she calls down the moon.

The woman stands with her feet wide apart and her head raised, eyes facing the moon outdoors, or indoors facing her through a window. If the moon is not seen, it can be visualized in the candle flame and still invoked. She holds her arms straight out at the shoulders, then lifts them reaching upward, palms facing, her body forming a chalice in salute.[14] In her hand, the woman holds the wand or athame of her choice, and uses it to trace an invoking (clockwise) pentacle over the moon's face, or indoors over her candle flame. Bringing the tool down to touch her heart chakra with its point,[15] the woman speaks the Charge of the Goddess or says,

---

[13]Marion Weinstein, *Earth Magic: A Dianic Book of Shadows*, p. 35.
[14]Selena Fox, "Ritual Gestures: Making Magic with Body Language," in *Circle Network News*, (POB 219, Mt. Horeb, WI 53572), Summer, 1985, p. 11.
[15]Marion Weinstein, *Earth Magic: A Dianic Book of Shadows*, p. 35-36.

Come to me and fill me with your light,
Enter me shining in your fullness,
That I may use your power for my good

And for the good of all.

The moon now part of her, the woman stands in its light, feeling herself bathed in moonlight, and the goddess' full moon radiance filling her body and spirit. She asks of this power coursing through her what she wills, the wishes for herself that are also for the good of all, and does this by way of affirmations.

Making herself comfortable outdoors or in front of her altar, under moonlight, and carrying the moon goddess' radiance, the woman begins her affirmations. These are a list of wishes voiced aloud and in positive-present terms. She states each wish as "I have" or "I am", and as she speaks each one, she visualizes herself having what she asks for. The image firmly in her mind's eye, she uses the full moon's radiant aura—that is her own radiant aura—to surround the picture with light, blesses it, then goes on to her next wish.[16]

Marion Weinstein suggests each third month as a "List Moon," when thanks and wishes are both named and visualized.[17] Some women who do affirmations do them with every full moon, on every night of the waxing phases, or even every night. When doing them at all, the visualization of wishes as already fulfilled is the important act, of seeing the affirmations in the present tense. Women remember in wishing, too, that "What goes out comes back threefold," and the other wise woman's adage that wryly warns, "Be careful what you ask for, you may get it."[18]

To complete her affirmations, the woman offers thanks and says,

I have all these things or their equivalents or better. I have them according to free will, for my good and the good of all, harming or manipulating none. I have these things and use them well, by the great mother, by Spider Woman and Yemaya, by the power of the full moon. Blessed be.[19]

[16]More on visualization and meditation is discussed in Ch. VI. For a wonderful book on the subject, see Melita Denning and Osbome Phillips, *The Llewellyn Practical Guide to Creative Visualization*, (St. Paul, Llewellyn Publications, 1984).
[17]Marion Weinstein, *Earth Magic: A Dianic Book of Shadows*, p. 37.
[18]Principle wiccan sayings.
[19]The concepts here are from Marion Weinstein, *Earth Magic: A Dianic Book of Shadows*, p. 36, and Marion Weinstein, *Positive Magic*, (Custer, WA, Phoenix Publishing Co., 1981), p. 208. ff

by the power of the full moon. Blessed be.[19]

The woman looks up to the moon, or visualizes her again in her candle. She thinks of how the moon shines on women everywhere, how the goddess is everywhere, and how women planetwide are invoking and wishing on her tonight. The priestess asks that her heart be open to other women in their full moon rituals, that she feels their presence and knows she is not alone.[20] She visualizes the women she knows personally who have drawn down the moon at this time, sees their faces in her mind, feels them invoking the goddess as she did, and feels her own pull of love toward women everywhere. Her heart chakra opened by the ritual, she channels the moon-lit energy of her love toward greeting her friends and feeling their greetings in return. Quietly and surely, she knows they are there. Then visualizing women everywhere, known and unknown, she sees the thousands of women of the earth who alone and in circles and covens, from Africa to Chicago to Belgium to South America to China, are drawing down the full moon. Radiating love from her heart, she touches them in greeting and feels their love and greetings in return.

Visualizing once again, the woman sees the earth from space, lit from afar by the goddess moon. She surrounds the earth with a rainbow of love and protection: red, orange, yellow, green, blue, indigo, violet and white. She imagines the beauty of the earth from space, turning on its axis through day and darkness, and the moon waxing and waning in her cycles. Sending her love and healing to the goddess moon and earth, the woman sees the planet strong and clear and filled with peace, then herself strong and happy in her place in the world.

Returning to that place of strength and happiness on earth, the full moon priestess salutes the moon once more. She draws the unbinding pentacle (counterclockwise) to open her circle, thanking the moon for her presence. She releases and thanks the directions and center, says, "So mote it be" to seal the ritual, and blows out her candle. Bending to the earth, returning to it on the earthly plane, she puts her hands on the ground and channels from her body any excess of full moon energy. She thanks the goddess and says, "Blessed be," and remains sitting with her palms to the earth until she feels present once more. Carrying a bit of the radiant goddess moon within her, the woman returns to her

---

[19]The concepts here are from Marion Weinstein, *Earth Magic: A Dianic Book of Shadows*, p. 36, and Marion Weinstein, *Positive Magic*, (Custer, WA, Phoenix Publishing Co., 1981), p. 208. ff

[20]Adapted from a full moon meditation from Light-Works, Tel-Empathy Network, 85 Bolinas Rd., #16, Fairfax, CA 94930

own life. She sleeps well, dreaming of moon symbols, ready to create or conceive if she chooses, and ready for the choices of daily life in the morning.

The Waning Moon

The waning moon is the ancient grandmother, the ending of cycles and the honoring of darkness. Fading and then unseen, she is the labyrinth of experience, wisdom, transformations and rebirth. Men fear the waning moon but women embrace her. She is both the brooding universe and the death, letting go and change that precedes new beginnings and renewals.

Hecate is the goddess of the last quarter moon, the Crone, Hermit, Shamans, Wisewoman or Death cards of the tarot. Rejecting conception and the Mother aspect, she is menopause and menstruation, the goddess as all-taker and changer. The daughter of the new moon, Persephone, becomes Demeter the Mother on the full and Hecate the Crone in the waning cycles. The time is a life passage and a second initiation, parallel to Persephone's menarche, the menopause rite of passage to a new life stage[21] or the menstrual letting go of new life.

Dark moon Hecate is the woman and the cauldron, the birth in death aspect, and the *sipapu* center of becoming. Snakes with their shedding and renewing skins, their closeness to the earth, their inwardness, are waning moon symbols.[22] All that ends is part of Hecate and all that begins, begins within her. The time of darkening is one of gathering-in, of walking within the power of the labyrinth. Knowledge enters the cauldron and foundations are made, roots extended downward toward the center. Women finish things begun on waxing cycles, follow up and follow through, plan, edit and lay new roots. After the new moon, these roots and root beginnings turn upward, to emerge, manifest and create. One thing becomes another in the inter-connectedness of life: the Wheel has no beginning and no end.

The waning moon is woman's body, the cauldron as womb. For ovulating women who haven't conceived, these are the premenstrual and menstrual days, the time when rejected conception is released and the cycle is renewed. There is an emotional let-down after the full moon's active and outward intensity, and women become more celibate by

---

[21]Helen G. Farias, "The College of Hera: The Beginning Lesson of the Pool," in *The Beltane Papers*, Eostre, 1985, p. 21.
[22]Lee Lanning and Nett Hart, *Ripening: An Almanac of Lesbian Lore and Vision*, (Minneapolis, Word Weavers, 1981), p. 54.

conscious or unconscious choice. Dreams for many women at this time are sexual and can be violent; the dreamer wants to deny them,[23] but waning moon violence seldom manifests. Not focused on lover or children, on outward others, the waning moon Crone of menstruation or menopause affirms her own needs. Self-acceptance in this phase, moving with and not against the lunar cycles, prevents depression and being 'premenstrual' or 'menopausal'. Honoring Hecate in oneself leads to a space of reflective calm, of heightened sensitivity and awareness. Introversion and spirituality are strong now, and this is a time of learning, of developing and using psychic skills.

Women's body is the source of life, whether she chooses to produce life herself or not, whether she is in her fertile years or not, and the moon as creative goddess, waxing and waning, is the cycle of women. The shedding of blood in menstruation and the letting-go of this shedding in menopause are part of the cycles of women and the moon. Patriarchy's parody of women's monthly bloodshed is war, and menstruation and menopause are war's opposites, an affirmation of peace and the goddess' life force.[24] The time of the Crone and the cauldron, the dark time of change, is women's greatest time of personal power. Menstruation's onset brings release and the start of a new cycle; menopause is the release from menstruation, from childbearing and raising, and another passage of the labyrinth. These are the aspects of Hecate, the serpent-symboled goddess, the darkening moon.

Women's waning moon rituals are healings and banishings, protections, letting go rituals, purifications for renewal and divinations. The time is a good one for past life meditations, for scrying to touch aspects of the earth or inner self, for breaking negative habits, letting go of past love affairs, and releasing people and needs that are gone. Discarding what is no longer useful opens up new starts. All of this is done gently, with love and without blame. As in the new and full moon rituals, emphasis is on women's loving themselves, valuing themselves and the beauty of their bodies, getting in tune with who they are in creative Be-ing, who they are as goddess. Waning moon rituals in women's spirituality affirm the hidden side of the labyrinth. They recognize and tap into women's power, making women aware of the grace and positivity of endings, of the darkness and depths within.

On a night of the last quarter moon, a woman takes a ritual bath

---

[23]Helen G. Garias, "The Gollege of Hera: The Beginning Lesson of the Pool", in *The Beltane Papers,* Eostre, 1985, p. 21.
[24]Helen G. Farias, "The Nine Precepts of the College of Hera", in *The Beltane Papers,* Beltane, 1985, p. 21. Also, Penelope Shuttle and Peter Redgrove, *The Wise Wound: Eve's Curse and Everywoman,* p. 68

and comes skyclad to her altar. She has begun menstruation,[25] and wears on her body a symbol of this, perhaps a crystal on a red cord[26] for her necklace or a red woven belt at her waist. On her altar she places white and red candles, a skein of black thread, a shell or dishful of dried beans, and a cauldron-bowl filled with fresh earth. She has on her altar other objects that are meaningful to her, especially objects of the earth element.

The bath is a purification and relaxant, and the woman increases this by lighting incense of sage, cedar, sandlewood or pine, and breath-ing the smoke surrounding herself and her altar with the fragrance. Sage as an incense is symbolic of protection and of rites of passage.[27] She casts a circle, only the white candle lit, then honoring Hecate, she blows the candle out.

Sitting comfortably in darkness the woman meditates on night and the waning moon, on the ending and beginning of cycles. She visualizes the dark as a velvet cloak,[28] comforting and warming her, healing her of all stress and worry. She feels herself held in the protection of the moon goddess, dark Hecate, the grandmother goddess of rest and peace. Going deeper and drawing the cloak in with her, the woman realizes she is safe within the goddess' womb, and that the goddess' womb is also her own. She feels the warmth and darkness of her body and pauses to honor it, and watches the process of change beginning within. The woman feels the firm roundness of red uterine walls and touches their living cushion of the blood of life. Becoming aware of color, texture, taste, odor, she affirms each of these, embraces them as wonders and good. When she has done this, she leaves the womb, the cloak of velvet darkness now within her.

Remembering her womb, the woman lights the red candle on her altar. She draws its light into her awareness and body, feels it filling her uterus with warmth and pleasing energy. Visualizing this, she sees menstruation beginning within her, the shedding of the old cycle. She watches the bleeding happen, watches it cleansing and renewing her light-filled body. Moments of endings are new beginnings, the lesson of Hecate's darkening moon.

---

[25]Women not menstruating adapt this ritual to their needs, as rite of passage for menopause or simply to honor the waning moon.

[26]Helen G. Farias, "The College of Hera: The Beginning Lesson of the Pool", in *The Beltane Papers*, Eostre, 1985, p. 22.

[27]Billie Potts, in *Dreaming: An Almanac of Lesbian Lore and Vision*, Nett Hart and Lee Lanning, Eds., (Minneapolis, Word Weavers, 1983), p. 87.

[28]Adapted from Diane Mariechild, *Mother Wit: A Feminist Guide to Psychic Development*, (Trumansburg, NY, The Crossing Press, 1981), p. 20, and Starhawk, *The Spiral Dance: A Rebirth of the Ancient Religion of the Great Goddess*, (San Francisco, Harper and Row Publishers, 1979), p. 121-122.

Anointing the red candle with a drop of her menstrual blood, the priestess says,

> Blood must be shed. Let the sacred mystery be acknowledged and honored. I shed my blood for renewal, that life may continue, my own and all the earth's, this waning moon.[34]

She takes the black thread from her altar and unwinds a strand from the skein.[35] Making a loop around the lit candle, the woman says,

"With this shedding I shed worry,"

and she ties a knot. Making another loop and knot, she says,

"With this shedding I shed fear."

She lists the things in her life that she wants to release, to banish and shed from her life, and with each statement she makes a loop of thread around the candle and knots it.

"With this shedding I shed insecurity."

"With this shedding I shed disharmony."

"With this shedding I shed scarcity."

"With this shedding I shed loneliness."

"With this shedding I shed pain."

As she ties each knot, she imagines her banishings tied into the cord, the things she wants to release from her life, and places a drop of menstrual blood on the knots. The candle continues to burn as she does her ritual, and as it burns down and burns the thread away, her sheddings and worries are gone in the flame.

While the red candle burns, the woman takes the shell full of seeds from her altar,[36] bean seeds that in the Hopi Powamu represent new life. Pouring them into her left hand, she says,

"These are my beginnings. I plant these things for growth when the moon is new."

She takes a bean in her right hand and says,

"I want to be loved."

Planting the seed in the bowl of earth on her altar, she says,

"I am loved."

Taking another seed, the dark moon priestess states another vision,

"I want to love myself,"

---

[34]Adapted from Helen G. Farias, "The Nine Precepts of the College of Hera", in *The Beltane Papers*, Beltane, 1985, p. 21. For women not menstruating, use olive oil, wine or pomegranate juice.

[35]Adapted from Darkfire, "Cord and Candle Healing", in *Circle Network News*, (POB 219, Mt. Horeb, WI 53572), Fall, 1984, p. 9.

[36]Adapted from Starhawk, *The Spiral Dance: A Rebirth of the Ancient Religion of the Great Goddess*, p. 166, and Lee Lanning and Vernette Hart, Eds., *Ripening: An Almanac of Lesbian Lore and Vision*, p. 19-20.

and planting the bean says,
    "I love myself."
With the next seed she says,
    "I want to see myself as whole,"
and planting the bean says,
    "I am whole."
She continues this for as many visions as she wishes, choosing first to want them then to make them real, and honoring both choices as her right.

Completing this, and her red candle with its threads burnt out, she takes a moment longer to honor her body, thanks Hecate for gentle endings, welcomes Persephone and new beginnings, and says, "So mote it be." She thanks the goddess, releasing the four directions and opening her circle, grounds the excess energy, and finishes the ritual by saying, "Blessed be." A cycle is completed, and a new one begins with the new moon.

6

Creative Visualization

Creative visualization skills and their use in meditation are the keys to inner work in women's spirituality. Everything from Sabbat rituals to moon magic, from altars and tools to the affirmations and banishings that effect inward change and daily life are based on creative visualization. Meditation's guided journeys through the subconscious are creative visualizations, as are past life and dream explorations and most psychic healing techniques. Use of visualization taps the power of the subconscious mind and brings that power into access of everyday reality. Visualization creates controlled dreams in the subconscious and brings them into the conscious to become real, connects spirituality, feeling and thinking, the inner selves, with the physical and material outer planes.

When a woman reads the goddess creation stories of Chapter Two, sees in her mind the goddesses and their stories, watches the universe happen, she is doing a form of creative visualization known to her since childhood. Words on a page become more than words, and the goddesses become real. The images change from a physical act (reading the words), to the emotional level (wordless pictures), to reach the intellectional plane of ideas. Goddess is no longer ink on paper, but something felt with inner senses beyond the intellect and made into ideas and thought processes. Creative visualization connects the word symbols to the emotional pictures and mental ideas, expands all three, brings the senses into feelings, feelings into ideas and concepts, and ideas into communication with the higher self.

Women are multi-leveled, as represented by the reading example and seen in the chakras,[1] and in the layered bands of light that are the aura. The human aura is divided into seven color layers, the seven colors of the chakras, that reflect the inner aspects of the psyche:

> The first ring reveals her state of health, the second her emotions, the third her intellectual makeup, the fourth her higher mind (imagination and intuition), the fifth her spirit, or the link between the individual and the cosmos, and the sixth and seventh reveal cosmic aspects.[2]

These or some of these layers are visible naturally to some women, and women can train themselves to see or sense auras by their colors, musical sounds or feel. The colors are the spectrum rainbow, in red, orange, yellow, green, blue, indigo and violet. The seven part aura is also divided into four bodies[3] or aspects, the physical, emotional (astral or etheric), mental and spiritual.

The physical body is at the starting level, the earth or material plane, mirrored by the first aura band (red). Women's body itself, her health and physical senses are reflected here, and the chakras are located at this level. The second aura body (orange) is the astral, emotional or etheric band, and the emotional body connects the physical woman with her mental and spiritual self. This is the seat of personality and emotional feeling. The third is the mental body . . . the source of the intellect, imagination, intuition and the rational mind. This body consists of two aura bands (yellow and green), the lower and higher mental planes,[4] with intelligence first and the world of inspiration and intuition above it. The fourth and highest body is the spiritual level, consisting of the fifth, sixth and seventh aura layers (blue, indigo and violet). These bodies connect the individual woman to the goddess universe, are the spirit, psyche or soul, and are represented beautifully in the crown chakra of Spider Woman's *kopavi* concept.

Women who can see or sense auras usually see the physical band as a cloud of clear or bluish light, the emotional/astral/ etheric body as a chameleon of rainbow colors changing with thoughts and emotions, and the mental body as flashing colored thought-forms. Color perceptions can vary with the individual, and the higher levels are less readily seen.

---

[1] See Chapter seven for chakra information, also the self-blessing ritual of Chapter Five.
[2] Diane Mariechild, *Mother Wit: A Feminist Guide to Psychic Development*, (Trumansburg, NY, The Crossing Press, 1981), p. 37.
[3] Keith Sherwood, *The Art of Spiritual Healing*, (St. Paul, Llewellyn Publications, 1985), p. 20-24.
[4] S.G.J. Ouseley, *The Power of the Rays: The Science of Colour Healing*, (Essex, L.N. Fowler and Co., Ltd., 1951), p. 23 ff.

Creative visualization is used to connect these bodies, the physical, emotional and intellectual woman with her spiritual goddess self. Inner change happens on all levels and connecting the levels puts inner change under individual control. Colors, symbols and images are used to do this, many of which have already been mentioned in Part I of this book. By use of visualization, rituals become powerfully real manifestations of goddess; affirmations and banishings (real magick) actually happen; healings and psychic skills like empathic links and telepathy come into focus; the tarot and I Ching function as powerful divination tools, and the goddess—with the goddess in woman's self—comes alive. Creative visualization is a skill, something to learn, and like muscle use or the development of any other skill, it opens up other learning and increases and grows with doing it.

Visualizing the creation goddesses of Chapter Two, watching them form the universe, is a beginning in creative visualization, as is making the material of Chapter One, goddess and women's herstory, have feeling, action and individual meaning. This is a reading skill learned early. The creation chapter includes universal symbols, and picturing these and their meanings in the mind are a start to visualization. In Chapter Three, take each process of ritual and make it real—give it sensual, emotional life by vision, sound and feeling, color, texture and odor. In invoking the directions, see, hear and touch them in images and symbols rather than in words. In purifications, make the cleansings happen. When grounding, feel the energy flowing out and being absorbed by the earth. In tracing an invoking pentagram, imagine the lines drawn in blue or red fire, the circle as a living force. All these and more are creative visualization.

The power of women's spirituality rituals, group or individual ones, is in bringing abstract ideas into the physical present. For each of the Sabbat rituals of Chapter Four, picture the goddess, what she is like and is doing, in personal terms. Then transfer that image to what's happening on the earth and in individual life. Not only does the ritual become real, but the woman visualizing this way becomes very aware of her place in the universe, in the season and the earth, of her interconnectedness with the cycle and with all that lives. This connecting of aspects with the self on the four levels, then connecting the self with the life force that is goddess is the power of creative visualization.

Images here are not only visual, but go beyond the reach of any single sensory experience. Though much is expressed here as visual imagery, sight and color are only beginning possibilities. Women who are sound or touch oriented use different images than visually oriented women, but the images bring them to the same place. A sight oriented woman's conception of a seashell is different from a sound or touch oriented woman's conception of the same shell, but each in her own terms creates an image that connects the physical seashell to her emotional, mental and spiritual aspects. Creative visualization involves many things. What works for the individual woman is what matters, and visual imagery is only one way of doing it.

When thinking of a dog, what's the immediate first impression that comes to mind? What the dog looks like (sight)? The warm softness of her coat (touch)? Or her bark (sound)? Different women are oriented naturally to different forms of sensory impressions or combinations of impressions. Where one might be sight oriented and picture the dog, another hears it and thinks in sounds, or feels it and works by touch. Use the orientation that fits the individual in doing creative visualization, and best yet, use all of the senses available.

In the individual rituals of Chapter Five, it is creative visualization that makes the woman become goddess in the self-blessing or in drawing down the moon. Likewise, it is the use of visualization to connect the sub-conscious to the conscious mind and both to the woman's physical actions that make affirmations and banishings manifest in daily life. Creative visualization is magick, real and natural magick, that connects the universe with the earth, the goddess with her woman priestess, the spiritual with the physical self. It's the root beginning of all wishes come true, of all inner change and inner and psychic growth in women's spirituality workings.

Part of the reason for the power of visualization comes from the concept of thought form. In the theory of aura and body levels, thoughts are real things. They are actual objects that manifest in non-physical planes before they have effect on physical levels. A thought originates in the mental body as a vibration pattern, and vibrations tend to reproduce themselves.[5] Once an emotion or thought pattern emerges, it continues to occur, and thoughts positive or negative have definite form to change the self through the four bodies. Women who can see or sense auras watch the colors or energy flows change continually with changes of thoughts or emotions in the second aura band. A thought affects the self at all levels, and an accepted thought changes lives.

A woman drawing down the moon creates a thought form that goes beyond words to affect her self at all four astral levels, the physical,

---

[5]Annie Besant and C.W. Leadbeater, *Thought-Forms,* (Wheaton, IL, Theosophical Publishing House, 1969, Original 1901), p. 11-17.

emotional, mental and spiritual. At mental levels, she creates a concept that her choice of imagery conveys to her emotional and spiritual self. She creates the thought form of herself as goddess, and feels and becomes goddess on each other level. Each of these levels receives from the one above it, and transmits energy and thought forms to the level directly below. The last level to be affected is the physical and material plane, and reaching that level, the woman as goddess expresses this in who she is and appears to be, in her body. She makes the ritual gestures standing tall, and draws the goddess from her own spiritual self, through the goddess moon. The idea affects her on all levels: when she goes to the office the next morning, she is strong and proud for knowing who she is. The changes are spiritual, mental, emotional and physical. Thoughts have power and form.

Creative visualization is thought form. It is the creation of conscious forms that manifest first in the mental body, extend upward to the spiritual and downward to emotional levels. The emotional body connects the mental and spiritual to the physical, so emotional changes have to happen before physical ones. Wanting something emotionally is necessary, not only intellectualizing it. By choosing what thought forms to use in changing the self, what desires, the woman who does creative visualization picks what she wants herself to be, then creates that self on all four levels. If she uses visualization to find a job, she pictures the best possible job in as much detail as she can. She pictures herself working there, taking home a good pay, enjoying the work, even what the location looks like or where it is. By using that image in her affirmations, rather than seeing herself jobless or in the image of just any old job, she creates a thought form. The woman designs a job for herself that is the best possible job and makes it happen. Women use visualization carefully, creating the thought form they really want, not settling for less or thinking they deserve less, and not creating thoughts they don't want to occur.

To go a step further, thoughts are not only things that affect the self, but are things that affect others.[6] Creating a thought makes it easier to repeat it, and thoughts are self-perpetuating and self-fulfilling. Create the thought of the ideal job, rather than present joblessness or an indifferent job, and use this thought form to affect the self and others. A woman who is depressed at her joblessness will make most of the women in a room with her feel depressed too, without the others often aware of what is happening. Likewise a hopeful woman makes others feel hopeful. If a

---

[6]*Ibid.,* p. 14-16.

woman uses creative visualization to find a job, her thought form of that job and her hopeful positivity affect the employers interviewing her. Those that have a job opening to match her image are attracted to her, and one hires her. With the image that this is the job she really desires, the woman continues her thought form visualizations, and physically makes the job into all she needs. Creative visualization brings conscious thoughts into realities—project the hopefulness and not the depression; project the best possible job and not a lesser one. "What's sent out comes back threefold."[7] In these ways, women use visualization to shape their lives.

Beginning to use creative visualization is simple, and the whole process is simple and natural. It's a skill free and available to everyone, and a skill that grows in power and ease with use. Meditation's techniques of deep breathing and relaxation are logical starting places, as calming the body and mind makes them clear and receptive. Meditation's entering of light trance connects the physical, emotional, mental and spiritual bodies for transmission of thought forms.

The time to begin is at night before bed, and a warm shower or bath sets the mood of letting go of the day's cares. A lit altar is a good place to be, sacred space in a room that's quiet and in darkness. Cast a circle if it feels right. Sit straight and comfortably on the floor or in a chair, or lie down flat on the floor without crossing arms or legs. Work barefoot and skyclad or wearing loose clothing. Use the floor or chair and not the bed to avoid sleep conditioning, but breathing and relaxation exercises are also good in bed to bring on sleep when desired. Using the same conditions every time, making a ritual of it, creates a pattern that makes visualization and meditation easier to learn and enter. Key symbols such as the candle flame or physical position become familiar, and are ways to reach the meditative state more quickly.

When seated or lying comfortably, still the mind and begin breathing in and out slowly, paying attention to the process. Air fills the lungs deeply but naturally and without forcing it, and the lungs empty completely when exhaling. Breathing is slower and fuller than normal, more rhythmic, and lower in the chest and diaphragm. At the same time, paying attention to it, draw calming in with every inhalation, releasing tension and worry with every exhaled breath. The cares acknowledged and let go of, use the inhaled breaths to draw peace within. As the process continues, peace enters with every breath and is exhaled with every breath, and this is the goal of the exercise.

---

[7]Principle wiccan saying.

Intangible concepts, such as calming and peace to keep, and worry to let go of are made real by giving them sensory attributes. For a touch oriented woman, calming, peace and worry have definite feelings, soft or warm for calming, light or free for peace, rough or prickly sharp for worry. These images vary with the individual. For a sound oriented woman, calming, peace and worry are musical tones that she hears and breathes. They can be bells or cello or whatever sound she chooses, individual notes on the piano. Visually oriented women see the qualities as colors, and these have universal correspondences: calming is green and peace is blue, worry is points of hard grey. Calming can also be the scent of new-cut grass, and peace the odor of lilacs. Symbols are both general and personal; experiment with them and use what works as the beginning of creative visualization. The breathing exercise takes only a few minutes and can be done anywhere, with reality changing effects on the mind and body.

Next, relax the physical body. There are several ways in basic meditation to do this, and all of them involve paying attention and continuing rhythmic breathing.[9] First, pay attention to your toes, visualizing where they are without looking at them, then tense and relax them. Keeping them relaxed, breathe peace into each toe inside and out, drawing the sound, color, fragrance or feeling of peace from the goddess earth. Move upward to the calves, paying attention to them, then tensing and relaxing the muscles. Breathe peace from the earth into the relaxed calf muscles, drawing it upward like a light velvet cloak or blanket that covers and protects, continuing upward from the toes in the color, feeling or symbol chosen. Tense and relax the knees, thighs, pelvic area, abdomen and lower back in turn, drawing by breath the peaceful cloak over and through them. Tense, relax and breathe peace into diaphragm, chest, breasts, back and heart, paying attention to and visualizing each organ.

From the heart upward, breathe peace into the body from the sky, the goddess universe. First draw the cloak over and into fingers, hands, elbows and shoulders in turn, tensing, relaxing and paying attention to each of them. Pay attention to, tense and relax the neck muscles, and draw the cloak of peace over and into the neck. Continue breathing peace, drawing it upward to the jaw and chin, lips, cheeks, muscles around the eyes, the forehead and scalp. Tense and relax each part,

[8]Paying attention is a concept of Keith Sherwood's in *The Art of Spiritual Healing,* p. 25.
[9]See Keith Sherwood, *The Art of Spiritual Healing,* p. 81-83; Melita Denning and Osborne Phillips, *The Llewellyn Practical Guide to Creative Visualization,* (St. Paul, Llewellyn Publications, 1984), p. 35-42; and Diane Mariechild, *Mother Wit: A Feminist Guide to Psychic Development,* p. 1.

visualizing and paying attention to each part, and breathing a cloak of peace that rises from the feet to the head.

When totally relaxed, feel lightly, gently and fully covered by a cloak or blanket of color, feeling or sound, a cloak or blanket of total peace. Remaining within it, continue rhythmic breathing, drawing peace into every part of the body from the earth and sky. Surrounded and filled with peace, visualize it entering from the earth through the left foot, travelling upward through the body on the left side to the heart chakra (breastbone), and crossing over to travel down the right side and leg, entering the earth again through the right toes. Then visualize peace from the sky, the goddess universe, entering the body through the *kopavi* (crown chakra), moving down the left side of the body from the head to the heart, crossing over at the heart chakra, moving upward through the right arm and right side of the body to the head again, and entering the sky through the *kopavi*. Allow the energy to move into and through continuously, inhaling and exhaling peace with rhythmic breath.

Two circles are formed here, peace breathing into and out of the body from both the earth and sky. Turn the two circles into one circle, a single flowing cloak of peace, the earth and sky connected. Breathe peace upward from the earth, through the feet and left side of the body, and draw it upward to the crown of the head, where energy releases to the universe. Breathe peace from the crown downward, from the sky down the right side of the body to the toes, releasing peace to the earth. Relax in the cloak of feeling, body floating and detached, mind clear and alert; savor peace in the flow of breathing it into and out of the body, through every part of the body and mind.

When there is enough of this, stop visualizing the flow of peace without trying to grasp or hold onto it. Rest under the velvet cloak a moment more, then allow the cloak to slowly fade. Peace remains within. Stay in position awhile longer, sitting or lying, and if rising move gently and carefully. Some dizziness may happen; that gradually disappears.

Rhythmic breathing and deep relaxation are the beginnings of most work in women's spirituality. Relaxing the physical body makes it receptive to connecting with the higher levels, the emotional, higher mental (intuitive) and spiritual. Allowing the feelings to happen without judging or rationalizing them, in symbols and without putting them into words, the divisions between the four bodies are bridged. Entering this state in ritual when casting and invoking a circle is called 'going between the worlds.'

In the two exercises, creative visualization is used to make intangible concepts (calming, peace) into realities understandable at non-cognitive and non-rational levels. Peace is a lower mental (intellectual) word concept given physical, emotional and spiritual form by taking it out of print and mind imagery and experiencing it as feeling, color or sound— as moving energy from the earth and sky. Relaxing the body by these means connects it to the higher self, to the astral/emotional and higher mental levels. These in turn reach the spiritual body, the silver thread *kopavi* that connects woman's spirit to the goddess.

The next step here, once entering this receptive state, is to choose and create careful thought forms to impress on the four connected levels. Thought-form affirmations define abstract or concrete wishes, and use all four bodies to make them happen by connecting the selves (physical, emotional, mental and spiritual) through visualization.

In the earlier example, the woman visualized the job she needed and found the job she visualized. She created the thought form carefully, in detail and without questioning her deserving. On finding the job, she continued affirmations/thought forms, and by this and her own actions kept it being the perfect job for her needs right now. The woman in the Chapter Five full moon ritual created the thought form of herself as goddess in drawing down the moon, and became goddess by doing so.

Affirmation wishes are sacred or mundane things, but are thought forms of power to be handled carefully. They can be used for prosperity, creativity, success, for finding the right job or apartment, for finding love. Once impressed on the four levels, they come true as real magick, in natural and often unexpected ways. The woman who asks for writing success in her affirmations, works hard at her actual writing, along with creating and visualizing the thought form. Her completed play is performed Off-Broadway. The woman who asks for a perfect job finds it logically in the want-ads, and her affirmations are fulfilled from within and without, from the bridging of the physical, emotional, mental and spiritual levels. Created as thought forms on the astral/emotional between-the-worlds plane and accepted in meditation's relaxed and receptive state, affirmations become actions that become physical realities.

In a simple example, a woman who wishes to hold a seashell in her hand does rhythmic breathing and deep relaxation to put her in a receptive state. Then she visualizes the shell she desires, its shape, texture, what it feels like to hold it, the sound when she puts it to her ear, its color and salty odor. If she continues this visualization nightly, she soon finds her seashell. Someone brings it to her from their beach vacation, she sees and buys it at a garage sale, or finds it long-forgotten in her own basement. When she sees the shell, she recognizes it immediately as her own, her desire is fulfilled, the thought form transferred from emotional to physical levels, and the object itself drawn to her from between the worlds.

Likewise, the woman who asks for personal clarity in her life first defines what this means to her, and puts it into emotional-symbolic terms, non-mental concepts. If personal clarity means the ability to teach others, the attribute might be symbolized by herself as high priestess of a circle. Creating this as a thought form, she does the rhythmic breathing and deep relaxation, then pictures, hears or otherwise visualizes her concept of the image. Appealing to her mental level, she speaks it aloud in positive present tense terms, and holding the visualization in her mind in repeated rituals, she works toward what it takes to become a high priestess. She becomes what her thought form creates. On physical levels, too, she participates in circle and coven work, learns all she can from books and other women, does rituals alone, and gains knowledge and understanding that women recognize and come to her to learn. She has created the thought form of herself as high priestess, seen herself leading women's circles in many affirmations, and the achievement happens for her naturally. The abstract quality of personal clarity takes on concrete meaning and action, and does so from the physical, emotional, mental and spiritual levels.

The ability to visualize and make use of creative visualization is a skill that gains in power with practice. A visualization done once could be enough to start the magick, but repetition nightly over a period of time increases, accepts and reinforces it. Along with formally ritualizing it, hold the visualization in the mind several times a day anywhere, briefly and even without the preparation, to reinforce the thought form. Speaking the wish aloud in "I have" or "I am" terms helps make it real, as does surrounding it with light and sending the light into it each time its visualized.[10] The light is obtained from within, by asking the goddess to fill the self with her own light, and sending that light as an aura to make affirmations real.

Since thought forms affect others as well as the self, never involve someone else in affirmations without their permission. To do so is manipulation and violates free will, however well-intentioned the thought form is. Women asking for love carefully create and visualize the perfect lover's attributes, but never a specific person as lover. Some forethought goes

---

[10]Melita Denning and Osborne Phillips, *The Llewellyn Practical Guide to Creative Visualization*, p. 124-126.

into this before the affirmations themselves, as this is a powerful thought form. To visualize a specific lover violates the other person's free will, unless that person agrees to it. And that person, too, may not be the perfect lover needed. With the wiccan warning of "Be careful what you ask for,"[11] gaining the wrong person's love can be something to deal with, someone whose love once gained is not so perfect after all.

When doing affirmations as healings,[12] and they are powerful healings, do them for others only with their permission, too. Everyone has the choice of their illness, and for whatever reason has the right to refuse. To use affirmations in this way, enter the receptive state and create the thought form image of that person in perfect health. Such visualization also works in self-healing and works well.

Women "casting spells" (as this work can be perceived), do only positive ones. No matter how much hurt they have experienced, they use only love in creating thought form affirmations. "What goes out comes back threefold,"[13] and hurt and anger sent out are hurt and anger returned. Release them in the rhythmic breathing and relaxation exercises before beginning visualization. If it is truly necessary to do affirmations against another person—and this is questionable—do them rather in a way to protect the self without harming anyone else. Create a shield of protection that rejects harm and invites love, or create an aura that, refusing negativity, returns it as love to the sender. Remember that walls created physically or psychically keep things isolated from within as well as protected from without, and that barriers refuse love as much as they do negativity. Remember too, that women's actions and thought forms have consequences; they are powers to be used well and carefully.

In banishing bad habits, use affirmations from their positive and healing viewpoints. To quit smoking, go into the receptive state and create the thought form of the self without a cigarette, in perfect health and happiness, fingers, lungs and teeth clear of nicotine. Don't imagine cravings for cigarettes, or even cravings overcome, as this creates the thought form of those cravings. Visualize perfect peace. If some other other habit is desired in smoking's place visualize doing that habit, jogging or whatever it may be, instead. To establish a positive habit, such as writing everyday or practicing the piano, create in the relaxed state an image of working at the typewriter or instrument. Surround that image with light from within, and hold that image in mind till it fades. Then go and do the writing or piano work, setting aside the planned amounts of time

---

[11]Principle wiccan saying.
[12]Chapter Seven is on healing.
[13]Principle wiccan saying.

for it every day and keeping to it. Also every day do the visualization that confirms the intent and created the thought form. Women take charge of their lives and responsibility for their actions; careful affirmations create the thought forms and dreams on higher levels, and dreams come true by actions on the physical plane.

One way of creating and getting in touch with the symbols to visualize is to use a wishing box.[14] Write three wishes on separate pieces of paper, wrapping a bay leaf into each piece and placing the pieces inside a small lidded box. Put the box on your altar. When doing affirmations, visualize the wishes in turn, first as the paper and herbs inside the box, next as thought concepts of what the words on the papers mean, and finally seeing the wishes as fulfilled. If one of the wishes is for an apartment, visualize living in the perfect apartment; if one is for healing skills, visualize holding a crystal and doing the healings with positive results; if one of the wishes is for a fine guitar, visualize tuning and playing it. For each of the wishes, create the thought form in feeling, sound or sight terms and hold the image in mind. Speak the image in words aloud, "I have the perfect apartment"; "I am a healer"; "I own the finest guitar." Send inner light to surround and circle the visualization, and hold the picture till it fades. Go on to the next wish in the box. As each wish is fulfilled over time, remove the paper and bay leaf and add another wish. A good time to review the wishes is at the full moon or on a "List Moon" (see Chapter Five). Realize too, that wishes and needs change, and accept and flow with the changes.

The process of doing creative visualization is to start with rhythmic breathing and a relaxation meditation. Then go to the affirmations themselves, which are often planned beforehand. As in the full moon ritual of Chapter Five, affirmations can be combined with other ritual work, and are the most effective on waxing or full moon phases. They are not limited to these phases, however, and can be done at any time and as often as wanted, and repetition works. To end affirmations, let go of the visualized images and watch them fade slowly. Return gently to daily consciousness or go on to another meditation or part of the ritual.

An Eastern meditation technique is to empty the mind totally of all passing thoughts, and this is easiest done when in a state of deep relaxation, a trance state. The technique is more difficult than it sounds, is only accomplished with much practice, but the results are startling and beautiful. Focus on breathing or concentrate on a candle flame, and

---

[14]"Mini-Spell: The Wish Box", in *Thesmophoria*, (POB 11363, Oakland, CA 9461 , Vol. 6, No. 6, Candlemas, 1985/9985), p. 3.

gently push aside the distractions, visions and thought forms that come. On emptying the mind totally of thoughts and sense perceptions, joy floods in, a peace so total and perfect as to only be called goddess and the goddess within.

Another Eastern technique modified is to create by visualization an image of the goddess herself. She is everything a woman needs in her, and in her thousand names has an image or symbol to appeal to every individual. The goddess is a mermaid, a weaver, a serpent, a woman. She is dark skinned or light, blonde or Afro-haired or grey-haired, small bodied or large, young or middle-aged or old, clothed in any way, in flowers or skyclad. She speaks in any language, or doesn't speak at all, or speaks in musical tones or in colors, or in ASL sign. She is doing any activity, from sitting still to giving birth to creating the universe, to hugging the woman who has visualized her presence and invoked her.[15]

The image of goddess visualized in all her beauty, the woman asks of her what she wills and waits to receive the message. She then sends inner light from her heart chakra to the thought form of goddess, surrounds the goddess with light and love, and draws the image into her own heart. The goddess is within and is part of her, and the woman returns to her present day awareness. She finishes the meditation filled with peace and love.

Other possibilities are the many guided meditations, visualized journeys, that are available in books and on tape or are created by the individual. Diane Mariechild's *Mother Wit: A Feminist Guide to Psychic Development,* (Trumansburg, NY, The Crossing Press, 1981) contains a series of these, and they may be read, memorized, outlined or taped beforehand. Use them freely, allowing the mind to travel where it fancies from the suggestions of the guided stories.

To end a session in creative visualization or meditation, let go of the images and slowly return to daily consciousness. If on a meditation journey, visualize coming home. Returning can be done by a formula of words, just as a formula of body position, words or candle use can make entering the meditative state easier. Opening the cast circle and thanking the goddess and directions, saying "So mote it be" to seal the intent, are ways of returning to earth plane reality. Always return slowly and gently, and once returned move slowly for awhile. Altered states of consciousness and deep relaxation affect the mind and body both. A process of grounding, placing the hands on the floor and releasing excess energy

---

[15]This meditation is on "Two Meditations" by Diane Stein, available from Llewellyn Publications.

through them, is a good idea. At the same time, use contact with the earth to return to her.

One ending invocation, based on Marion Weinstein's work,[16] goes like this:

> I have these things or their equivalents or better. I have them according to free will, harming or manipulating none, for my good and the good of all. I have these things by the great mother, by Yemaya of women's wishes, and I use the gifts wisely and well.
>
> So mote it be.

Placing hands on the ground and visualizing excess energy leaving through them, thank the goddess and say, "Blessed be."

Another ending formula is that of Melita Denning and Osborne Phillips, who visualize each line of the following as an arm of the five pointed star:[17]

> Blessed are the laws of the goddess.
> Blessed is her bounty.
> Blessed is the swiftness with which all is wrought.
> Blessed is the total good with which all is achieved.
> Blessed are my desires, even now fulfilled.

These formulas are subject to personal needs and women's creativity, but words spoken aloud are good returns from any meditative state. The change from emotional level symbols to physical and intellectual wording is a gently grounding return. When doing visualization anywhere and throughout the day, or doing them without the relaxation process, a simple change of physical position returns the mind to the present.

Creative visualization is a powerful tool in women's spirituality. It's the means of connecting the physical daily self with the higher self, the emotional, intuitive and spiritual mind. By the connecting of realities and levels, a thought form in the higher self is brought to bear on the lower, and wishes, change and desires come true. Visualization is the heart of ritual, of all of women's magick. It's the root of healing work, as is seen in the next chapter, of relaxation and physical well-being, of meditation, divination and altered states. Like any other skill, creative visualization is something that is learned, and once learned comes into constant use. Women use it positively and channel its power well.

---

[16]Marion Weinstein, *Positive Magic*, (Custer, WA, Phoenix Publishing Co., 1981), p. 208 ff. Adapted.
[17]Melita Denning and Osborne Phillips, *The Llewellyn Practical Guide to Creative Visualization*, p. 153. The lines are slightly adapted.

7

Healing

Women have always been healers, and the knowledges of healing—of aura work, colors, herbs and homeopathy, reflexology, midwifery, massage, crystals and trance states—have always been part of the goddess' mysteries. Healing in the matriarchies was women's work, connected to birth, death and the life force, and this only changed with the submergence of women's culture, women's political, religious and personal power, under patriarchy. In the Inquisition, when the new male medical establishment (not very scientific at the time), took healing away from women and made a business of it, women died for the sin of having the healing knowledge medicine lacked.

> The rise of the experts was not the inevitable triumph of right over wrong, fact over myth; it began with a bitter conflict which set women against men, class against class. Women did not learn to look to an external 'science' for guidance until after their old skills had been ripped away, and the 'wise women' who preserved them had been silenced, or killed.[1]

Where women's concept of healing was and is that of mutual sharing, male medicine began and remains in competitive exclusiveness. Medicine was and is a business; healing is not. Medicine was and is knowledge hoarded and hidden, dispensed only to those who can pay for it and held as power over women, children and the poor, over all minorities. Healing, by contrast, belongs to all who want to learn it, and is taught, learned and

---

[1] Barbara Ehrenreich and Deirdre English, *For Her Own Good: 150 Years of the Experts' Advice to Women.* (New York, Anchor/ Doubleday Books, 1978), p. 33.

practiced among women in openness.

> The triumph of the male medical profession . . . involved the destruction of women's networks of mutual help—leaving women in a position of isolation and dependency—and it established the model of expertism as the perogative of a social elite.[2]

Healing knowledge went underground with wicca and women's culture, but like the goddess and women's Be-ing survived the assaults. Devalued, persecuted, degraded and burned, healers and their skills were repressed but not totally lost. The traditional techniques are being re-claimed today by an awakening population that is relearning the power of the female principle, and women are dis-covering the long submerged knowledge as part of women's spirituality and the goddess. The knowledge is being used where it's most needed, as an at least partial and preventive alternative to the increasingly dehumanized big business medical profession. Along with regained skills is the rewebbed networking and sisterhood sharing that women's healing and community involve.

Healing is caring and nurturing, the ability to reach out and love others, the interconnectedness of all life. Its basic models are those of mother and child and of women who are sisters, who share each others' knowledge in freedom, openness and trust. Women's healing is very different from patriarchal medicine. Compare a session of women's massage and aura work, done one-to-one at home with time and concern, to a visit at a hospital clinic. The surroundings at the clinic, after a long and nervous wait, are fully automated and sterile. The doctor doesn't know the patient's name and is judgmental of her life, and raw science and interminable forms do little of comforting. The doctor writes a prescription for chemicals to mask the woman's symptoms or cuts some body part out, if the woman can afford to pay for it, and the experience is physically and emotionally traumatic. The field of patriarchal "mental health" is even more invasive. No healing—in the sense of easing fear and pain or the causes of pain and disease, in the sense of giving comfort or sharing human warmth, love and understanding—has occurred.

The women who share the massage have a better and more validating experience, participating in power within rather than submitting to patriarchal power over. The healer receives healing as much as her patient

---

[2]*Ibid.*, p. 34.

does, in a non-alien comforting setting, and touching, deep relaxation, the feelings of nurturing and love, the power of polarities and crystals, result in real and gentle changes. Pain is gone, and with it the inner emotional fear and stress that caused or aggravated it. All healing is self-healing, only channeled and made safe by the healer, and deep peace occurs for both healer and healed. Healing is personal respect and sharing, not invasive or judgmental, and is done between equals. Healing is what witches do.[3]

There are a number of skills and fields involved in healing, and witches are associated traditionally with midwifery and herbs. Midwifery is the bringing of new life into the world, the care of pregnant and delivering women and young children. The skill also includes abortion and contraceptive needs, and in some cases the care of animals, but it was for the easing of women's labor pain that midwives were killed during the Inquisition.[4]

Herbs and homeopathy are another key field of the wisewoman or woman healer. Acting gently and in natural ways on the body, inexpensively and without side effects, plant material was the first medicine and the pre-chemical basis of all prescription use. Herbal medicine was early a women's field, with Hildegarde of Bingen's twelfth century work still a classic. It was mainly a women's oral tradition of worldwide scope until taken over by male experts. Homeopathy and flower essences are related skills, with much research being done by women, and herbal knowledge, along with midwifery, is being studied and regained in the women's spirituality community.

Reflexology, acupressure and acupuncture involve the relief of pain by stimulation of mapped nerve centers that relate to the organs and glands of the body. An aspect of massage and often used with it, reflexology or zone therapy especially uses energy centers in the hands and feet, can be done as self-healing, and involves no drugs or side effects. Massage is full body work, using touch, stroking, the kneading and stimulation of muscles, skin and energy centers to increase circulation, release blockages and pain, shape body tone and invoke deep relaxation. The transmission of caring is intrinsic in this skill, as in other women's skills, and massage requires two partners. Use of aura work, polarity balancing, colors and crystals, turn massage into psychic as well as a physical healing skill.

---

[3]Patriarchal law requires that I make this disclaimer: no attempt is made in this book to claim cures. In time of illness, see the care-giver of your choice.
[4]Barbara Ehrenreich and Deirdre English, *For Her Own Good: 150 Years of the Experts' Advice to Women*, p. 35-36.

While all women's healing knowledge is vital and only a few skills are even mentioned here, the main focus of this chapter continues the work of Chapter Six. The trance states of deep relaxation and creative visualization, of color work and auras, form the basis of psychic healing, and are what is most often referred to in women's spirituality as healing skills. The work described in this chapter is done as self-healing, and is also done with a partner. The goal is to increase wellness as much as to ease discomforts, to gain, regain and stimulate the natural energy balances of well-being.

Colors have been mentioned often in *The Women's Spirituality Book,* and color work and visualization are major in women's healing. The seven chakra colors, the aura rainbow of red, orange, yellow, green, blue, indigo and violet are basic healing forces. As in their other uses, each color can be translated into other sensory qualities—degrees of warmth or feeling instead of visual imagery, or musical tones. When using colors in the healing that follows, use what works, and this is true in most craft or healing skills. While the system of chakras is known as learning from the East, it is also a system developed by Tibetan and Native American peoples, is used particularly and fully by the Hopi.

The seven chakra colors correspond to the seven aura bands and are energy centers located in the first aura band, the physical aura body or etheric double. The emotional level of the four bodies connects the physical with the higher self, and the chakra centers are instrumental in this. Each color represents a physical position, ductless gland center, musical notation, sound syllable for chanting, and energy attributes.[5] The energy attributes, made use of by color, sound or touch correspondences, are what are used in psychic healing to right imbalances, change moods, release blockages and pain. Receptive deep relaxation states allow color healing to connect the four bodies, the physical, emotional, mental and spiritual, and manifest changes that stimulate well-being and balance throughout the individual.

The first of the physical centers, the root chakra, is the color *red.* This is the sexual genital area, the gateway of birth, the delta, and red denotes heat, the life force, strength and vitality. Its sound correspondence is C-major, sound syllable Ooo, ductless gland is women's ovaries,[6] and position on the spinal column is at the coccyx or base of the spine. For women who can see or sense auras, the presence of red shows strong

---

[5]Correspondences here are from the work of Kay Gardner, "A Chart of Color, Sound and Energy Correspondences", in *The Rose Window,* (Healing Through the Arts, Inc., POB 399, Stonington, ME 04681), Spring, 1983; and S.G.J. Ouseley, *The Science of the Aura,* (Essex, L.N. Fowler and Co., Ltd., 1949), p. 17-25.
[6]Where Gardner and Ouseley disagree on gland correspondences, I have chosen Gardner's. Sources, correspondence and colors vary.

will and mind, ambition, sexuality, physical strength and affection. Red is used in healing to send warmth, and increase blood circulation and vitality.[7] It's used for reproductive area healing, for infertility, depression, anemia, poor nutrition, chills, cold exposure, frostbite, neuralgia and paralysis. Red is a hot color and the sending stimulates heat, passion and the life force. It should not be used where there is inflammation of any sort, or where there is emotional anger, over-excitement, fever or overheating.

The second chakra color is *orange,* located in the lower abdomen and corresponding with the pancreas gland. Its musical tone is D, sound syllable Oh, and spinal location the first lumbar vertebra. Orange is a warm color, expressing the brightness of solar energy. The feelings, emotions and appetites are involved at this belly chakra level, and a person with orange in her visible aura is an active, energetic woman, an outgoing leader and woman of personal pride. In healing uses, send orange to energize, and for any lung problems, asthma, bronchitis or coughs, as well as for epilepsy, depression, depletion and exhaustion. Orange intensifies emotions, cheers, and is good for kidneys, stomach cramps, rheumatism and arthritis.

The third chakra center is the solar plexus, the warm color *yellow,* located above the navel. The corresponding ductless glands are the adrenals, the musical note E, sound syllable Aw, and spinal location at the eighth thoracic vertebra. The solar plexus is the seat of mentality, of clear thinking, studying and learning. Vitality, psychic awareness and protection, nervous and physical activity are yellow's emotional attributes. People with yellow appearing in their auras are highly intellectual, optimistic, psychic and capable in business. They are high spirited and sometimes tend to ungroundedness. Use yellow in healing as a tonic, for physical and mental stimulation for exhaustion and burnout. This is not a color to use in healing ungrounded people or before sleep; use violet instead, but it is excellent for students and writers to aid learning and retention of knowledge, including psychic knowledge. Yellow is the color of personal power and self-confidence, and its uses in healing include mood elevation and dispelling fears. Use yellow also for nausea, stomach upsets, the liver, diabetes, skin problems and constipation.

The next two colors, green and blue, are cool colors and the most widely used colors in healing. *Green* is the heart chakra, located at the center of the chest under the breastbone, and is correspondent with the thymus gland. Its musical note is F, its sound syllable Ah, and its spinal

[7]References for healing uses are mostly from S.G.J. Ouseley, *The Power of the Rays: The Science of Color Healing,* (Essex. L.N. Fowler and Co., Ltd., 1951), p. 69-80. Chakra material is expanded and revised in Diane Stein's *The Women's Crystal Healing Book,* forthcoming from Llewellyn Publications.

location is the first thoracic vertebra. Green is the seat of love, of healing, empathy, caring,and is the color of the healing arts. The heart chakra is the connecting link between the lower three and higher three chakras, connecting the physical to the spiritual aspects. Women with green in their auras are individualistic, sympathetic, successful and caring. They are independent, versatile, intelligent and thoughtful. Green is the color of growth, of ideas and new life, and is representative as well of the higher mental band in the aura, that of inspiration and intuition. In healing, use green to balance, refresh and soothe, to bring harmony and peace. Heart ailments and headaches are treated with green, as well as tension, loneliness and love-loss. Green is a cooling, antiseptic color for infections, ulcers and eye problems, and is usable in most healings. Use green first in healing sunburn, then use blue. The woman who sends green in a healing sends empathy, caring and love.

Blue is the coldest color, another of the two most widely used healing shades. The fifth chakra is located at the throat and is the center of communication, hearing, speech and creativity. Its ductless glands are the thyroid and parathyroids, its musical range is G, and its sound syllable Eh. Spinal location is at the third cervical vertebra. The blue here is light blue, the color of the daylight sky, and it is known as the color of the moon and the female, as well as the oriental shade of good fortune.[8] Blue is a goddess color, associated with Mary and Isis, with Yemaya and Kwan Yin. Women who show blue in their auras are artistic, creative and spirituality oriented. They are loyal and sincere people, reliable, sometimes too intense, with varying degrees of self-confidence and strong self-reliance. Blue in healing is sleep and peace inducing, cooling and very calming. Use it powerfully against any inflammations, pain, tension, swelling, throat diseases, fevers, burns, diarrhea, headaches, spasms, menstrual cramps and infections.

Indigo, the color of the night sky in summer, is the third eye or brow chakra, located at the forehead between, slightly above and behind the eyes. Its sound tone is A, sound syllable Ih, gland pituitary, and spinal location the first cervical vertebra. The third eye is the center of insight and higher intuition, perception, self-realization and comprehension, psychic skills such as clairvoyance, clairaudience, telepathy/empathy and ESP. Its temperature is electrical and magnetic, rather than either hot or cool. Women with indigo in their auras are highly evolved spiritually, with integrity, wisdom, loyalty and sincerity in their natures. They are

---

[8]S.G.J. Ouseley, *The Science of the Aura,* p. 22.

idealistic, trusting and often very open. Indigo in healing is used for the senses, the eyes, ears and nose, as well as for mental and nervous imbalances. The color rejects negativity and helps in building a clear mind and positive outlook; use it for finding inner strength, for self-validation and for inner peace. Indigo is used with orange in easing lung problems and pneumonia, for the spleen and upset stomachs, by itself for convulsions, and by women seeking artistic inspiration, self-image or psychic growth.

Violet or purple is the seventh and highest chakra color, the color of the *kopavi,* the magnetic or electrical chakra located at the crown of the head. The chakra is correspondent with the pineal gland and has no spinal location; its musical note is B and its sound syllable Eee. The color and chakra are the thread of Spider Woman, the link of creative substance that attaches the individual to the goddess. It is the color and location of highest spirituality, not often seen in individual auras, and is the oneness of all life, the goddess in the woman and in the universe. Violet is the color of power within and influence without, of spirituality, wisdom and greatness, of spiritual transcendence. The color in healing is used for sleeplessness, mental disorders, brain and scalp function, tumors, and to ease stress, tension and ungroundedness. Ouseley uses it for cataracts and eye disorders as well. Calming and higher understanding are violet's attributes, the realization of self on the Wheel of Life, self as goddess and the goddess as the earth and the stars, the deep inner calm that these realizations bring. Violet is peaceful, inspiriting and stimulating at once, useful in women's quest for identity, spirituality and interconnectedness with the life force. Use in healing where yellow is indicated, but the person being healed is too tense for it. Use for neuralgia, rheumatism and epilepsy, to stimulate the nervous system, to calm and awaken the soul.

Kay Gardner's work is unique in listing an eighth chakra, the transpersonal point located several inches above the crown and beyond the physical limits of the body. The color here is *white,* the blending of all colors of light, and the sound is silence, the blending of all sounds. Attributes of this chakra are "Divine liberation, love and light,"[9] the soul and the universe/goddess. White light is used, and perhaps over-used, in women's spirituality for protection, healing, energizing and just about anything else. It's the aura color first and most readily seen or sensed by women who perceive auras, a color present in everyone's aura as the combination of all the aura level colors. Use at the beginning of healing

---

[9] Kay Gardner, "A Chart of Color, Sound and Energy Correspondences," in *The Rose Window,* Spring, 1983.

Color Correspondences

	RED	ORANGE	YELLOW	GREEN	BLUE	INDIGO	VIOLET	WHITE
Chakra	1. Root	2. Abdomen/belly	3. Navel	4. Heart	5. Throat	6. Third Eye	7. Crown	8. Trans-personal point
Spinal Location	coccyx	1st lumbar Vertebra	8th thoracic vertebra	1st thoracic vertebra	3rd cervical vertebra	1st cervical vertebra	(none)	(none)
Ductless Gland	ovaries	pancreas	adrenals	thymus	thyroid parathyroids	pituitary	pineal	(none)
Musical Tone	C	D	E	F	G	A	B	Silence, all sound
Syllable	Ooh	Oh	Aw	Ah	Eh	Ih	Eee	Om
Attributes	life force heat strength will ambition sexuality affection	solar energy emotions appetites pride	intellect rational mentality learning psychic center nerves personal power self-confidence	love empathy healing individualism success higher intelligence	communication speech creativity artistry spirituality loyal sincerity	intuition perception psychic skills spirituality idealism	spirituality goddess transcendence power influence	"Divine liberation, love & light" the soul
Healing Uses	to warm circulation depression infertility bring on menstruation anemia frostbite neuralgia paralysis	lungs coughs exhaustion intensify emotions stomach cramps rheumatism mood elevation epilepsy kidneys	stimulation vitalizing learning mood elevation dispel fears constipation exhaustion	nervousness ulcers eyes sunburn (then blue) love loss/ loneliness harmony and balance soothing heart ailments antiseptic headaches refreshing infections	cooling burns pain sleep calming headaches inflammations infections swellings throat fevers menstrual cramps	ears eyes nose mental and nervous negativity mind clearing inspiration pneumonia psychic growth self-image inner peace	sleep inducing stress nervousness cataracts & eyes calming mental disorders scalp and skull tumors	clearing making rapport vitalizing protection unifying
Temperature	hot	warm	warm	cool	cool	electric	electric	electric

References are from Kay Gardner, "A Chart of Color, Sound and Energy Correspondences", in *The Rose Window*, (Healing Through the Arts, Inc, Box 399, Stonington, ME 04681, Spring, 1983; and S.G.J. Ouseley, *The Science of the Aura*, (Essex, L. N. Fowler and Co. Ltd., 1949), p. 69-80.

when making initial contact and rapport, for energizing and clarity, and at the end of healing to complete and unify the color session. White is all colors, but greater healing effects are made when definite colors are sent, or when white light is broken down into its rainbow colors and used in a color sequence. Black is also the blending of all the Chakra colors, as pigment, and work needs to be done on its healing uses. It's the positive color of the goddess Earth.

Colors have to be experienced to become meaningful, understood in their attributes before they are used as healing tools. A basic way to do this is through color meditation, which is also a basic healing technique. Sit, stand or lie in a quiet place as in the meditations of Chapter Six and begin deep breathing. Once breathing is established, relax fully, and use creative visualization to experience the crown chakra as a shining spiral of white light.[10] Continue rhythmic breathing, feeling the light intensify with each exhaled breath. Pay attention to the chakra and its light. Inhaling, draw the light as a glowing white aura down the front and back of the head to the third eye, the brow chakra, light remaining strong at the crown as well. Breathe deeply and slowly, intensifying the light at both chakras and the light of the enveloping halo that connects them. Pay attention to the third eye. Inhaling again, draw the aura down further, lighting the throat chakra with a shining spiral of white brilliance, and continuing the light in the crown, third eye, and in the glowing aura that connects them. On the exhaled breaths, intensify the brightness and pay attention to the brilliance of the third eye.

Inhaling again, draw the shining aura down further to energize the spiral of the heart chakra, and use exhaled breaths to intensify the white light. Pay attention to the heart. Continue deep breathing, and on an inhaled breath draw the aura from the heart to the solar plexus, down front and back of the body. Exhaling, brighten and visualize the spiral of light at the solar plexus, pay attention to the solar plexus, and brighten and intensify the light of the other chakras. Inhaling, draw the aura of glowing whiteness to energize the spiral of the belly chakra in the lower abdomen. Use exhaled breaths to vitalize the light and pay attention to the chakra, to maintain the brightness of the other chakras and of the aura that encloses them. Inhaling, draw the light to the root chakra. Intensify the spiral glowing at the root chakra, the light of the other chakras, and the light of the aura on exhaled breaths. Pay attention to the

[1]Melita Denning and Osborne Phillips, *The Llewellyn Practical Guide to Astral Projection,* (St. Paul, Llewellyn Publications, 1984), p. 73-76. Adapted for color work. Available on tape, "Two Meditations" by Diane Stein, Llewellyn Publications.

root chakra. Again inhaling, draw the aura of shining white light down and around the body to the ground between the feet, noting the smaller spirals of light at the feet themselves. The soles of the feet and palms of the hands contain lesser chakras.

Visualize the aura of glowing light extending from the crown to the feet. Visualize it as entering the body from the sky, moving through the chakras from crown to feet, and returning to the earth at the feet. Then visualize the glowing spirals of light at each chakra, moving in order from the feet to the crown, changing from white to their colors, within the shimmering glow of the aura. The root chakra is red, belly chakra orange, solar plexus yellow, heart green, throat blue, third eye indigo and crown chakra violet. Experience this, then change the colors back to white light spirals again, moving the energy from crown to feet.

Next take each chakra color in turn, starting with red and drawing red from the earth through the glowing aura and into all of the chakra centers, including the hands and feet. Note what red feels like. Some of the sensations are of heat, sexuality, vital intensity, affection. Symbol connotations come to mind, perhaps as flames or hearts. Sounds, touch, odors occur, and these correspondences vary with the individual. At the crown, release the color to the sky. Do the exercise with each chakra color in turn, going next to orange, then yellow, green, blue, indigo and violet. Continue deep breathing throughout and do the exercise without rushing it. After reaching the violet crown chakra, the *kopavi,* change the colors again to white light, begin drawing the white light aura from the sky, into the crown and through each chakra to its return to earth at the feet. Do this for several inhaled and exhaled breaths, then stop the flow, allow the light to fade, and slowly return to daily awareness. Make notes of the color impressions, of the changes in moods and feelings that each color invokes. Another form of this is to simply breathe each color in turn, drawing the color from the earth, through the body and chakras, and releasing it into the sky from the crown *kopavi.* Or do it in reverse, drawing from the sky and beginning with the crown, to release the energy to the earth at the feet. Note the differences between starting at the sky and ending with the earth, and starting at the earth to end with the sky.

Once understanding what the colors mean and do, they are available to use for healing. In the case of a headache, for example, begin the meditation with white light, then draw blue (or green) from the earth in and through the chakras, releasing the color to the sky. When the flow is steady, visualize the headache itself and see it breaking into pieces that leave the body with the color's flow. Continue until the headache pieces (visualized in whatever way is personally meaningful) have all left the body, and continue the flow in pure blue (or pure green). When enough color healing has taken place, change the flow to white, then allow it to fade. Use the process for other forms of healing and mood altering. In times of exhaustion, use yellow; for sunburn use first green and then blue; for sleeplessness or worry, use violet. The hot colors (red, orange, yellow) are the least often used, and the cool ones (green and blue) the most frequent. In using colors be aware of their emotional connotations as these are powerful. Red, orange and yellow are hot and rousing; green is soothing; blue, indigo and violet are sedating. For lethargy use red or orange, not the violet that sedates; for nervousness and stress use violet, not the yellow that increases tension.

These color choices reflect the principle of complementary colors. A color's opposite or complement is used for balancing, for reducing "too much" of a quality by adding its dual opposite to the aura. Green and red, blue and orange, violet and yellow are complementary color pairs. Using violet to sedate reduces the amount of yellow in the aura, balances the nervousness of an over-active solar plexus by stimulating the crown and third eye. Using yellow for exhaustion activates the solar plexus, decreases the effects of the violet third eye or crown chakra. Using orange decreases blue to warm and vitalize, as using orange's complement blue reduces the belly chakra activity to calm and cool. Green, the heart, calms and soothes the physical and sexual intensity of the red root chakra, and sending red excites and stimulates the life force. Opposites attract and also bring each other into balance, and balance is peace, harmony and health in emotional, physical and spiritual ways.

Colors can be used in other than meditation for healing. A violet light bulb shining as the only light in a room for thirty minutes[11] has the healing effects of the color violet; use it to overcome sleeplessness. A green light bulb is antiseptic in cases of infection. Colored light concentrated for fifteen minutes on the exact area to be healed, blue on the swelling of a sprained ankle, for example, is localized color healing. Unfrosted colored light bulbs are available in hardware stores and supermarkets inexpensively, and they come in various colors. Colored cellophane over white bulbs works as well, but be careful of overheating. The light bulbs are plugged into any lamp. They never physically touch the body, only their radiating light does. Try colored candles, too.

---

[11]S.G.J. Ouseley, *Color Meditations, With Guide to Color Healing*, (Essex, L.N. Fowler and Co., Ltd., 1949), p. 74.

Aura healing begins with the use of magnetized cloth or water,[12] and this is the place where healing extends beyond the self to begin the healing of others. Using deep rhythmic breathing and relaxation techniques, visualize the aura of light through the chakras in the color desired.

When the flow is established, hold both hands, open and palms downward, over the mouth of a clear glass of water. Hands do not touch each other, the glass or the water itself. Continue deep breathing and visualize the color flow leaving the body through the palms of the hands, entering the water. A sense of vibration, heat or cooling depending on the color being sent, of electricity, magnetism, pressure or polarity results from the centers of the hands. Do this for about five minutes, or until the feeling of energy flow fades from the palms. Used by drinking, the water contains and is able to transmit the colors sent into it.

In magnetizing a cloth with color, the process is similar.[13] Using silk or cotton sprinkled with a few drops of water, and visualizing the flow of color in a healing meditation, hold the cloth flat in the left hand, left palm upward. Using the right hand, hold it palm over but not touching the cloth, a couple of inches away from the cloth surface. The sensations of electricity or polarity, of heat or cooling, vibration, sound or magnetism occur again in a few moments, and when they fade after several minutes the cloth is invested with the healing properties of the color visualized and sent into it. If no color is sent, direct aura energy and white light are transmitted into the cloth (or into the water in the last exercise). Use a cloth whose color matches the color being sent, or a white cloth other-wise, and use cloth of natural fibers. Cotton balls held in the hand are good for this, even a cotton menstrual pad. Place the magnetized cloth on the area to be healed, and the color and vibrations sent into it are transmitted.

Both the water and the cloth can be used as self-healing or for healing others. The colors are sent intentionally, visualized, and the electricity, vibration, magnetism or polarity, heat or coolness are aura energy transmitted through the small chakras in the palms. In doing this, and in the healing that follows, make very sure to draw the sent energy from the earth or sky, not from the body of the sender but through it. When com-pleting the process of magnetizing the cloth or water, return to daily awareness, then shake the hands off freely to remove the last energy,

[12]*Ibid.*, p. 81.

[13]*Ibid.;* also, Dolores Krieger, *The Therapeutic Touch: How to Use Your Hands to Help or to Heal,* (New Jersey, Prentice Hall, Inc., 1979), p. 27-30.

and wash them for several moments under cool running tap water. This is very important in all healings.

The energy involved in magnetizing is the aura energy used in what is variously called laying on of hands, psychic healing, faith healing or therapeutic touch. Schools of thought and practice such as Touch for Health and Reiki Healing have developed from it, and Therapeutic Touch as a skill by that name is being developed and taught by Ph.D. Dolores Krieger in nursing school programs. Krieger's book *Therapeutic Touch: How to Use Your Hands to Help or to Heal* (New Jersey, Prentice Hall, Inc., 1979) is a good beginning guidebook.[14] Deep work in this form of healing is used by body workers and massage therapists as psychic massage or polarity balancing techniques.[15] The principles of healing combine color meditation and transmission with aura transference, utilize the healing effects of color with the power of auras to create changes both in the healer and in the person experiencing healing. Aura healing is the use of energy, color and polarity to fill imbalances, release blockages and relieve pain—in effect to return a state of disharmony or imbalance to harmony and equilibrium, to health and participation in goddess Being.

The woman who has done the water and cloth magnetizing exercises has used aura energy, and if she understands the attributes of the colors and chakras, she is ready to heal. Establish deep breathing and relax as much as possible, using or not deep body relaxation. Visualize the white light aura and the spirals of glowing light at the chakras, then establish a flow of color from sky to earth, or earth to sky through the chakras. Hold the hands palms apart facing each other, four to six inches apart and not touching at any point, and send the color out through the palms. Continue deep breathing and visualizing the color of choice. If the color feels uncomfortable, or the flow of energy doesn't happen within a few minutes, change the color. The feelings noticed when magnetizing water or cloth occur in one or two minutes, and these feelings of pressure, temperature, vibration, polarity, electricity or even sound are stronger than in the earlier exercises. When the sensations fade and then stop, the exercise is over. Remember to draw the color from the earth or sky, allowing it to flow through you as a process of entering and leaving, and at the end of the exercise remember to shake off the hands or ground by touching the earth to release excess energy. Run both hands under cool tap water. Experiment with various chakra colors, individually and in a

---

[14] Krieger's work has influenced my own healing and this chapter greatly.
[15] See Roberta DeLong Miller, *Psychic Massage*, (San Francisco, Harper Colophon Books, 1975), and Robert Gordon, *Your Healing Hands, The Polarity Experience*, (Santa Cruz, The Unity Press, 1978).

rainbow series, noting the differences in their qualities.

With women working together, have one place her hand between but not touching the palms of a woman doing the color and aura exercise. Notice the sensations and compare impressions. Responses vary with individuals, but become familiar reactions. If the woman placing her hands between another's palms has a cut on her hand or is arthritic, have her take notice of the hurts before and after the exercise. Her pain is less at the end, or is gone. Healing has noticably progressed in the case of the open cut, and in arthritis there is freer movement. When the person placing her hand between another's palms has a hurt to be healed, take careful notice of the colors used. For a wound, use blue or green, but for arthritis use a warm color. Take turns holding the palms apart and building up the polarity, and take turns holding a hand inside the energy field. When the exercise is finished, ground it by shaking off or touching the earth, and in running water before going on to the next exercise or using healing on another person. Take note of the healer's physical state after using healing. The healer notices changes in herself: she is calm, relaxed and grounded; her movements and voice are slower in tempo; she feels at peace, interconnected and one; she has entered a state of empathy with the woman she has healed.

Women doing healings are aware of what's actually happening, and examine their own egos. Healing energy is a force of the earth, of the goddess, and available to all. The woman doing a healing is not healing someone herself, she is only channeling earth energy and goddess through herself and her own aura. Take no credit where none is earned. The person being healed uses the energy available to her as she wills, accepting or rejecting it and effecting her own healing by it. Perform healings only with love, and perform them also only with permission, as expressions of mutual free will and sharing.

As the next step, build aura energy between the palms without visualizing a color flow. Visualize white light or simply allow the energy polarity to build of itself, and use rhythmic breathing while doing this. Spread the palms wider apart, and starting at the head of a partner, run the palms slowly over the aura of the other person.[16] Do not physically touch the person, only her aura; stroking with long sweeping strokes from head downward, four to eight inches away from her physical body. Touching her aura is immediately recognizable, and the energy flow established between the palms continues to build. The feeling of touching

---

[16]Dolores Krieger, *The Therapeutic Touch: How to Use Your Hands to Help or to Heal*, p. 52-55. Krieger calls this process "unruffling the field."

another person's aura varies with individuals. The sensations may be of electricity, vibration, temperature, pressure, polarity, springiness, color or sound. If there is color, notice what the colors are, as this is a beginning to aura sensing. As hands travel along the length of a partner's body, moving from top to bottom, notice changes in pressure or sensation at various locations. There may be one or several of these changes that appear as cold spots, vacuums, spots where the vibration lessens or increases, spots where the colors change. Ask the partner about these spots; they are usually pain or tension areas, sites of old accidents or surgeries. A common one occurs in the lower abdomen as menstrual cramps.

The woman who has used her hands is the next woman whose aura is read, and the exercise is repeated. Discuss impressions as the exercise continues and afterwards, and don't forget to ground. Discuss the physical changes that result from experiencing the exercise by each partner. Next balance the "rough spots" in the auras. Build energy between the palms of the hands, and visualizing white light, hold the palms close together but not touching over the tension areas, one area at a time. Where possible, move one hand to each side of the area, front and back. On wider surfaces, place the hands side by side, but not touching each other or the person's body. Allow aura energy to enter the rough spot until it fades, then move to the next spot, moving through the aura. Reading the aura again, the rough spot is gone or lessened. Rough spots can also be balanced by a process of stroking the aura over the spots. Ask the woman being worked on to describe what she's feeling, both during and after the exercise. Take notice as healer of physical changes in the self. The partners experiment with this on each other, not forgetting to ground at the end of the exercise, shaking off and holding the hands under running water or placing hands to the earth, and stopping before becoming over tired. Always remember to ground.

This, in basic, is what healing is. The chakra and aura polarity of the hands develops in strength with use, as in any other skill. The ability to visualize and send colors also develops and grows. Once familiar with the process, the altered state of consciousness in healing requires very little preparation. Deep breathing can be enough to enter it, a process of simple centering. With practice, sending colors does not require full color work meditation, but only visualization of the needed color. When in doubt about what color to use, send white or green as neutral, or colors in a series until response is felt. Work closely with the person being healed and be very sensitive to her reactions and needs. Remember the temperatures of the colors. With experience on various types of discomfort and knowledge of colors, the color to use often comes to mind spontaneously when reading the aura or hurt spot. The technique does wonderful things for headaches, menstrual cramps, sore joints, swollen ankles, skin wounds, and any sort of physical or emotional tension. It draws heat from burns or sunburn and adds warmth to arthritis or frostbite, sends calming or energizing, relaxation, cheering or sleep.

The person experiencing a healing may or may not feel energy sensations from the healer's palms. She may or may not feel an immediate relief from pain, and is often unaware that pain is gone until the healer asks her. In some cases, there may be no decrease in pain immediately, or even an incease in pain, but a great difference is noticed later or the next morning. In some cases there is no change at all, and a woman being healed can consciously or not block the healing. The person experiencing healing may show mood changes after, usually physical and emotional calming and relaxation, sometimes a need to sleep. Though it can be done anywhere, choose calm and quiet places to perform healings, places of least distraction, for ability to enter the trance state and strongest results.

The healer feels changes, too, as described above, becomes more relaxed physically and emotionally, deeply peaceful. If she feels drained at the end of a healing, she is revitalized by sitting or lying on the ground for a moment and drawing energy back to herself from the earth. She may need a few moments quiet, or be hungry and need to eat something naturally sweet like fruit (no white sugar) for energy. None of these effects are serious or last long. Vegetarians have easier times learning to sense and channel energies for healing, and use of alcohol or smoking can prevent or lessen healing ability in some people. When there are aftereffects to the healer, drained feelings or hunger, the cause is usually a need for drawing healing from the earth and sky, rather than from the self, and this can be an ego problem. Remember to channel the healing *through* and not *from* the healer's body, to visualize the flow this way. When feeling aftereffects, take a moment to visualize the white light chakra exercise, as this energizes. If the healer experiences the pain of the person she is healing, she learns to let it flow through and out of her. Grounding at the end of every healing, shaking the energy off of the palms and running the hands under cool water, removes this sensation. Women doing healings, too learn to know when to stop, and stop before becoming tired.

When doing healing where the hands can't be placed opposite

each other, its important to be aware of how energy flows through the small chakras of the palms. Energy enters the body through the left side in most women and leaves through the right. The woman doing an aura reading receives more sensation into her left hand; when healing, she sends more energy out through her right hand. Both hands are needed, however, as what is being used here is a polarity situation, a state of energy tension between the plus and minus poles of the electrical aura.

Gain experience in doing healings by experimenting on house plants, and watch them burst into growth and blooming. Use green, of course. Experiment on the dog or cat, it can help and never harm them, though some animals get annoyed with the sensations. Practice healing on receptive others, on children, or with anyone who is learning the skill. Take it seriously, but enjoy doing it. The person experiencing healing doesn't have to believe in it for it to work. The technique of watching pain break up and leave the body is a valuable one. Visualizing an energy circuit running between the hands, into the left and out the right through the healer's body in a circle, is helpful. Stroking the aura and balancing rough spots is enough in some healings; hands held over the pain area are all that is needed in most situations. Remember the charged water and cloth.

Healing can be used on others or used for work on the self, and can also be done for someone not physically present. Creative visualization is the key here, and when doing absentee healing, pre-plan a day and time and ask the person being healed to visualize with you. Enter the trance state formally, by deep breathing and full body relaxation. Do the aura visualization with white light, then visualize the women to be healed as completely as possible. See her in a normal state, not ill, standing or sitting normally before you. Visualize doing an aura reading, first filling the woman's aura with white light through your hands.[17] Stroke her aura, moving from head to foot and locating the rough spots. Visualize using white light through the hands to balance the rough spots, then fill the person's aura with color, either a rainbow sequence (red, orange, yellow, green, blue, indigo and violet in turn) or a specific healing color carefully chosen for her need. Visualize placing hands over the hurt area, energy and color entering the woman from the palms, pain breaking up and leaving her body with the color flow. Remember to channel the energy from the earth or sky, and have it return to the sky or earth when it leaves the woman being healed, when it leaves the healer as well. See

[17]Keith Sherwood, *The Art of Spiritual Healing,* (St. Paul, Llewellyn Publications, 1985), p. 77-88.

the person totally well, an aura of full energy, beauty, health and peace surrounding her, a smile on her face. The flow of color changed to white, send the woman blessings, thank the goddess, then allow the flow to fade. Return slowly to daily consciousness and ground yourself.

Healing is one of the wonders of women's spirituality, perhaps the greatest of the mysteries. It is available to any who choose it, a skill available for self-care and for helping others. Like all forms of power, healing comes with a choice. Use it freely and with responsibility, refusing none who ask for it and manipulating none, respecting all, including the choice to refuse it. The healer channels energy from the goddess' earth and sky; the person experiencing healing uses the energy as she chooses and heals herself with it. A healing is something shared equally and in trust by two people, or is done for oneself in love. When the situation happens to do a healing and it feels right to do, then go ahead and use the skill. It's a gift to use wisely, lovingly and for the good of all.

8

Crystals and Gemstones

Crystals and gemstones are healing tools, with uses in meditation and
creative visualization, in color work, protection and energizing, psychic
healing and biofeedback, in rituals and goddess altars, divination and in
psychic communication skills. Their beauty and great power have made
them a major interest in women's spirituality, as well as in Western New
Age and wiccan groups, and in Eastern, African, Egyptian, South
American and Native American healing. The legendary crystal work of
past civilizations like Atlantis and of this civilization's sages and psychics
is being re-claimed and redefined today, and much of the work is
happening in the women's community. Where patriarchal interest in
crystals has focused on computers, telemetry, lasers and weapons, New
Age use focuses on mind power tools and interplanetary broadcasting.
Women's spirituality concentrates on healing and psychic skills, on re-
forming and dis-covering the matriarchal knowledge and peace net-
works within and among women on goddess earth.

Women everywhere are using crystals and associating them with
women's spirituality work and the goddess. They are obtaining stones
by trading for them, purchasing them at women's music and goddess
festivals, from lapidary dealers at home and by mail, mining them,
receiving and giving them as gifts. Women are learning about clear
quartz crystals particularly, carrying them with them, wearing them,
discussing them and using them for healing, sleeping with them for
dreamwork. Other gemstones are being re-cognized and explored,
books and learning dis-covered, understood and written, and research
into gemstones as healing tools is happening with increasing interest

and excitement. Women are dis-covering garnets and amber, amethysts, peridots, moonstones and rose quartz, lapis, aquamarines and others, learning what they are, where to find them, and how to use them. Much is known, much is being learned and relearned every day, much knowledge is being gained and shared—and there is much much more to come.

Natural quartz crystal is known chemically as silicon dioxide (SiO_2), poetically as petrified water.[1] Water is the source of life and its power fossilized resonates with the life force. Crystals and minerals are of earth element origins, formed by the geologic combining of earth, air, fire and water over thousands of years' development. Formed within the earth, sand (silicon) and O_2 (oxygen) are transformed from cooling magma into crystalline forms. All the four elements of weather—wind/air, geologic changes/earth, volcanic and chemical action/fire and the flooding-freezing-thawing of water—take part in the formation and shaping process.[2]

A quartz crystal takes 10,000 or more years to form, and crystals are over a third of the earth's composition. Quartz crystal absorbs both magnetism from the earth's core and radiation from the sun, and emits that energy. Kirlian photography has recorded this energy emission, which appears in photographs as a white light aura radiating from a blue star center.[3] The energy radiant from clear quartz and other cyrstals is resonant with the human aura, and this, scientifically called its piezo-electric effect, is its healing attribute. The resonance occurs rapidly, within a few moments of holding a crystal or gemstone in the hand. "Energy from crystals passes through and penetrates all bodies of matter,"[4] penetrating even into human cellular structure. Crystal energy transmission is a magnetic polarity similar to the natural aura polarity used in laying on of hands. Its strong ability to match aura energy and resonate with it makes crystal a powerful healing tool. While all of the gemstones discussed in this chapter contain healing properties, clear quartz contains the greatest human resonance and the ability to transmit any color, to focus a chosen strand of its rainbow white light spectrum and use it to transmit, store, duplicate and magnify color and aura polarity.

The hexagonal, symmetrical shape of crystal is a basic form in

[1] DaEl, *The Crystal Book*, (Sunol, CA, The Crystal Co., 1983), p. 13.
[2] Thelma Isaacs, *Gemstones, Crystals and Healing*, (Black Mountain, North Carolina, Lorien House, 1982), p. 1-5.
[3] Michael G. Smith, *Crystal Power*, (St. Paul, Llewellyn Publications, 1985), p. 137.
[4] *Ibid.*, p. 137-138.

geometry, physics and atomic theory,[5] and is a universal, perfect form in the structure of matter. This is a scientific way of saying what witches and wisewomen already know—that crystal, though technically inorganic, participates in the life force, in goddess earth, and can be used by Be-ing women to radiate, focus and balance their own earth energies, as well as to help heal others. Magick and physics move closer everyday, as do magick and psychology, and Native American healers call crystals "living stones."

Crystals magnify, store and focus energy, are used to transmit and direct energy, healing and color in resonance with the aura. Used with creative visualization, their applications and uses are beyond any now-known limits. Crystals are used to relieve pain, to stimulate healing, to transmit color. They focus and clarify dreams, are the original biofeed-back machines, cast protective auras and circles, increase intellectual and psychic powers, change moods, enhance meditation skills, create calming and deep physical and mental relaxation states. Kept with a tarot deck, runes or I Ching, crystals enhance the power of divination tools, and are divination tools themselves. They increase and focus the power of altars and rituals in group or individual work, stimulate astral projection, psychic links with receptive others, and cause chosen deep psychological changes. DaEl suggests their use in refrigerators and gas lines to increase fuel efficiency,[6] and classifies crystal attributes into: amplification and clarity, transforming, storage of information and energy, focusing, energy transference, and altered states of consciousness.[7] Virtually all work in women's spirituality is made more powerful by use of crystals.

The first step in beginning crystal use is to obtain the right crystal for the woman using it. Vendors at goddess and women's music festivals are first choices for finding cyystals to purchase, but most cities have lapidary stores and societies, or museums with gift shops that sell raw stones. Mail order is a possibility, and lapidary and women's spirituality journals advertize crystal and gemstone dealers, but buying by firsthand touch is preferable. New Age bookstores and magick and occult shops sometimes sell crystals and gemstones, or know of a private dealer for them. Crystals as gifts, given or received, are gifts of love.

Women who live in an area where crystals or gemstones grow can mine or find their own. Most clear quartzes in the United States come from Arkansas, and Brazil is the second major source of clear quartz.

---

[5]For technical material on crystals, see Ra Bonewitz, *Cosmic Crystals: Crystal Consciousness and the New Age,* (Great Britain, Turnstone Press, 1983), p. 24-84.
[6]DaEl, *The Crystal Book,* p. 28. I haven't tried this.
[7]*Ibid.,* p. 14-15.

Concern is growing over industrial strip mining techniques being used in Arkansas to obtain computer chip crystals, and no healer participates in a rape of goddess earth. Crystals are sold by the pound from some mining areas, and individually by many ethical dealers. Quality healing amethyst comes from Canada, deeply purple, and amethyst also occurs in Brazil, Ceylon and Mexico. Turquoise is found in the American Southwest; lapis in Colorado, California and where there are gold mines, and garnets grow in Arizona and Colorado, as well as in Greenland.[8] Peridots and Herkimer diamonds (a form of quartz crystal) come from New York State, and peridots also from Canada, South Africa, Siberia and England. Rose quartz is mined in California, Maine and Brazil; citrine quartz in Brazil, France and the USSR; and smoky quartz in Pennsylvania, Colorado, Scotland, Brazil and Switzerland. Non-jewelry topaz is found on Pikes Peak in Colorado and in Canada, and aquamarines, moonstones and agates are found in several US states.[9] Despite the geographies and distances, uncut crystals, minerals and gemstones are rarely expensive to buy, with most stones of two inch size ranging in price from two to ten dollars. The stones used in healing and women's spirituality work are natural stones only (and not lead crystal which is glass), are uncut, unmounted, usually unpolished raw stones, with some of the gemstones tumbled. Many are not jeweler's quality, and have no need to be.

In picking a crystal or gemstone, the best way is to handle and hold it, being sensitive to how it feels. Appearance is secondary and unimportant. Pick a stone by attraction, by being drawn to touch it, then hold it in the left hand loosely. Let it rest against the palm chakra and notice the impressions, colors, sounds, mood feelings that go with the stone. No two stones are the same, even the same type of stone or crystal, and crystal resonance feels different to different women. The feelings are similar to what aura energy in healing feels like, and the two energies are closely related. Sensitivity to crystals grows with use, but the woman knows which stone is hers. Look for a stone that resonates with the individual's aura, and regardless of size, shape, color, clarity or jeweler's quality, it's this subtle polarity impression that is meaningful. The stone feels alive in the hand, vibrates or radiates—it feels good. A tiny quartz no bigger than a thumbnail can be powerful and effective. Look for pleasing colors and unchipped points, symmetrical shapes, but these appearances are secondary to the energy vibrations. Crystals select their owners, and if a woman has to have a particular stone or crystal, for any reason or no

[8]William T. Fernie, MD, *The Occult and Curative Powers of Precious Stones*, (San Francisco, Harper and Row Publishers, 1973), p. 156 ff.
[9]Various encyclopedias and sources.

reason, it's her stone.

Stones should be picked by the user, but can be ordered by mail if necessary. When ordering from a spirituality source, state what the stone is for. If it's for healing or ritual work, tell the dealer so in a brief handwritten note with the order to help her to match the right stone. Do visualizations before mailing the letter; hold and impress the letter with the request for a perfect crystal. Ask in affirmations for the crystal that's the right one, then mail the order. Do visualizations for the perfect stone until the crystal arrives. When ordering from other types of dealers, do the same visualizations without writing to the dealer what the stone is for. Ask wisely and clearly to receive what is visualized. When choosing a crystal for someone else, visualize her picking a stone, then pick the stone for her by attraction and first impressions.

Quartz crystals come in a range of colors, each with their healing uses. Smoky quartz is wonderful as a mood raiser; rose quartz opens the heart; and citrine quartz sharpens perceptions and sexuality. Clear quartz crystal, however, is the stone with the most power, aura resonance, versatility, healing use and attraction. Sizes range from minute Herkimer diamonds to hundreds of pounds in weight for a single stone. One that fits comfortably in the hand is best for healing and most uses, from an inch to four inches in length; and for wearing choose crystals of about an inch, unpierced and uncut in the mounting. There are no rules except what feels right to the individual.

Quartz is single or double terminated. Single terminated means a point at one end; double terminated is less common, more expensive, and has a symmetrical point at both ends. Double terminated quartzes are powerful, they channel the energy in both directions, but a single terminated stone can do anything that's needed, too. Double terminated crystals are good for channeling group energy, for meditation, rituals, astral projection and for healing uses, but may be too strong to wear as a necklace or to carry every day. Single terminated crystals are used for balancing, healing and psychic work, for any crystal use, and their energy is more grounded. Crystals also come in clusters and chunks, and are clear, translucent or milky in shades. While some experts say that a crystal with a chipped point is undesirable, this is not always the case. Know by holding it and sensing its vibrations.

The first thing to do with a new crystal is to cleanse it, clear it of other people's energies. Since crystals absorb and store energy, this is important in making the stone yours, and is done periodically as well. Crystals often need clearing after handling by others, always after use for healing, and any time they become sluggish or feel overloaded. There are several easy ways to do it. Salt water is traditional for purification in women's spirituality: soak a new crystal in a solution of sea salt and water overnight to clear it. Running the crystal under cool tap water is another way; the method of grounding used in aura healing for the healer. Use only cool water, as hot can shatter a fragile quartz, and point the crystal downward, visualizing negativity running out of the stone and down the drain. Other ways to clear and cleanse a new or over-loaded crystal are to bury it in the ground for three days or to set it on the earth in direct sunlight for an afternoon. Soak crystals in dry sea salt, sage, frankincense or dried rose petals—roses are the nicest and gentlest but take a longer time—and these herbs are cheaply available from food cooperatives and herb stores. A cleared crystal feels cold to the touch and vibrant when held in the hand. The length of time this takes depends on the method used, on how overloaded it is, on personal sensitivity, and on the phase of the moon. (Use clearing with visualization to *gain* clarity on the waxing moon, to *banish* negativity in the waning phases.) It may take a couple of hours to clear a crystal outdoors in the sun, or three days or a week for a very overloaded stone in the earth; running water takes only a few minutes, if it's the right method for the occasion. Salt is harsh and should be used with care; it can strip a crystal of all liveliness and bonding, at least temporarily, and is best used on new crystals only.

Placing a crystal in a positive energy environment—on a goddess altar during private or group ritual, on the stage through a women's concert, in the center of a spirituality circle workshop, or next to the bed when making love—are good ways to vitalize and clear it. Crystals absorb and store the energies they are exposed to. When clearing a stone or working with it, use creative visualization to energize and program a crystal. For a new crystal, visualize it made new, clear, pure and yours alone. Consecrate it to the goddess, to healing, to any positive use as a magical tool, to the highest good. For a crystal that's already consecrated and bonded, clear it by visualizing negativity leaving it and the positive things, the rituals, music and love its experienced, remaining. When making a ritual of this clearing, visualize the crystal's aura and your own Be-ing simultaneously cleared and energized. Use with meditation and altars, and in the self blessing.

Proceeding in crystal work, the next thing to do with a new and cleared crystal is to make it the user's own. Bonding a crystal is done by handling it and keeping it with you. Place it in a left-sided pocket and carry it there everyday, putting it on an altar overnight and during spirituality work. Hold it often and get the feel of its vibrations, colors or sound, energy and changes, as absorbed through the chakra in the left palm. This is extremely pleasant and cheering. Visualize the flow of colors through it, held in the right hand to send colors out. Gradually and over a period of days and weeks, the crystal becomes tuned to the user's aura, bonded to her in growing power, attraction and versatility. No one else should touch the crystal in this period, or sometimes even after this period. It may be necessary to keep it hidden from others to prevent this, as everyone is attracted to crystals. Allow others to handle a personal crystal only if it feels right to do so, and it may need clearing afterward.

As the crystal becomes tuned to its user, begin working with it for healing and ritual. Experiment slowly and move gradually into crystal use. Crystals are the original biofeedback tools, and work powerfully with creative visualization for mood and body changes. When feeling cold or chilled, hold a crystal in the left hand and draw warmth. Do this in a color meditation with deep breathing, drawing the energy in as red through the left side of the body, in a circuit that releases it from the right side to the earth or sky. Continue doing this for several minutes and get warm, and it works for cooling with blue as well. For cheering, draw yellow in this way; for calming draw violet or indigo. Do the color meditations of Chapters Six and Seven, holding a crystal, and note the differences with and without the stone, with the stone in the left and right hands. Body metabolism and heart rate can be raised or lowered by this, an effect already familiar with deep breathing. Use crystals in visualizations, affirmations, rituals and on altars to amplify and intensify the work. Use in the left hand to receive energy, in the right hand to send it, but this can be the opposite in some women. Experiment and learn what works best.

Crystals relieve pain magickally. In another self-healing exercise, hold a crystal in the left hand, feel the energy polarity build from it, then put the right hand gently on a pain area and hold it there.[10] The headache, body pain or menstrual cramps dissolve within half an hour, usually less than half an hour, and particularly faster when used with color. Set the crystal directly on the pain area, hold it flat in the palm of the hand with the thumb, or grip it between the fingers point downward, to use both hands with a crystal in aura healing. When receiving color or energy, hold the crystal in the left hand; when using the stone to send energy away (to draw out pain), hold it in the right. Crystals held in the right (sending) hand, increase and amplify the power of magnetizing cloth

---

[10]DaEl, *The Crystal Book*, p. 67.

or water. Place a crystal in the water point up while magnetizing it, as well. Crystals held in the left hand draw colors in for self-healing and energizing.

Hold a crystal in the right hand, or one in each hand, to do psychic healing for others, increasing the power of laying on of hands or therapeutic touch. In doing this, try rotating the hand holding the crystal clockwise in a spiral over the pain area, crystal point facing the area to be healed. Use colors and other visualizing as usual. Use in massage over chakras and tension areas to release blockages, over the entire body to balance, vitalize and soothe energy flow. Tape a crystal to a pain area overnight for three nights running on the waning moon. A small crystal chip is fine for doing this. After the third night, take the crystal and bury it outside in the ground, visualizing the pain gone into the crystal, and the earth and moon phase banishing it. The pain wanes with the waning moon and is gone by the new, and the crystal unretrieved is exchanged for health.[11]

In aura reading, hold a crystal in the left hand to receive impressions, in the right moving in a clockwise spiral or stroking motion to clear rough spots. Hold a crystal in the left hand, or one in each hand, for the chakra balancing exercises and self-blessing of Chapters Five and Seven, placing the crystal over each chakra in turn being energized. For direct or absentee healing, visualize the rough spots and pain areas entering the crystal. See the stone turning grey with the illness it's absorbing, the person's aura being cleared of pain, brightened and energized; then release the illness from the crystal into the earth, transforming it to energy the earth needs. Visualize the stone clear again, and cleansed.[12]

After using a crystal in healing, clear it as you clear your hands. Run it under cool tap water, point downward, and visualize all pain or illness leaving it, being changed into positive energy as it returns to the earth through the water. Where running water is unavailable at the time or not wanted, blow "through" the crystal strongly, from base to point, visualizing again and transforming the negative energy given to the sky into positive symbols. When running under water or blowing, visualize illness and negativity leaving, but the positive things remaining in the stone. Use a visualized image or symbol to represent these things. See the crystal as clear and cleansed, bright, sparkling, cold and renewed.

Some healers prefer to use other crystals for healing than the ones they keep with them and use otherwise. Crystals grow in power with use, however, grow in bonding and resonance to the woman using them.

[11]Tyshe Moonfeather, from her workshop at the Michigan Women's Music Festival, August, 1983.
[12]Uma Sita Silbey, "Natural Quartz Crystal Healing Ritual", in *Circle Network News*, (POB 219, Mt. Horeb, WI 53572), Fall, 1984, p. 13.

Just make sure to ground and clear them after healing and whenever else they need it. Distinguish healing energy from ritual, psychic or other work, do it verbally or by visualization and symbol when starting to use the stone each time. Use crystals as a channel, in the many ways that the human aura is also a channel, sending and receiving energy from the goddess earth and sky in a variety of circulating flows.

Crystals are powerful in ritual and psychic work, as well as in healing, and the possibilities are boundless for their uses. Use a large crystal as an athame, or made into the tip of an athame or wand,[13] to cast circles, invoke the directions, channel power and to draw down the moon. Use a crystal or crystal cluster to represent the north direction, the earth correspondence, and also place on altars to amplify the power of any ritual. A double terminated crystal or crystal cluster in the center of a circle increases every aspect of group work and channels group energy, harmony and the raising of power. A crystal garden, crystals arranged point up in a circle or clockwise spiral in a shallow bowl of sand, is a powerful ritual transmitter. A crystal can be used to clear auras in ritual purification, but remember to cleanse it afterwards before using it again. Take a journey into a crystal as the group's beginning meditation,[14] and learn wisdom from the grandmothers, goddesses or womanspirit guides inside it.

In the menstrual ritual of going within the womb, hold a crystal in the left hand and move it clockwise over the abdomen while visualizing.[15] To enter meditative states, hold a crystal so the altar's candle flame is seen through it, but not so close as to burn or overheat the stone. Focus the eyes on the glowing, candlelit crystal while doing deep breathing as a key for entering trance. For scrying work, continue using the crystal in this way, in the flame or in a dark colored bowl filled with water to stimulate psychic images: this is the principle of the crystal ball.

Crystals amplify and intensify any form of meditation and visualization, and tuned to the user's aura they open the psychic and healing centers. They transmit this absorbed and stored energy when directed to or held, and hold it otherwise for later use. They facilitate in entering and channeling altered states. Hold a crystal in the left hand, or one in each hand, for meditation in any form. Double terminated crystals are good for this, and also stimulate astral projection work, but single terminated stones—

---

[13]For information on making psychic tools, see Michael G. Smith, *Crystal Power*, (St. Paul, Llewellyn Publications, 1985). I cannot condone Smith's non-peaceful uses for crystals, however.

[14]DaEl, *The Crystal Book*, p. 33.

[15]Bonnie Holbrook, "On the First Night of Menses", in *WomanSpirit Magazine*, (2000 King Mountain Trail, Wolf Creek, OR 97497-9799), Issue No. 39, Spring, 1984, p. 15.

any bonded crystal of any size—work well.

Focusing on a crystal in reaching out to others (the full moon exercise), intensifies the power of the link and does so in other telepathy/empathy linkages. To reach someone receptive psychically, enter the trance state by breathing and deep relaxation, and visualize the woman's face in the crystal. Never force this type of link, only open to it and allow it to come if it happens. Be open and loving to the impressions, receive them, and send a message in return. Before withdrawing from the touch, send love, sisterhood and caring. Store tarot decks and I Ching books with a crystal on top of them to increase their strength as psychic divination tools. The crystal tunes them to the user's aura.[16]

Hold a crystal in the left or right hand to induce sleep, and during sleep for remembered, symbolic and precognitive dreams. A crystal becomes natural to hold in the hand while sleeping; after a few nights it remains there and seldom moves away or gets lost in the blankets. This is an important tool for women interested in dreamwork, and worth developing. Psychic links while dreaming increase with crystals used this way.

In jewelry, wear crystals for balancing, calming, protection, energizing and in ritual. Wear a crystal necklace in coven work, point upward for raising power, or a double terminated crystal as a necklace, mounted horizontally, to tune fully with the energies of the group. Some intense psychic links can happen here, and both of these are too powerful and "spacey" for everyday use. A crystal held in a headband over the third eye, stone touching the skin, induces psychic experiences.[17] When wearing a crystal daily, wear a single terminated crystal point downward for balancing and grounding. Use crystals as jewelry with silver chains and mountings, glued or pronged rather than drilled. Experiment with necklaces for chain length to find which chakra a crystal is best held over, close to the throat, over the heart chakra at the breastbone, or lower near the solar plexus. Try wearing it on the right or left; try a ring with the stone exposed at the back of the mounting to touch the skin. Avoid metals other than silver, gold or copper for jewelry. Copper is a merging of earth and sky energies, and is suggested by Smith for psychic inducement. Gold's energizing properties can be too hot with a crystal for some women to wear. Silver cools, calms, balances and flows like water, and adds these properties to what the crystal absorbs and amplifies. Silver is a lunar, goddess and feminine form.

---

[16]Chapters on tarot and I Ching follow.
[17]17Michael G. Smith, *Crystal Power*, p. 55-63.

The suggestions here are only a beginning of the uses for clear quartz crystal, and basics for using other gemstones in healing and mood altering follow. The possibilities are limitless and new women's spirituality uses for crystals are being dis-covered and tried daily. Experiment and work with aura bonded crystals and keep them with you. New ideas emerge on an on-going basis, new information to experiment with and to share with others, to use and heal with. The results are exciting, magickal and healing in every way.

Clear quartz crystals and diamonds, which are also crystals, are stones of the highest chakra level, the transpersonal point. Their color is white, the blending of all colors, and their uses are versatile as they contain all colors of the rainbow spectrum, which can be separated into individual colors for use. Diamond induces courage, daring, strength and long life, rejects evil and encourages trust, joy and faithfulness in relationships.[18] *Clear quartz crystal* amplifies all healing, is electrical, channels all the chakra colors, induces intuition, psychic development and meditation states. It's an all-use stone for all purposes.

While other gemstones are less versatile than clear quartz, their healing properties are powerful and not to be overlooked. They are a traditional interest in wiccan and occult healing, and newly being dis-covered in women's spirituality, which has focused heavily on clear quartz. Colored quartzes—smoky, citrine, green, amethyst and rose— are being studied, and minerals and gemstones that are not crystalline, that are technically called massive forms, and that come to the healer as raw chunks or tumbled pieces. These are being experimented with for their colors, healing and mood properties, for chakra correspondences, and much is being learned.

Gemstones are held in the hand for healing, worn as jewelry particularly over the chakras, used in magnetized essences, or even ground up and taken internally. (No ground up uses are made in this chapter.) Use in laying on of hands or therapeutic touch has been covered in the healing and clear quartz sections, and is done in the same ways with other gemstones. Gem use as jewelry is similar to that for clear quartz, following the correspondences for individual stones.

Magnetized essences or elixirs are water polarized by aura healing

[18]Healing uses of gemstones are from the following sources: DaEl, *The Crystal Book,* p. 61; Thelma Isaacs, *Gemstones, Crystals and Healing,* p. 30 ff; Jim Knight, "Healing Uses of Gemstones, Minerals and Metals", in *Circle Network News,* Fall, 1984, p. 12; Julia Lorusso and Joel Glick, *Healing Stoned,* (Albuquerque, Brotherhood of Life, 1985 ed.), p. 27 ff.; Rhiannon McBride, et al., "Occult Uses of Gemstones", in *Circle Network News,* Summer, 1982, p. 12; and J'aime Schelz, *Crystal Essence,* (NY, Gemstoned Ltd, Inc., 1984), unpaged.

and with a gemstone. A chosen stone is placed in a clear glass of water, and aura energy with corresponding color is sent into the water. The magnetized water is used by drinking in

> doses of a wineglassful every half hour for the first day, every hour for the second day, and a wineglassful three times a day to finish the treatment.[19]

Prepared gemstone elixirs are available from some New Age sources and make use of this process in homeopathic ways, using colors, gemstone energies, sun or moonlight, and sometimes the energy of ley lines and other natural power spots. A preservative base is added, and the essences are bottled and sold. Dosage is in drops under the tongue or in a glass of water, or used in massage oil or the bath.[20] The development and principle is similar to that of the Bach Flower Remedies.

Various stones are used for healing other than clear quartz, for aura work and essences, and aura work is emphasized in this chapter and book. *Amethyst* is the most familiar of these, a stone found as crystals or in chunks and geode clusters, a form of crystalline quartz. Amethyst corresponds to the crown chakra, the violet color band in the spiritual aura. Worn as a necklace point downward, the crystals are used for calming, grounding and balancing over the heart and solar plexus particularly. They are known as the sobriety stone, and are a symbol for many recovering alcoholics. A chunk of Canadian amethyst placed under the bed induces sleep and is a remedy for insomnia. Amethyst also soothes sexual urges, and should be removed during lovemaking. For stress and tension, a crystal of Canadian or Brazilian amethyst held in the left hand and used to draw violet inward is calming. Use amethyst in healing for all mental and nervous disorders, except those caused by electro-chemical imbalances. It eases anxiety and depression, transforms habits, is a spiritual cleanser and stimulant, stabilizes kundalini energy, and is effective wherever violet is called for in color work. Amethyst opens and balances the crown chakra, the individual's connection and relationship to goddess, and raises sound and other vibrations to spirituality levels.

For the crown chakra also, though not violet in color, is the *moonstone*. Stone of lunar goddess energy and correspondent to the pineal gland, moonstone heightens psychic sensitivity and trance states. It is

[19]S.G.J. Ouseley, *The Power of the Rays: The Science of Colour Healing*, (Essex, L.N. Fowler and Co., Ltd., 1951), p. 66.
[20]J'aime Schelz, *Crystal Essence*, unpaged pamphlet.

144

sedative and soothing for sleeplessness and stress. A form of feldspar, moonstone is a hope stone, cheering to use and strengthening. It aids in psychometry and astral balance, lessens over-reaction, keeps near things nearer, and is a psychic mirror for emotions already there. Because of its reflective qualities, moonstone should not be used during negative or ungrounded states of mind, but to amplify affirmations, positivity and groundedness. It works well with amethyst, sapphire and rose quartz, and is a stone of inner work and growth, of balance, spirituality, healing and peace.

A stone for the third eye, the brow chakra is *blue sapphire.* Use it for insight and perception, clarity, joy, introspection, to focus meditation, and for psychic protection. Called the "supreme gem"[21] sapphire attracts the goddess' favor, brings peace, enlightenment, spiritual wisdom, induces courage, devotion and instant knowing. Its healing uses are for inspiration and the senses, and like amethyst it raises vibrations to spiritual levels, induces positivity and a positive self-image. Use sapphire for the eyes, ears and nose, for mental clarity. Use it with moonstone, and remember that these are uncut stones. Most healers feel that their power is lessened greatly by commercial faceting.

The legendary *lapis lazuli* is a stone for the throat chakra, as is aquamarine. Lapis is the healer's stone, the gemstone of the Egyptian sky goddess Nuit or Nut and of Isis. Using it gains sensitivity to higher auras and spiritual vibrations. Lapis opens the chakras, strengthens and balances, and induces psychic experiences. It regains lost love, cheers all moods and ills, and is useful for incest recovery. Worn as a necklace, lapis opens the throat to articulate speech and energizes all the mental and communicative faculties. Use it in healing for cooling and calming, for all infections and inflammations, burns, fevers and pain, for all throat ailments, earaches, and as a general energizer and toner for the body. It stimulates creativity, artistry, speech, sincerity and meditation. The stone is not a crystal, and compared to other gemstones is harder to find and often more expensive when located, depending on origin and quality. It has a lovely mid-blue color, streaked with gold, is massive and comes tumbled, polished or in raw chunks.

Aquamarine is another throat chakra stone, a stone of sea water and sea goddesses, soothing and calming. A crystalline, aqua form of beryl, aquamarine is used in healing for throat, mouth, stomach and liver problems. Its strongest properties are in mood easing, for tension and

---

[21]Rhiannon McBride, Louise Devery, Charlene Deering and Amber K, "Occult Uses of Gemstones", in *Circle Network News,* (POB 219, Mt Horeb, WI 53572), Summer, 1982 p. 12.

tension headaches, for migraines. It works well with clear quartz and in white gold settings. Some sources list aquamarine as correspondent to the thymus (heart chakra), while others list it as correspondent to the throat and thyroid. The stone enhances psychic sensitivity, love, lunar energy, inner peace and flowing, protects travellers at night, and is thought to banish fear, cure laziness and stimulate intelligence. Aquamarine is a stone of self-understanding and tranquil acceptance.

The heart has several gemstones, not all of them green for the chakra color, stones that connect the lower with the higher chakras and open sympathy, empathy and the emotions. Peridot, rose quartz, emerald and turquoise are some of the stones. *Peridot* or olivine is crystalline, a green translucent stone used for protection, prosperity, happiness and clarity of mind. Peridot draws these qualities, and is used for healing as well. It calms, balances and purifies, and is good for digestive, emotional and spleen difficulties. *Rose quartz,* a massive form of quartz, opens the heart, particularly if worn as a necklace or in a bag over the breastbone. Emotional release results from this, and the healing that follows this release. The stone is also used for a loving, positive outlook and emotional state, for forgiveness, self-acceptance and cheering. Rose quartz stimulates a feeling of oneness with the goddess' universe. In healing, use rose quartz for heartache and emotional pain, for dis-ease of the throat, ears, nose and sinuses, for the kidneys and high blood pressure and for adults recovering from abused childhoods.

Emerald, another stone for the heart chakra, is a crystal of prophecy and psychic experiences. It draws beauty and love, protection, and is healing for the eyes, heart, spleen, pancreas and gall bladder. Like peridot, emerald draws prosperity and peace, also bringing strength in old age, emotional healing and aura balancing. *Turquoise* is called skystone by Native American healers, with the property of connecting the earth to the sky, the lower to the higher chakras and bodies. Like other heart chakra stones, turquoise is used for healing the heart and emotions, for all-round healing, balancing and grounding, and for knowing the ways of the earth. Turquoise draws and sends love and courage, prosperity, luck, soothing and protection. A massive stone, use it in healing for the eyes, for fevers and inflammations, to ease tension and emotional shock. It draws peaceful relationships, increases breast milk, releases psychic and physical blockages, draws wisdom and empathy. Use all four of these stones: peridot, rose quartz, emerald and turquoise, in heart chakra healing, for success, higher mental and earth wisdom, empathy, balancing and prosperity, for heart healing and healing love-loss and loneliness. They are powerful and positive stones with great healing effects.

The yellow stones—amber, citrine quartz and topaz—are healers for the solar plexus chakra. Topaz and citrine are crystalline. *Amber* is fossilized pine resin and unique among stones for its vegetable origins. Use it against disease and infections of all types, for ear and vision problems, for ulcers and burns, rheumatism and protection. It is used for healing the digestive system, stopping bleeding, for calming, the teeth, and for the endocrine system. Amber is solar vitality, strengthening the aura and drawing out pain and negativity. It balances yin and yang energies within the individual woman. *Citrine* is a yellow form of quartz crystal, strong for uses in sending and receiving colors. It's a toner and stimulant of both psychic and sexual energy, enhances trancework and meditation, raises clarity and perception, and connects the higher and lower mental levels. Use citrine in healings for urinary infections (cystitis), for the colon, gall bladder, kidneys and liver, for digestion. Citrine strengthens the will and eliminates toxins.

Topaz is another yellow chakra stone, a crystal sometimes confused with citrine quartz, but very different in energy and uses. Topaz in healing helps tension headaches, insomnia and depression, and banishes fears. A stone of trust, strength and protection, it eases death and establishes protective auras, is a mood elevator. This is a strongly magnetic stone, said to change color (as does emerald) near poisons. Topaz in healing is used for urinary tract infections and the kidneys, as a blood coagulant, stimulant for exhaustion, and aids sexual functioning. Where amber is calming and citrine energizing, topaz is a heavier, more electric and volatile stone.

Carnelian and red coral are two stones for opening the belly chakra, the color orange. *Carnelian* is electromagnetic and energizing and aids the digestive system, mental abilities and the liver. It stops bleeding and hemorrhages, and is a good stone for painful menstruation or heavy flows. Use carnelian in purifications, cleansings and renewals of all sorts, for learning about past lives, to deepen concentration, and to harmonize fire and earth as elements within. *Coral* in the red-orange shades, valued by Native American healers, is a stone for fertility and physical wisdom, a negativity repellent that protects psychically and physically against violence and attack. A warm stone of animal origins, use it for attunement to nature and the animals of the sea, to the physical body and material world, to the sexual world. Use it for enhancing creative visualization and meditation states. Coral is said to cure madness, remedy poisons, bring physical tranquility. In healing, use red coral for the blood and circulation, to warm, for arthritis and rheumatism and for calcium deposits in the joints.

Red stones for the root chakra include garnet, ruby and bloodstone. *Garnet* draws happiness, power, possessions and peace, and aids in patience, persistence, sexuality and purification. Offering friendship, loyalty and sometimes more, garnet protects against nightmares and brings quiet sleep, aids in health and travellers' protection, brings peace, balance and inspiration. Use garnet to ease birth and life passages. It balances polarities and kundalini energy, aids the blood and is used in healing for arthritis, rheumatism, calcium in the joints, and fertility problems.

Bloodstone offers courage, constancy, endurance and harmony, corresponds to the root chakra, and is used in healing to stop bleeding. A form of chalcedony and of massive form, bloodstone or heliotrope helps in decision making. Use it in healing for iron deficiency in the blood, for moving kundalini energy, and to invoke all-around peace in women who are drawn to it. The black stone *hematite* has many of these attributes also.

Ruby is the hottest of the red root chakra stones, crystalline and a correspondent to the sign of Aries. Use it to gain strength and riches, sexual fulfillment, courage, invulnerability. This is not a stone to wear or use under emotional stress. The vibrations of ruby are extremely electrical and strong, with energy flows released in intensé and fiery bursts. In healing, use ruby to bring on menstruation, for infertility, to warm and to energize. Use in exhaustion and depression where no ungroundedness or anger are involved, in blood circulation disorders, for red blood cell growth and physical energizing and rebuilding.

As in the material on clear quartz, the above is only a beginning of the healing uses of gemstones. A few of the many stones not even mentioned here are smoky quartz (great for raising depression), the agates and jaspers, pearl, malachite, jade, fluorite, the tourmalines, onyx, obsidian, and dozens of others.[22] Women who are healers are exploring this field of knowledge, using crystals, gemstones and combinations of stones and metals and of healing techniques in their work. Experiment and learn, and enjoy the fascination of the learning. Teach others, heal and be healed in women's work with "living stones."

---

[22]Work continues on gemstones and crystals, and includes the uses of black stones, in *The Women's Crystal Healing Book,* by Diane Stein, forthcoming from Llewellyn Publications.

The Uses of Healing Gemstones[23]

Stone	Color	Chakra	Healing Uses
Ruby	Red	Root	fertility, bring on menstruation, warmth, exhaustion, depression, blood circulation, energizing, sexuality, kundalini energy
Bloodstone	red	root	courage, constancy, endurance, harmony, decision making, stops bleeding, iron deficiency, moving kundalini energy
Garnet	red	root	happiness, power, possessions, peace, patience, sexuality, persistence, balance, inspiration, cleansing, renewal birth, menstruation and life passages, blood, fertility, arthritis
Smoky Quartz	black	root	raise depression, lifts emotional pain, clears aura, positivity, grounding, menstrual cramps, eases fear or panic, breaking habits, tranquilizes, drug-stress, for intestines, stomach and digestion
Coral	orange	belly	cure madness, remedy poisons, physical tranquility, visualization, the blood, fertility, protection, sexuality, arthritis, joints
Carnelian	orange	belly	digestive system, mental ability, the liver, bleeding, past lives, painful menstruation, heavy menstruation flows, purification
Tiger Eye	gold/ brown	belly/solar plexus	eases ideas into reality, karmic recognition, past lives, certainty, will, protection from things without, decision making, perspective
Topaz	yellow	solar plexus	tension headaches, insomnia, depression, fear, eases death, protection, mood elevator, urinary, kidneys, blood, stimulant
Citrine Quartz	yellow	solar plexus	color work, toner, stimulant, psychic and sexual energy, trancework and meditation, clarity, urinary, colon, gall bladder, kidneys, liver, digestion, toxins, the will
Amber	yellow	solar plexus	disease and infections, ears, vision, ulcers, burns, bleeding, teeth, calming, pain, negativity, yin/yang balance, stimulant
Turquoise	green-blue	heart	emotions, healing, balancing, grounding, earth energy, love, courage, prosperity, soothing, protection, eyes, fevers, inflammation, tension, emotional shock, breast milk, wisdom
Emerald	green	heart	prophecy, psychic development, eyes, spleen, pancreas, gall bladder, prosperity, peace, old-age strength, aura balancing
Aventurine	green	heart	heart, heartache, emotions, soothing, acceptance and self-acceptance, calming, cooling, flowing, healing, peace-within

The Uses of Healing Gemstones (Continued)[23]

Stone	Color	Chakra	Healing Uses
Peridot (Olivine)	green	heart	protection, prosperity, happiness, clarity of mind, calming, healing, balancing, purification, digestive, emotional
Rose Quartz	pink	heart	heart, emotions, release, acceptance, love and self-love, warming, positive outlook, forgiveness, joy, oneness, emotional pain, throat, ears, nose, sinuses, kidneys, hypertension, heartache
Aquamarine	green/ blue	heart/ throat	sea water, soothing, calming, mood easing, tension, love, inner peace, flowing, lunar energy, travelers, banish fears, mouth, throat, stomach, liver, intelligence, self-understanding
Lapis Lazuli also Sodalite	blue	throat/ brow	healing, sensitivity, spirituality connector, strength, balance, psychic experience, lost love, cheering, incest recovery, speech, communication, mental, cooling, infections, calming, burns, fevers, pain, throat, inflamations, toner, creativity, voice
Blue Sapphire	indigo	brow	insight, perception, clarity, joy, introspection, meditation, psychic protection, divine favor, peace, enlightenment, wisdom, inspiration, the senses, eyes, ears, nose, mental clearing
Amethyst	violet	crown	calming, grounding, sobriety, transforming, spirituality, insomnia, balancing, mental and nervous, stress, depression, stabilizes sexual energy and solar plexus, spiritual cleanser
Moonstone	white	crown	psychic sensitivity, trance, sedative, soothing, psychometry, astral balance, over-reaction, mirror, spirituality, peace
Clear Quartz/ Rutilated Quartz	white	transpersonal point	all-purpose, all healing, amplify, focus, direct energy, color work, meditative states, aura work, laying on of hands, all chakras
Diamond	white	transpersonal point	courage, daring, strength, long life, rejects evil, trust, fidelity, joy, long relationships, wealth, infinity

[23]Sources: DaEl, *The Crystal Book*, (Sunol, CA, The Crystal Co, 1983), p. 61; Thelma Isaacs, *Gemstones, Crystals and Healing*, (Black Mountain, NC, Lorien House, 1982), p. 30 ff; Jim Knight, "Healing Uses of Gemstones, Minerals and Metals," in *Circle Network News*, Fall, 1984, p. 12; Julia Lorusso and Joel Glick, *Healing Stoned*, (Albuquerque, NM, Brotherhood of Life, 1985 ed.), p. 27 ff.; Rhiannon McBride, *et al.*, "Occult Uses of Gemstones," in *Circle Network News*, Summer, 1982, p. 12; and J'aime Schelz, *Crystal Essence*, (New York, Gemstoned, Ltd., Inc., 1984), unpaged pamphlet.

9

Transformational Tarot

The woman who experiences *The Women's Spirituality Book* through each chapter, from "What Is Women's Spirituality?" through "Healing" and "Crystals", sees changes occur in her Be-ing and transformations in her life. From an awareness of women's place in herstory and history to an awareness of female divinity and creation (Chapters One and Two), she learns women's real place on earth and in the universe as the source and life force. In Chapters Three and Four, she learns the power of women in groups, working together to create, direct and change reality, to choose among realities, learns the living symbolism of ritual, and in Chapter Five she begins to learn the individual power of herself and women's Be-ing—to take charge of her own choices and direct her personal life. Chapters Six, Seven and Eight, the Part II material on creative visualization, auras, colors, the chakras, healing and crystal work, put to use the principles of women's Be-ing learned in Part I. They dis-cover a beginning of women's great power, her active and knowing abilities to heal and change herself and others.

Women are healers, shapers and changers, "the changer and the changed."[1] In women's spirituality, not only do women choose and direct their own lives, participate as goddess in active, creative Be-ing in the world, but also heal themselves, their sisters, daughters, mothers and the earth of the pain and damage of the patriarchal past and present. There is no healing that can ever erase the realities—the centuries repressed loss of the goddess and women's autonomy, the pain of

---

[1] Cris Williamson, "Waterfall", on *The Changer and the Changed,* (Olivia Records, LC904, Box 12064, Oakland, CA 94604, 1975). The song and album are a women's music classic.

alienation from women's strengths, daughters and each other, the loss of our healers and leaders to silencing, degradation, book burning and the Inquisition. No healing can erase the facts of women's lack of civil rights and freedom in virtually every culture, her abuse in every culture, and the abuse of goddess earth since the overthrow of female divinity. No one can deny and women won't forget. Yet these are the situations that spirituality's Be-ing women, the women of the civil rights, anti-nuke, disability rights, feminist, lesbian and other women's movements are changing and being changed by. Women's healing has begun to understand and may one day forgive the past. The healing works actively to reclaim women's future, to change it and be changed by it, individually and for all in the now.

Women are transforming themselves and the world. In doing so, in dis-covering women's Be-ing, women's power, women choose the now of transforming the goddess earth. Re-claiming the knowledge of the goddess, the knowledge of herstory, of the foremothers, is part of the way to women's Be-ing. Re-claiming the goddess is a vital way, for the goddess principle re-cognizes and re-claims women, the vital, creative female of the earth and universe that has always been the first principle of the life force.

Women who participate in goddess are re-claiming the earth, themselves, and all women of all times. The process of dis-covery is more than women's growth; it's total individual transformation that creates women who re-cognize the needs, along with their own power to meet the needs, for planetary changes and healing. The process of women's Be-ing is the highest real magick this way; it affects the quality of life on all the earth. This process is the difference in Be-ing a woman undergoes between who she was at the beginning of dis-covery and who she is now, who she becomes by the changes invoked through her awareness of the goddess within. A woman who knows the power of women and the goddess dis-covers her own power, and she lives accordingly in her life and in the world. A woman who experiences divinity as female and herself, who does the self-blessing, draws the moon into her Be-ing, understands her womb, links psychically with others, is someone new from who she was before experiencing these things. A woman who does a healing or experiences one and chooses health never sees herself as powerless again. A woman who chooses a dream in her life and makes it come true by her own actions and affirmations, experiences an irrevocable and exhilarating independence and freedom, something that changes who she is, who she wants to be and who she chooses to become. With the awareness of herself as powerful, she is powerful, and uses her knowledge to create change beyond herself and for the good of all. These are the power of the goddess, of the female principle in the creative universe, the goddess and Be-ing principle within every woman.

The material of this book uses outward actions, knowledges and realities to create inward changes, inward positive transformations that in turn affect outward actions even more surely and strongly. The process is a ping-pong effect, a chain reaction set in motion that sets other things in motion. The motion is women's Be-ing, women's change, and women who experience it become the leading edge to change the planet. The following chapters on tarot and I Ching continue this ping-pong effect, but they do so from the inside outward, by turning the process around. The remainder of *The Women's Spirituality Book* works from the inside, defining, understanding, sorting out and assimilating women's transformations by new skills. Tarot and I Ching are divination tools, are skills of seeing from within, and are some of women's oldest wisdoms. Like the other skills of women's spirituality, their power is within every woman and is goddess. They bring the transformations of inner growth out to consciousness and to active in-the-world choice.

Tarot is a women's skill never lost or lost sight of during patriarchy, but not untouched by it. It is one of the earliest skills re-claimed in women's spirituality, with an interest among women that gains and continues steadily. Origins and era unknown, the tarot may have come from the goddess religion in Africa or Egypt, as is evidenced by tarot art in the pyramids. It may have developed much earlier than the pyramid era. Eden Gray links it to Egypt, but also to China, the "gypsies" that brought it to eastern Europe from India, and to the Hebrew Kaballah. 1390 AD is the date of the earliest known still existing deck in Europe.[2]

Z. Budapest and Eden Gray, in books published nineteen years apart, both give the following story that Z. heard from her mother Masika:

> Mother said it was originally designed about four thousand years ago, when Alexander the "Great" burned down the matriarchal libraries. Scrolls of knowledge and ageless wisdom perished in the flames, especially at the largest library, in Alexandria. The existing scientists, partially matriarchal and partially (new) patriarchal, gathered at a conference to resurrect the living knowledge still in their heads. Being from different

---

[2]Eden Gray, *The Tarot Revealed*, (New York, Signet Book, 1960), p. 11.

153

parts of the world, they had a language problem; so they
devised the tarot deck to commicate with each other through
symbols they all had agreed upon.[3]

The symbol system developed into a picture key of twenty-two cards and
life forces, and these became the major arcana. The fifty-six cards of the
minor arcana, divided into four suits representing the four elements and
daily existence, the numbers and court cards, developed later, and were
the forerunners of modern playing cards. The minor arcana is believed
to have developed in "Saracen Lands," countries in the geographic
areas of Morocco (Africa), Italy or Spain, with Greek and Hebrew influences,
and brought to Europe via returning crusaders.[4] With the major and
minor arcanas of different sources, the major arcana or both from pre-
patriarchal times, and with even the meaning of the word "tarot" lost, no
one knows whether the cards of either arcana were originally developed
for divination, or when divination with either or both arcanas began. The
great popularity of card playing in the Middle Ages was a strong factor in
saving the tarot, a remnant of goddess matriarchal wisdom and the
Alexandrian libraries, for today's women's use.

Repressed by Judaism and the Catholic and Protestant churches
as heretical, the tarot was seen as a threat to patriarchal institutions. It
was an element of goddess worship, the old religion of women's
dominance that patriarchy had to erase. What the original tarot deck
looked like is lost to women, as is the collection of matriarchal wisdom
and literature of the burnt libraries. Much of the symbolism of traditional
decks is traceable to Egyptian "mythology" and the mythologies of the
past are the remains of the goddess religion everywhere. Given even this
sketchy background, it is safe to guess that the original tarot was goddess and female. Evolved over the centuries by artists' interpretations
and the addition and loss of knowledge, by the influences of Judaism and
the churches, by artists' media and geographic cultures, the tarot lost
much but not all of its goddess and female orientation in favor of the ruling climate, patriarchy. Like the rest of goddess craft and women's
spirituality, tarot was illegal and went underground, emerging with new
openness in the last two hundred years since the decline and ending of
witch burnings.

The best known traditional (turn of the century) tarot deck of the

---

[3]Z. Budapest, *The Holy Book of Women's Mysteries, Part I*, (Oakland, CA, Susan B. Anthony Coven, No. 1, 1979),
p. 90-91. Barbara Walker comments that the Alexandrian library was in fact destroyed in 389 AD by Christians.
(Personal communications).
[4]Melita Denning and Osborne Phillips, *The Magick of the Tarot*, (St. Paul, Llewellyn Publications, 1983), p. 4-
5.

many available today is the Smith-Waite deck. Also called The Rider Tarot, it was developed by symbol interpreter Arthur Waite (1857-1942) and drawn and painted by Jamaican designer Pamela Colman Smith of the British Order of the Golden Dawn.[5] The publication and great popularity of this deck has done much to regain interest and spark Western learning in the tarot, particularly among members of traditional witchcraft. The best known deck in the women's spirituality movement, one of several impressive tarot decks that re-claim women's values and the goddess, is Vicki Noble and Karen Vogel's Motherpeace (1983).[6] This colorful round deck and fascinating book are a culmination of ten years of women's work in goddess spirituality, and are a new beginning and building bridge in women's tarot scholarship.

The first written women's re-claiming of tarot was by Sally Gearhart and Susan Rennie. *A Feminist Tarot: A Guide to Intrapersonal Communication* was self-published in 1976,[7] and later reprinted by Persephone Press. The work was daring for its time, a first beginning and breaking open of the field that made more and further advances possible. The book used the Smith-Waite deck in a revised interpretation, but was basically and philosophically still traditional (patriarchal) tarot. Women's tarot books and decks since,[8] interpretations by writers, witches and artists such as Billie Potts, Susun Weed and River Lightwoman (Amazon Tarot and New Amazon Tarot, decks and book), Gail Fairfield (*Choice Centered Tarot,* book and tapes), Vicki Noble and Karen Vogel (Motherpeace, deck and book), Ruth West (Thea's Tarot, deck), Jean Van Slyke, Shekhinah Mountainwater, Ffiona Morgan and Kate Taylor (Book of Aradia Tarot Deck, Daughters of the Moon Tarot, deck and book, and Shekhinah's Tarot, not yet released) Mary Greer (*Tarot for Yourself,* book), and Barbara Walker (tarot deck and *Secrets of the Tarot* book), have followed to re-claim tarot and tarot decks as a women's spirituality skill. These women's works have returned the goddess and the goddess within to tarot symbolism and use, and made tarot relevant and real for women everywhere. Major differences between these books and decks and traditional wiccan tarot is in their emphasis on personal power and transformation, on female and goddess images of all races and cultures, and on women's spirituality symbols and philosophies. The tarot used

[5]Stuart R. Kaplan, "Introduction", *The Rider Tarot Deck Instructions,* (New York, Samuel Weiser, Inc., 1971), p. 1-7.
[6]Vicki Noble, *Motherpeace: A Way to the Goddess Through Myth, Art and Tarot,* (San Francisco, Harper and Row Publishers, 1983). The Motherpeace Round Tarot Deck is available from Llewellyn Publications.
[7]Sally Gearhart and Susan Rennie, *A Feminist Tarot: A Guide to Intrapersonal Communication,* (Venice, CA, Pandora's Boox, 1976). Now reprinted by Alyson Publications, Boston.).
[8]Amazon Tarot (decks and book), Hecuba's Daughters Press, Bearsville, NY, Book of Aradia (deck), Aradia Press, Berkeley, CA, Daughters of the Moon Tarot, (deck and book), Ffiona Morgan, Willetts, CA, Gail Fairfield, *Choice Centered Tarot,* (book and tapes), Seattle, WA.

with women's decks and books is a meditation and divination tool for all women, a lunar goddess key to the always feminine subconscious, a tool for women's spirituality.

Tarot is a divination skill, a way of seeing within rather than of foretelling the definite future, a way of understanding what influences and predispositions exist in an issue to be followed through with or to change. Inward knowledge (higher, spiritual or subconscious) is expressed to mental consciousness through the "random" selection of cards that unlock the connecting emotional level symbols. The theory of synchronicity is invoked, that nothing is accidental, and the symbols are in pictures, seventy-eight of them in the full tarot deck. The major arcana's twenty-two life force cards are used alone in some women's tarot decks, and major arcana spreads from full decks or spreads using both arcanas can be used. Most women use both major and minor arcanas, the full tarot deck in their readings, with the major arcana representing universal forces and the minor cards daily situations. The symbols of the cards are familiar to women who practice creative visualization, do dreamwork or healings. Through a tarot spread, the subconscious influences of a question or issue are brought to conscious analysis. What is already within is brought to light. The woman reading the cards is made aware of the influences in relation to her question, then decides what to accept or change, what to make manifest by her actions.

The process of tarot reading is a reverse affirmation with the same results as affirmation. In doing creative visualization work, a woman chooses what influences to impress on her higher levels, what to manifest above and below by the thought forms she creates. She chooses these on the conscious mental level and impresses them through her emotional subconscious on her higher and lower realities. In tarot divination and I Ching, the subconscious affects the conscious, the outer level moving inward, and the woman reading the influences in her tarot cards uses or changes them consciously. This is transformational tarot, subject to free will and cleared of its patriarchal predestiny, chauvinism, racism and judgmental attitudes.

To use the tarot, the woman first chooses a deck and does so with the care of picking any other spirituality tool, from her altar objects to her crystals. With the many decks available, both traditional and women's, there are lots to choose from. Become familiar with tarot decks through seeing others use them, through articles and pictures in women's spirituality periodicals or books, through seeing them in magick and occult shops or at women's festivals. If the artwork of a particular deck is individually appealing and attracting, look further into it. If the philosophy of a particular tarot book that goes with a deck is appealing, the woman can choose both book and deck, or use the book with other decks. Most decks can be used with a variety of tarot books and philosophies, and most decks with a variety of books. The ultimate test is what emotions, symbols, thought correspondences and feelings a particular deck unlocks in the individual sensing it. These individual feelings, openings of the sub-conscious higher levels, are what are used in tarot readings. Women unfamiliar with tarot can learn the basics from books, but tarot is individual and comes from the labyrinth of the inner mind. Choose a tarot deck that opens these feelings, whose symbols lead to other symbols.

Some decks are in brilliant color and contain the full deck (Mother-peace, Barbara Walker's tarot deck and most traditional decks), some are full decks in black and white (Thea's and Amazon Tarots), and some are full decks to be colored in by the user (Daughters of the Moon and Shekhinah's tarot). A few women's tarot decks, such as The Book of Aradia, are done in black and white and contain the major arcana only. Some decks are rectangular (Amazon Tarots, Thea's, Barbara Walker's, and most traditional decks), and some are round (Motherpeace, Book of Aradia, Daughters of the Moon, Shekhinah's). Select the deck appeal-ing to the individual.

In beginning to use a new deck, get to know it first, handle it and impress it with the user's aura. As with a crystal, others handling the deck may not feel right. Spread the cards out on a table or floor and look at them, becoming familiar with their images. Do this in a quiet place, in front of a lit altar and unhurriedly. Shuffle the deck and spread the cards out again, handling and sensing them. Allow the images they invoke to come.[9]

Hold your hands over the deck, over all the cards. Build aura polarity, healing, and use it on the deck, impressing it with the user's aura. Place a crystal on top of it while doing this. Empty the mind of all thoughts, and allow a question to come, a simple one for the first few one-card readings. Shuffle the deck holding the question in mind, cut into three piles moving to the left, and use aura polarity on all three stacks. Sensing with the left hand, choose a stack, and turn the top card upward to view. Study the card, allowing the picture impressions to unlock ideas and symbols. Refer to the booklet that comes with the deck, use the tarot guidebook of your choice, but always give the most weight to first impressions and intuitions. Try other one-card readings,

[9]Suggestions from Vicki Noble and Karen Vogel, "Instructions", The Motherpeace Round Tarot Deck, (New York, US Games Systems, Inc., 1981), p. 5. Also see Mary Greer, Tarot for Yourself, (N. Hollywood, CA, Newcastle Publishing Co., 1984).

shuffle the deck and begin again. Try readings using only the major arcana, even if the deck is a full one. Move into the use of full spreads and full decks when familiar with the cards, when the deck feels bonded and known. This process of bonding can happen quickly or take time, but individual cards, selected one a day in sequence or at random, are powerful in both meditation work and in bonding.

Always store a tarot deck in its own pouch or decorated box, wrapped in a soft scarf or cloth. Things handmade are the best, cloths and storage boxes of beauty and personal meaning, filled with the energy of the user. Keep the deck on an altar and rest a crystal on top of it when not using it, for clearing and continued bonding. If the deck becomes overloaded, in the way that crystals do, clear it by spreading the cards in the sun, placing them exposed on a lit altar, sprinkling them with dried roses, salt water or frankincense pellets, or by using aura healing.

A full tarot reading begins with knowledge and understanding of the symbols and pictures of the deck. Any number and form of spreads are available, or design your own, from the traditional Celtic Cross formation of eleven to thirteen cards, to a full life reading using the entire deck. There are three card layouts for past, present and future, or the single card readings used in beginning work. Prepare for the reading by lighting a candle, casting sacred space, having a cleared mind relaxed of anything but the question being asked, and use aura polarity and crystals to impress the cards before laying out the spread. Ask the goddess for wisdom and guidance, select by sensing which stack to use from the shuffled and cut deck, and turn up the cards. Use a similar process when doing readings for others; let the other person's subconscious do the card selecting by the method of your choice. Doing tarot work as ritual brings powerful results, but rituals are not required. Deep mind concentration on the question being asked is the necessary factor.

The most popular traditional spread is the Celtic Cross, adapted to a wheel in the Motherpeace and Book of Aradia tarot systems. The cards are as follows, laid out in a double circle, but how they are physically placed is a matter of choice if the cards are drawn and read in sequence. The Motherpeace version of this spread is:

1. Significator: who you are, especially right now.
2. Atmosphere: the place from where the question emerges.
3. Cross Current: the obstacle facing you, the challenge.
4. Root: the unconscious mindset, the foundation.

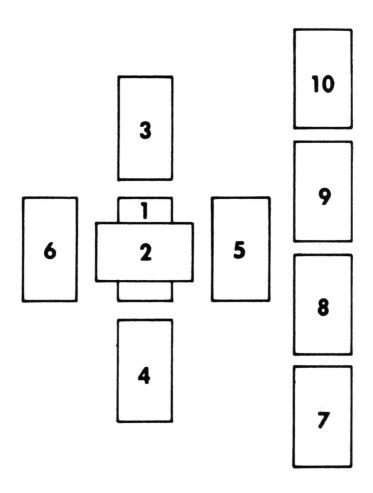

Standard Celtic Cross Spread.

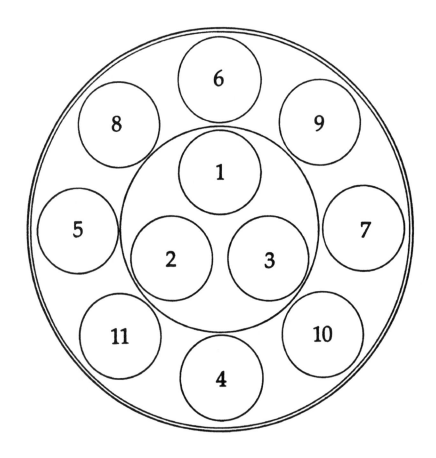

The Motherpeace Wheel Formation.

5. Recent Past: what has happened.
6. General Sky: what is conscious, the mind.
7. Near Future: where things are moving.
8. Self-Concept: self-image in relation to the question.
9. Hopes and Fears: what you hope for, you also fear.
10. House: environment, is close to you.
11. Outcome: resolution.[10]

If the final card is a major arcana card, the reading stops there. If the outcome is a minor card, the reading can also stop, but can go on for two more cards, stopping when a major arcana card appears. If no major arcana card appears in three cards, the results of the reading are seen as in process and not conclusive at this time.[11] Take the messages of the given cards as aspects of an answer, and try again when some time has passed. This is not an issue when using the major arcana only in a spread, or a major arcana deck. At completion of a reading, turn up the next card in the deck, asking for clarification or a summary. Women get what they ask for, and this final after-outcome card can be the message of the reading. Interpret and understand the original layout before doing this.

Gail Fairfield in her book *Choice Centered Tarot* describes several different layouts, and directs tarot readers to design their own. A simple layout is a three card reading:

1. past as you remember it.
2. present, as it stands now.
3. future, as it will probably unfold.[12]

Also described are a Celtic Cross spread, similar but laid out differently (traditionally) from the Motherpeace wheel, and a circular horoscope reading involving twelve cards, one card for each astrological house. Fairfield's tarot work with children and dreams is extremely interesting, as is both women's work with tarot group readings. Where Fairfield and Mary Greer are involved with women and psychology and use any deck, Noble's book is goddess oriented and goddess awakening, and uses the Motherpeace deck she co-designed. Fairfield includes material and meanings for reversed cards, but Noble does not.[13] One way of dealing with reversed images is to call them a "need for" the qualities of the card when upright.

[10]Vicki Noble, *Motherpeace: A Way to the Goddess Through Myth, Art and Tarot*, p. 233. Slightly condensed and abbreviated.
[11]*Ibid.*
[12]Gail Fairfield, *Choice Centered Tarot*, (Seattle, Choice Centered Astrology and Tarot, 1982), p. 145.
[13]Reversed card meanings for Motherpeace are now available in *The Motherpeace Tarot Playbook*, (by Vicki Noble and Jonathon Tenney, (Berkeley, Wingbow Press, 1986).

In interpreting the layout, look to the symbolism and meanings of each individual card in turn, in its position in the reading. Then notice relationships, the repetition of a particular suit, number, idea in the cards. Suits in the Motherpeace minor arcana are discs (earth, pentacles, the physical-material world, the earth plane); swords (air, ideas, the mental and conscious level); wands (fire, energy, activity, sexuality) and cups (water, emotions, the subconscious, higher realms, feelings). Discs in the Motherpeace deck portray Native American women and wands are women of African descent. The use of multi-racial and multi-cultural images is a feature of women's decks. Fairfield's use of the suits is similar to Noble's, adding the concept of self to the wands.

Numerology in the tarot is another key to meaning, useful in both the major and minor arcana. In the minor arcana, the numbers progress from one through ten in each suit, then go into court cards, in traditional decks the Pages, Knights, Queens and Kings. In the Motherpeace system, the court cards are Daughters, Sons, Priestesses and Shamans, and Fairfield and Noble define the numbers as follows:

Number	Noble[14]	Fairfield[15]
Aces	Gifts	Beginning
Twos	Balance	Affirming
Threes	Synthesis	Planning
Fours	Fixity	Manifesting
Fives	Struggle	Adjusting
Sixes	Exuberance	Repeating
Sevens	Inner Work	Imagining
Eights	Change	Organizing
Nines	Completion	Integrating
Tens	Transformation	Hesitating
Daughters/Pages	Youthfulness	Risking
Sons/Knights	Male Polarity	Focusing
Priestesses/Queens	Sacredness	Fulfilling
Shamans/Kings	Experience	Releasing

A woman who draws the Ace of Wands in a reading, in the position of her Near Future, might be about to experience a new beginning or gift, perhaps the gift of a new love. A woman who draws the Five of Swords

[14]Vicki Noble, *Motherpeace: A Way to the Goddess Through Myth,* Art and Tarot, p. 158-201
[15]Gail Fairfield, *Choice Centered Tarot,* p. 46-76.

in the position of obstacles or Cross Current, may be warned of a coming struggle that mentally challenges her goals. The appearance of the Nine of Swords, Nine of Wands and Nine of Discs in a spread, or major arcana card IX the Crone, indicate that a process of completion or integration of experience is taking place, a withdrawal. The numbers progress in depth and inner evolution from beginnings to ending, from newness of understanding onward in a wheel that begins again at its end. The progression is a developmental process and early numbers are the simplest ideas, while later numbers gain in complexity as accruals of all that's gone before. Either system, Gail Fairfield's or Vicki Noble's, reflects this.

Building on this idea of progression, Shekhinah Mountainwater, in a personal communication (October 13, 1985) offers the following number musings for the tarot minor arcana. In her conception, the court cards are Maiden, Mother and Crone and the cycle begins with zero:

0 – The goddess, parthenogenic, self-perpetuating, self-birthing, whole unto herself. Potential, cosmic egg, prior to manifestation.

1 – Zero gives birth to the first spark of manifestation.

2 – One divides to become two, like cellular growth of the embryo, creating a reflection, an Other, for interaction, love and dynamic movement.

3 – Two get together and give birth to three, a new circle or universal egg of Maiden, Mother, Crone.

4 – A new factor is birthed creating a square out of the circle, giving stability, maintenance, linearity, control.

5 – The square is made to spin anew—Maiden, Mother, Crone now expands to earth, water, fire, air and spirit. Five shakes up four.

6 – Beauty and flow as the odd and even blend in harmony.

7 – Equilibrium, a plateau; time to contemplate the mysteries.

8 – The four is doubled, keeping its stability and linearity, yet now is multifaceted as in the eight great Sabbats.

9 – Fulfillment, culmination of 0's potential.

10 – And the cycle begins again with zero and one.

Maiden, Mother, Crone – 1, 2, 3. A circle or egg that encompasses 1—10. Beginning, middle, end; me, us, you; initiate, perpetuate, dissolve.

The major arcana, composed of twenty-two cards from 0 (The Fool) to XXI (The World) are a similar progression of experience and wisdom. The Fool is the child, new and innocent, with all potential before her for the taking. The World is the other end of the scale, everything attained that a woman could wish for, and is also the ending of the cycle. Each major arcana card represents a cosmic, goddess or life force concept, and the numbers are the process a woman takes from The Fool to The World in her development. The steps on the path are open to interpretation, and different tarot decks define and portray the steps differently, though similarly. Card XIII of the major arcana is *Death* in Noble and Fairfield, *Transformation* in The Book of Aradia. The card rarely means or predicts a physical death, but usually an ending and letting go. Card XII is *The Hanged Man* for Gail Fairfield, *The Hanged One* for Vicki Noble, and *Reversal* for Shekhinah Mountainwater, Ffiona Morgan and Jean Van Slyke.[16] The Book of Aradia and Shekhinah's tarot consider the major arcana to be the tarot's fifth suit, adding aether (spirit) to earth, air, fire and water, and the major arcana deck contains only twenty-one cards, deleting The Devil, The Hierophant and The Emperor to add Pan, a new and positive male god.

The Fool, card 0 in Motherpeace and *Choice Centered Tarot,*[17] is the beginning of the progression, the innocent child. She is portrayed positively in women's decks and books, perjoratively as the joker or wastrel in traditional ones. In The Book of Aradia she is the Self. The Fool is at the start of her journey and begins it with faith and total trust in the universe. Whatever her direction and her errors on the way, she faces the path in purity. She can choose to become anything and is protected, helped and aided on her path by the goddess. Fairfield, Noble and Mountainwater/ Morgan/Van Slyke agree closely on this card.

Card I is *The Magician* in Motherpeace and Choice Centered tarots, and is *The Witch* in The Book of Aradia. In Motherpeace she is a woman with the power to channel energy, to heal, achieve, transform and manifest her chosen realities. For Gail Fairfield, The Magician discerns between and chooses among realities, along with creating her own. In The Book of Aradia, The Witch is everywoman, she who shapes and creates reality and destiny. She is the woman of power, of women's spirituality, in running her own life.

Major arcana card II is the *High Priestess* or *Priestess* in the three

---

[16]Shekhinah Mountainwater, "Instructions for Using The Book of Aradia Tarot", (Oakland, CA, Aradia Press, 1984).
[17]Interpretations are a comparison of Motherpeace, The Book of Aradia Tarot Deck, and Gail Fairfield's Choice Centered book and systems.

systems, the feminine intuitive consciousness in most decks and tarot sources. She is the lunar goddess within, involved with attunement to the universe, interior transformations of watery, hidden modes. Harmony with the self is her message, paying attention to the rhythms and flowing with them, letting reason take a back seat to the goddess within.

Card III is *The Empress* for Fairfield, Noble and Vogel, and is *Maya* in The Book of Aradia. The card represents the great mother, all-giving, all-nurturing, sensual, and is shown here and traditionally as pregnant or giving birth. She is the full moon, the life force healer of the universe and herself, the abundant, sustaining and caring mother aspect.

Next is IV, *The Emperor,* a male boss or power figure, the patriarchy. A confrontation with an authority figure, or with the authority training in the self, is at hand. The question here is in who a woman chooses to give power to. Gail Fairfield sees the issue as aligning by choice with the system for whatever reasons. In The Book of Aradia deck, this card is *Pan,* the divine son-lover of the goddess, the New Age positive male and feminist man.

Card V is *The Hierophant* in Motherpeace and Choice Centered Tarot, and is hierarchal, patriarchal religion, the fundamentalism that represses others with its rigidity and power-over, that extends beyond religion to all parts of life. A conflict with the system may be happening here, or a conflict with the repressing aspects in the self. Someone is repressing or oppressing the self or another, and it needs looking into. The card is deleted in The Book of Aradia.

The Lovers is card VI of the traditional and Motherpeace decks. Union and love on many levels including self-love from within is the issue, two forces brought into harmony by a third aspect. Gail Fairfield interprets the card as the power of cooperation, not as a merging, love affair or marriage. For Shekhinah Mountainwater, Ffiona Morgan and Jean Van Slyke, the card is V, *Aphrodite,* the risks and joys of love.

Card VII of the major arcana is *The Chariot* for Fairfield and Noble, replaced by *Boudicea* (card VI) in The Book of Aradia deck. The Chariot is winning and taking control, immersion in fast-paced events and changes, self-discipline and victory on the physical plane. Boudicea was a woman warrior, and is the power of choice and the will to make positive changes with centered, decisive strength.

Justice is card VIII (reversed with XI, *Strength* in Fairfield and in some traditional decks). The concept in Motherpeace is that of the connectedness of Be-ing, the oneness and inter-relatedness of all that lives, woman's awareness of her place on the universal Wheel of Life.

Choices have responsibilities, and Justice in Choice Centered Tarot is balance and equilibrium, being fair, mediating and understanding all the aspects. In The Book of Aradia, the card is XI, Athena—conscience, natural justice and the karmic balance and protection of the inner mysteries.

Card IX, *The Hermit* in Fairfield, is feminized to *The Crone* by Vicki Noble and Karen Vogel, and in The Book of Aradia. The Crone is the third aspect of the three-form goddess, the grandmother, wisewoman Hecate. In all three tarot systems, she is the solitary witch and healer, the woman who knows the mysteries and participates in the labyrinth. Temporary withdrawal is the message here, a scholarly pulling-in to validate the inner growth of self.

The Wheel of Fortune is card X in the Motherpeace and Choice Centered major arcanas, and is called *The Moirae* in The Book of Aradia. The card in all three systems delineates karma and fate, and the Moirae are the three fate goddesses of Greek mythology, shown as Maiden, Mother and Crone. Vicki Noble and Karen Vogel represent fortune as the Wheel of Life and the zodiac. In Choice Centered Tarot and Motherpeace, The Wheel of Fortune is something "fortunate" set in motion, something already begun. There is nothing to do but wait for the outcome, as everything possible is chosen and taken care of. In Motherpeace, the card is the coming manifestation of something long awaited, a positive high point, joyous and remarkable. In The Book of Aradia, The Moirae are new cycles, new beginnings and endings in the spiral goddess universe.

Strength is card XI in Motherpeace, card VIII in Fairfield, and VI, *Power* in The Book of Aradia. Strength is the mother goddess, the matriarchal female consciousness, the originator of civilization. She is instinct as opposed to intellect, able and ready to survive and achieve in grounded, caring, sensual ways. Protection and nurturing are available and affirmations come true. Power for Shekhinah Mountainwater, Ffiona Morgan and Jean Van Slyke is taming the forces within by character, oneness, gentleness and strength.

Card XII of the major arcana is *The Hanged One* in Motherpeace, *The Hanged Man* in Choice Centered Tarot, and Reversal in The Book of Aradia. Vicki Noble's interpretation is in letting go, allowing a loss of control and trusting in the wisdoms of the universe for positive outcomes. Gail Fairfield says to wait until the time is right before taking action. The Book of Aradia interpretation is closer to that of Noble's, letting go of personal ego and control to trust in the goddess universe.

Death is the lunar number XIII for Motherpeace and most tarot decks. Shekhinah Mountainwater calls the card *Transformation*. Rarely physical death, the card is more the ending of a cycle, a conclusion and releasing. Fairfield calls it total change and transformation, something to be surrendered to. In The Book of Aradia Tarot Deck, death is rebirth, with the concepts of all three systems matching closely in this card. Endings are beginnings on the Wheel of Life.

Card XIV is *Temperance* in all three interpretations, and is a particularly colorful card in the always colorful Motherpeace deck. Temperance for Vicki Noble and Karen Vogel is "an integration of emotional forces with the physical—a blessed union of opposites within and without."[18] The interpretation is much the same for Gail Fairfield and in The Book of Aradia. The card in a reading means balance and reaching, using talents and resources to their maximum power and effectiveness.

The Devil is card XV in the tarot major arcanas of Motherpeace, Fairfield and most tarot systems, and is card VIII, *Oppression* in The Book of Aradia. The card is the negativities of patriarchy, refused and rejected in women's spirituality for positive boundaries set from within. The Devil is denying the spirit or abusing power in Motherpeace, setting limits in Choice Centered Tarot, the differences between power-over and power from within. In The Book of Aradia, Oppression is negativity and the crushing abuse of power that destroys.

Card XVI is *The Tower* in Motherpeace, Fairfield and most tarot decks, and *Lightening* (a deliberate pun) in The Book of Aradia. Its meaning is radical change, the shattering of old structures. The three tarot systems agree closely here that change is necessary and can happen traumatically, but is an enlightenment that proves for the best. Illusions of false power are destroyed, basic ingrained attitudes, and a whole readjustment results. Fighting the process only makes it harder.

The Star is card XVII in all three tarot systems, perhaps the loveliest card in Motherpeace and in The Book of Aradia both. The goddess is the sweet abundance of the universe, and she pours her healing gifts upon the woman pictured on the card or doing the reading. Gail Fairfield interprets The Star as a new flow of energy, resources and inner power; Vicki Noble as grace and an opening to the goddess peace, blessing and beauty. She is the muse for Shekhinah Mountainwater, the healing of inspiration and meditation. The Star is oneness with the goddess and with universal love.

Major arcana card XVIII is *The Moon,* the labyrinth of women's

---

[18]Vicki Noble, *Motherpeace: A Way to the Goddess Through Myth, Art and Tarot,* p. 107.

mysteries. The card is number XV in The Book of Aradia. In Mother-peace, The Moon is the positive darkness, the inner realms of the powerful female subconscious. Trying to understand it on mental levels gains nothing; the woman can only flow with it and accept where it takes her. Shekhinah Mountainwater, Ffiona Morgan and Jean Van Slyke agree with this, as does Gail Fairfield. "Harmonious moon energy is ecstasy."[19]

The Sun, card XIX, is rebirth and emergence on conscious levels (Noble), and the card is XVIII, *Amaterazu* in The Book of Aradia. An interpretation of joy, childlike energy and exuberance is in all three tarot systems for this card. Fairfield emphasizes redirected growth, Mountain-water/Morgan/Van Slyke creation and expansion, and for Vicki Noble and Karen Vogel the card is the self and conscious awareness. This is a positive and happy card to draw in a reading.

Card XX of the tarot major arcana is *Judgment* in Motherpeace and Choice Centered tarots and card XIX, *Celebration* in The Book of Aradia. Noble sees this card as Healing the Earth, a return of the life force, Gaia, the great goddess. Judgment is peace, and the joy that comes with full awakening. Transcendence, interconnectedness and oneness are achieved. In The Book of Aradia, the women contact the goddess in themselves, raise energy together in a ritual. The Mother-peace image for this card and concept is the ankh and chakra rainbow. Maturing into the New Age is Gail Fairfield's interpretation.

The World is the final card of the tarot major arcana, card XXI in Motherpeace and Choice Centered Tarot and card XX, *Nut,* in The Book of Aradia. The consciousness of complexity and ability to deal with it is Fairfield's concept for this card. For Motherpeace, the card is the attainment of a cycle, transcendent understanding of the body, mind and spirit. The pictured dancer is the oneness of the self with goddess, within and beyond time, the transpersonal point in the chakra system. The World is the woman of women's spirituality, the leading edge for positive change to heal women and the planet. Shekhinah Mountainwater and the Book of Aradia call the card beginnings and completions, *The Sacred Year.*

The progression in tarot from birth (The Fool in the major arcana or the Aces in the minor) to enlightenment and oneness (The World in the major arcana, The Shamans in the minor) is the progression of an individual woman on her Road of Life. It mirrors the year and Sabbat cycle, and the Wheel of beginnings and completions in any issue or question that the tarot reader asks. By paying attention to the meanings of the cards, their numerical positions and positions in the layout, the

---

[19]Shekhinah Mountainwater, "Instructions for Using The Book of Aradia Tarot", card 15, Moon.

168

mix of major concepts with daily realities (major and minor arcanas), and the cards' relationships to each other, a woman reading tarot qets a comprehensive discussion of the issue she asks the cards to answer. In interpreting the cards she interprets her subconscious, brings the knowledge of her higher levels to conscious light, her inner moon out to the bright daytime sun. By doing so, she gains awareness of her own personal growth and inner changes, an impetus for further growth and positive choice and change.

Women's tarot decks and interpretation systems vary from traditional tarot in this basic outlook. Women's decks use female imagery and non-violence, and recognize and honor the racial and cultural differences among women. The decks are goddess oriented, using goddess images and women's spirituality symbols. Judgmental and patriarchal bible morality is removed from women's tarot; women make their own choices and decisions in ethics as they do in every other aspect of directing their energy and lives. The only rule is to harm none, and is all encompassing. Where patriarchal mentality is filled with limits and warnings, with "no," women's spirituality and women's tarot is bounded only by limitless abundance for all and by individual choices for achievement. Patriarchal values of hierarchy, rule, status, punishment, indifference and money as measure of inner worth are nonexistent. Women's spirituality and women's tarot are positive and affirming, respecting and validating of women's equality, of all women's worth and paths. They are based on giving and receiving, on joy, caring and on the oneness of body, mind and spirit.

Woman carries the responsibility for life on earth, for creation and survival of the planet and life force. Her first responsibility is to herself, to realization of who she is, of what powers within she holds and channels to determine, create and choose her way of living. The woman who is goddess, the Be-ing woman of women's spirituality, takes her own empowerment and freedom seriously. In creating her own life, she gains the influence, skills and power to help others in their quests for self-creation. She unites her power with her sisters' and companions' power to change and make positive the oppressions, wrongs and abuses of her world.

> The role of women today is the same as it always has been: to nurture, to make strong, to carry the seed of wisdom. Woman has the gift and the mind that can forgive. And we in our hearts, can make this planet better.[20]

---

[20]Dhyani Ywahoo, "Woman's Role in Planetary Transformation", in *Woman of Power,* (POB 827, Cambridge, MA 02238), Premier Issue, Spring, 1984, p. 4.

The concept of transformational tarot, of all of the skills being learned, re-claimed and created in women's spirituality, are parts of this realization of who women are, what they can do and are doing to re-claim and dis-cover Be-ing, the goddess and the female earth. Tarot is another way of understanding that transformation, that process of returning women's power, that women's spirituality offers. Tarot's understanding and re-visioning by women reflects the transformation process, and its use by women reflects the changes that women are making today. This chapter is only a beginning of tarot use and what tarot is, as *The Women's Spirituality Book* is only a beginning in women's spirituality work. Every beginning opens the process, however, the process of women's growth in herself, in all women, and in women's worlds.

10

Women's I Ching

Women's spirituality is a means of re-claiming and dis-covering women, women's skills and wisdoms, women's creative and inner Be-ing. Part of the process is in un-covering of the matriarchal past, sifting and separating patriarchy's repressions from women's culture and learning, under-standing and using women's positive power independently from it. This dis-covery and re-visioning has occurred in all facets of women's spirituality, from finding the stories of goddess creation, to developing women's rituals, to women's use of healing, gemstones and tarot, to the reaffirming of women's bodies, harmonies, minds and psychic intuitions. Finding women and women's culture where the only view is male is a creative and revolutionary act, and the word "revolution" means the turning of the wheel again. Women exist in male culture, though are seldom mentioned by it in any but trivializing and negative ways. Ignored by mainstream patriarchy, women are the underground foundations of culture, male or otherwise.

Much of patriarchal rigidity in society and religion is a reversal of women's experience, women's art, healing and knowledge. How medicine was taken over by the male elite establishment, and how the patriarchy changed it from what it was under women is a good example. The work of Mary Daly, particularly in *Gyn/ecology* (Boston, Beacon Press, 1978) discusses this phenomenon of reversal, and the idea is very evident in religion in Merlin Stone's work, *When God Was A Woman* (New York, Harvest Books, 1976). Starhawk has defined the concept comparisons of women's power-within versus patriarchal dominance and power-over in *The Spiral Dance: A Rebirth of the Ancient Religion of the Great*

Goddess (San Francisco, Harper and Row Publishers, 1979). All of these writers and thealogians (the word "thea" means goddess), have made women aware of the loss, knowledgeable of the process that women's spirituality is a key to changing. Re-asserting women's realization of the creative life force in herself and in her Be-ing, re-claiming women's role in religion (female goddess divinity), re-claiming birth and women's bodies that have been called unclean under patriarchal fear, re-claiming women's skills and women's lost or submerged knowledge, the heritage of women scholars, leaders, healers, artists and priestesses of the now and past are all parts of the re-cognition. Each and all of these are ways of re-turning women's identity and force in the universe. Aware and Be-ing women, women who in goddess spirituality learn about their own and other women's traditional and present power, are making the changes and re-claiming what has been lost. They are seen as revolutionary; they are turning the wheel. In dis-covering the work of other women, their literature, art, healing, religion, philosophy and lives, women dis-cover themselves. They begin to realize that not all learning is male and aimed at teaching men, and that much that comes under male scholarship is women's own wisdoms, reversed or with women written out of them.

The Inquisition, churches, Judaism and patriarchy submerged but did not destroy the goddess, submerged but did not destroy women's Be-ing. The abuses of women's experience worldwide, her denial of education, her poverty and ownership as chattel everywhere, her suttee in India, footbinding in China, burning at the stake in the West, have not destroyed women or women's power, or given men control of the life force that women are. Herstory is being re-claimed by women in every wisdom from anthropology to biography, from spirituality to architecture, from poetry and music to medicine and science. Be-ing women are re-storing the learning of matriarchy, rebuilding and re-filling the Alexandrian Libraries, dis-covering what has been so long hidden but has never been totally lost. Religion that was only male for centuries is being re-cognized as once female; medicine that is now male was once female; women who for centuries were refused education are re-membered as the earliest sources of civilization, of art and human knowledge, and women are regaining their place there today. Any science or philosophy that seems too totally male is suspect by women of once being female, perhaps totally female, and women are becoming aware of this, are delving for the roots. The female principle and the goddess are re-turning, and the wheel of life revolves into a new age. Women's religion and women on earth are being re-claimed, and with them the respect for life and birth, the healing, herstory, psychic and other skills that are parts of women's culture and heritage. "Hera" is the root word in "heritage", Hera the great goddess whose name means "womb."[1] Any art, science or philosophy that is totally male, that ignores, excludes or degrades women and women's power, bears looking into in this light. Reversals seen through are being turned around.

The Chinese I Ching or Book of Changes is a totally male system that bears looking into and turning around by women. While the tarot has retained its female character through all its centuries and evolution, and has drawn women's re-visioning early, the I Ching was translated into English relatively recently, in male-dominated ways, and is only beginning to reach the re-claiming of women. Interpreted through patriarchal religious values by missionaries, excluding women and women's roles as was conventional in the Eastern and Western scholarship of its time, and without regard for its culture or use in divination, what is known as I Ching in the West is only a shadow of what the system is or perhaps once was. Yet even in this far removed form, the Chinese Book of Changes is a powerful divination tool used by women and men, and a force for women's spirituality to dis-cover and re-claim. The goddess was not unknown in ancient China, nor were matriarchy, the strength of women and the patriarchal changeover, and I Ching is perhaps another example of reversal for women to re-turn.

The I Ching is a written tarot at least four thousand years old. It is composed of sixty-four passages called hexagrams, as compared to the seventy-eight cards in a tarot deck. The sixty-four passages are believed in Chinese philosophy to encompass the full range of human situations, wisdom and experience, as is similar in the tarot's seventy-eight cards. "Hex" means "six", and the hexagrams are found by casting coins to make a pattern of six lines, two groups of three lines called trigrams, composed in turn of a sequence of broken (—— ——) or unbroken (————) single line patterns. Each possible six-line pattern, made by the tossing of three two-sided coins six times, matches a written passage. Both line pattern and written passage are called the hexagram. The lines themselves are the oracle, the broken or unbroken binary code, and are found by invoking the concept of synchronicity.

When asking a question of the I Ching, a woman concentrates on her question, meditates on it, throws three coins a total of six times, and the six throws or lines' pattern indicate a written hexagram. A key to

---

[1]Penelope Shuttle and Peter Redgrove, *The Wise Wound: Eve's Curse and Everywoman*, (New York, Richard Marek Publishers, 1978), p. 19.

matching these is given in the book. She reads the written hexagram passage and receives an answer to or discussion of her question. The process of throwing the coins is similar to shuffling, cutting and laying out a tarot spread, and reading and analyzing the passage is similar to interpreting the tarot cards of the layout. The oracle is in the lines of the I Ching, as it is in the individual tarot cards; the written hexagrams are the layout, the relationship of the lines. The written work is also a matter of bias and translation, as is the artwork in tarot, and this is the final area of women's re-claiming and re-visioning in I Ching dis-covery.

In its earliest beginning, the I Ching was based on the two primary lines,[2] instead of on the six-line hexagram. The unbroken line (———) read as yes, yang, the bright, active and creative, and the broken line (—— ——) was seen as no, yin, the dark, receptive and passive principles of existence. These concepts are opposites, dualities named in a thousand ways, and a basic principle also in goddess philosophy. In the Chinese, as well as in women's spirituality, the dualities were and are known as opposite but complementary and positive parts to every whole. They are the original concept of yin and yang, which meant much more than male and female.[3] No and yes, yin and yang, dark and light, moon and sun, female and male are not good or bad in value—nothing is complete and whole without both aspects. Summer does not exist without winter, or life without death, the active without the receptive, in goddess and ancient Chinese philosophy. All life contains both sides within it and both at once. The opposites are each and both, are one, are the circle and the wheel of life, and in the world order of the original Chinese this principle was intrinsic in the I Ching. The concept is known in China as T'ai Chi, or oneness.

> The important part of the yin/yang symbol is not the black part or the white part or the way they balance or contrast with each other. The important part is the circle that unites them.[4]

It was in the patriarchal translations that brought an evolved-to-male I Ching to the West that connotations of yes/male/yang/ good and no/ female/yin/bad were imposed on the cosmic dualities to separate, limit and confine them, to judge them in ways and attitudes they never before meant. The opposites intrinsic in goddess spirituality, in ancient Chinese thought and the I Ching were reversed and submerged under

[2]Richard Wilhelm and Cary F. Baynes, *The I Ching or Book of Changes*, (New Jersey, Bollingen Series XIX, Princeton University Press, 1950 and 1967). This is considered the definitive scholarly translation.
[3]*Ibid.*, p. lv-lvi.
[4]Gail Fairfield, *Choice Centered Tarot*, (Seattle, Choice Centered Astrology and Tarot, 1982), p. 30.

Western patriarchal values and dimmed greatly by patriarchy in the east.

The early concept of a two-line oracle was gradually expanded to six lines in China over the centuries. Where yes and no (————) and (——— ———) have two possibilities, and yes and no used in two pairs have more, six lines in all their possible combinations of yes and no have a total of sixty-four possibilities and become the sixty-four hexagrams. Yes and no as expressed here illustrate equal opposites; they are not judgmental values. An oral tradition in the beginning, the increasing number of factors and possibilities made the I Ching into a written book, and limited its use to those who could read, to men.

Chinese history paralleling that of other cultures, the goddess and women's matriarchies were overthrown and submerged through the centuries, women's dominance destroyed. Chinese goddesses Kwan Yin, Hsi Ho and Nu Kwa were devalued to a male emperor hierarchy, with the living emperor as god, and human (male) worth rigidified into nearness of rank to the emperor and his court. Women were removed from government and influence (legends of the Chinese woman warrior still exist), eventually denied education (some of the East's great early poets and writers were women), and footbound in known times to total dependence and silence. Where once it was only a woman who could directly approach Kwan Yin and be heard, now only males were gods and oracles and it was men who read the I Ching.

Vicki Noble, in her Preface to *The Kwan Yin Book of Changes*, (Diane Stein, Llewellyn Publications, 1985), the first women's full re-claiming of the I Ching, illustrates the change. She writes that in pre-dynasty China, as in pre-patriarchal cultures worldwide, women were the teachers, shamans and healers of every village. They were called the Wu, which meant healer, and the ancient symbol for these women looked like a woman holding two dancing children by the hand. The modern character for wu, its female meaning removed, is something quite different, an alphabet symbol not a picture, and its women and children gone.

Figure 1

Figure 2

175

This abstraction of what was once pictographic corresponds to the gradual and complete replacement in Chinese culture of the Wu by men who took over the arts of healing. By the time of the Han dynasty, we read that the Wu were no longer allowed in the courts.[5]

It was male scholars that developed the I Ching as a written oracle, and women and the goddess were written out. The process took thousands of years. The concept of the eight major trigrams with their patriarchal family roles was in effect as early as 2205 BC.[6] Male court philosophers such as King Wen (1150 BC) and Confucius (551-479 BC) shaped the I Ching into court and patriarchal terms, what later Western missionaries and travelers saw. James Legge's first translation of the I Ching into English, published in 1894, completed the erasure and reversal of women's and goddess values, adding non-Eastern bias and some fire and brimstone besides.

As the binary code of broken and unbroken lines were given in translation good or bad judgmental meanings, so were the eight major trigrams (three-line units and the major arcana of the I Ching) given in Eastern changes and Western translation patriarchal, nuclear family and male dominated roles. From neutral forces of nature, the eight basic trigrams reinforced the court and family system—yes/male/yang/good and no/female/yin/bad. The sexism in the trigram attributes from Wilhelm/Baynes is evident:[7]

Trigram	Name	Attribute	Image	Relationship
	Ch'ien, The Creative	strong	heaven	father
	K'un, The Receptive	devoted yielding	earth	mother
	Chên, The Arousing	inciting movement	thunder	first son
	K'an, The Abysmal	dangerous	water	second son
	Kên, Keeping Still	resting	mountain	third son
	Sun, The Gentle	pentrating	wind/wood	first daughter
	Li, The Clinging	light-giving	fire	second daughter
	Tui, The Joyous	joyful	lake	third daughter

[5]Vicki Noble, "Preface" to *The Kwan Yin Book of Changes* by Diane Stein, (St. Paul, Llewellyn Publications, 1985), p. xi.
[6]Richard Wilhelm and Cary F. Baynes, *The I Ching or Book of Changes*, p. lviii.
[7]*Ibid.*, p. 1-li.

176

According to this, the father is the creative principle and the only one. His wife (male ownership of the family is implicit here), is not goddess who creates but is she who receives passively from the male. Their sons are movement and action, youthful creation and power in training, while their daughters are passive, devoted and following—learning to be receptive mothers. In the light of the re-cognitions of women's spirituality, the reversals need re-turning.

In the original pre-patriarchal concept of yin and yang, of the goddess' dualities in matriarchy and women's spirituality, all of the eight trigram's concepts are present in every individual and action, all are positive attributes, and all are goddess. The creative, receptive, arousing, dangerous, resting, joyous, penetrating (dark-giving) and light-giving are all one and are parts of a whole. K'an, The Abysmal water is the intuitive, female lunar depths; Ken, Keeping Still is the waiting earth, the patience and strength of mountains; and Ch'ien, Heaven and K'un, Earth (above and below) are both the goddess and goddess Be-ing. Ch'ien, The Creative is elemental air, the Labyris life force; K'un, the Receptive is elemental earth, the Pentacle and mother; K'an, The Abysmal becomes the Chalice, the waters of life and birth; and Li, The Clinging is elemental fire, the wand of power in the life force. These four elements are also the four suits in the tarot. The remaining four of the eight major trigrams, Mountain, Wind/Wood, Thunder and Lake (Ken, Sun, Chen, Tui), are also earth, air, fire and water—the four directions of casting a wiccan circle repeated a second time.

Patriarchal ownership and sexism are removed by this re-turning. Judgmentalism, negativity and Christiam brimstone and blame are removed, and "no" is dropped from the attributes. Where the trigrams are the four elements and four directions, the roles of all women, the goddess and the self, the matriarchy of an original and lost I Ching begins to emerge.[8] The I Ching is relevant to women's spirituality, powerful and re-claimable: yin and yang are both at once, and are goddess.

Instead of the god/emperor/yang/father as the creative principle split off from the goddess/lunar/yin/mother, why not combine them and call them both goddess? The role on earth then would be the Mother. Above, the Mother is the goddess of creation, the all-giver who birthed the universe, the heavens and the planet. On earth and in women, the Mother is a leader of matriarchy, birth-mother or not, but a

[8]The concepts of re-claiming here are all from Diane Stein, *The Kwan Yin Book of Changes*, (St. Paul, Llewellyn Publications, 1985).

mother among her women. She is the organizer, peacemaker and facilitator, the coordinator of the community (never the ruler in consensus matriarchy), the woman who knows how to gain action and cooperation from groups and individuals. She is the capable, competent business-woman, the manager, homemaker, networker, activist and senator. In the tarot she is The Empress, the mother aspect of the three-form goddess, the full moon. What she does is done with love and nurturing, with caring and with skill.

Replacing the hierarchy of the first and second son, Chen, The Arousing (inciting, movement, thunder) and K'an, The Abysmal (the dangerous, water) in matriarchal I Ching is the role of the Priestess. The Priestess arouses and awakens women psychically and artistically, incites the movement of Be-ing, of energy and power in the circle and individual, and connects women to their inner depths, to goddess. She represents not danger but excitement. Her role in matriarchy is to connect the forces of the goddess universe to the goddess within women and on earth, and she does this in the circle or in writing, painting or onstage. The Priestess channels power, unites women in understanding and learning to channel their own power, the power of goddess Be-ing, and never forgets that she is only channeling herself. She is the singer or musician who performs in trance, the painter-weaver-poet-writer of women's mysteries. The High Priestess in the tarot, she is one with the women she directs, their force is her force, and she uses it for the good of all.

The trigram roles of the third son and first daughter, of Ken, Keeping Still (resting, mountain) and Sun, The Gentle (dark-giving, penetrating, wind/wood), is re-turned in women's I Ching to the role of the Wise-woman. She is The Crone in the tarot, the waning moon, the Hecate aspect of the three-form goddess. The aged-one has strength and peace, the wisdom and knowledge of experience. As one at the ending of life, she accepts death, the change and transformation that leads to rebirth. The Wisewoman is the healer, midwife, counsellor and teacher of the matriarchy, the sage and solitary woman who chooses to work inwardly and validates working alone. Any she teaches are blessed by her, and her daughters and students are the Mothers and Priestesses that follow her to lead.

The final two roles in traditional I Ching are the second and third daughters, Li, The Clinging (light-giving, fire) and Tui, The Joyous (joyful, lake). These roles in women's re-turning become the Daughter, the joyous brightness of new life, the child. The Daughter can be young, Persephone playing with her mother Demeter, the waxing moon. She can also be a woman of any age, anyone who comes to a Mother, Priestess or Wisewoman (also of any physical age) to learn. The Daughter is lively and curious and all the world is open and new to her. She wants to know and understand everything, has no fear, and is protected in her innocence, is guided gently and positively in her experimenting and growth. She is The Fool in the tarot, the maiden of the three-form goddess roles. In matriarchy she is given "yes", and is made free to grow and learn with joy.

Any and every woman can be each of the above roles, or all of them, either simultaneously or at different stages in her life. All of the roles of Mother, Priestess, Wisewoman and Daughter are positive roles and equal in their power, in their contributions to the matriarchy of the women's re-visioned I Ching. They make the patriarchal translations of the eight major I Ching trigrams look dull and stuffy in comparison, and make the I Ching relevant again to women. In diagram, the eight major trigrams, the major arcana of the new I Ching, look like this:[9]

Trigram	Name	Attribute	Image	Relationship
	Ch'ien, The Labyris	Be-ing creativity	universe air	Mother (Hera, full moon)
	K'un, The Pentacle	birth nurturing	planet earth	Mother (Demeter, full moon)
	Chên, The Awakening	arousing channeling	thunder air/fire	Priestess (Ishtar, new moon)
	K'an, The Chalice	depths labyrinth	water womb	Priestess (Yemaya, new moon)
	Kên, Keeping Still	waiting patience	mountain earth	Wisewoman (Spider Woman, waning moon)
	Sun, The Gentle	penetrating dark-giving	wind/wood air/earth	Wisewoman (Hecate, waning moon)
	Li, The Wand	light-giving warming	fire	Daughter (Persephone, waxing moon)
	Tui, The Joyous	joyful flowing	lake water	Daughter (Gaia, waxing moon)

[9]Ibid., also a trigram for each Sabbat, beginning with Ch'ien at Candlemas and ending with Tui at Yule.

When the binary code lines are re-turned to both-at-once dualities, and the eight major I Ching trigrams are re-turned to women's roles, the I Ching is given the basis for a women's re-claiming and re-vision. The second half of the process is in re-turning, re-volving and re-cognizing the sixty-four written hexagram passages, the poetry, prophecy and wisdom of the ancient, pre-patriarchal Chinese I Ching.

The I Ching is called the Book of Changes, and its basic characteristic is change and movement. The principle is that of the circle, a line that moves continually but has no beginning or end. As in the wiccan Wheel of the Year, when some aspect, issue or process begins, it travels in a waxing phase to its peak, then declines to an ending. Endings are new beginnings. When the wiccan year ends with death at Hallows, the seed of the new year, the new daughter, is in the mother's womb. When the moon wanes and fades, the new moon and waxing follow. Births are followed by growth, maturity, aging and death, and death is followed by rebirth. There is the spring, summer, fall and winter—then the spring again; the waxing full and waning moon are followed by the new cycle; life is followed by death that is followed by life.

When a woman asks a question of the I Ching, her answer comes from the basis of change. She receives the wisdom of the moment, knowing that in a day or week the factors have changed, time has passed and the wheel proceeded, and the answer may be different. The answer she receives is the aspect of the moment, and the future is subject to her choices. As in transformational tarot and differing from traditional I Ching, the reading is an indication of direction and influences, not pre-destiny; the woman makes of them what she wills, and changes them if she wishes them changed.

The focal point of the reading in traditional I Ching is the superior man, who is only superior when acting wisely. When acting foolishly or not succeeding, he is the inferior man instead. Success and achievement are approach and nearness to the emperor/god. In women's I Ching, the focal point is female, and every woman is the Superior or Spiritual Woman. There is no inferior role in women's I Ching, as all the roles are valued equally and no woman is inferior. This is consistent with the re-turned eight major trigrams, and the concepts of the roles and the Superior or Spiritual Woman are reflected in re-volving the Book of Changes to a wiccan Wheel of the Year in its sixty-four written hexagrams.

The I Ching that has come to the West mentions women only a few times, and the wife is seen walking behind her husband, "knowing her place." In Hexagram 54, the etiquette of the concubine is discussed, the husband's second wife, a sexual servant. In Hexagram 28, the married woman past child-bearing age that "flowers out of season" is scorned. In Hexagrams 17 and 58, denoting the youngest daughter, the qualities of her following and of inner joy are discussed. In all of these the viewpoint is that of the male, the superior man, "he", as ruler, owner and sage.

Women in the east have used the I Ching since time began, going to I Ching readers when the oracle was taken from their direct use. In the West, women are drawn to the book's poetry and wisdom, compelled by its beauty and divinatory power to return to it again and again, even through its off-putting sexism. Feminist and wiccan women rearrange the pronouns, know the superior man as themselves and the "he" of the oracle as "she." They translate the negativity, misogyny, agism and predestiny into positive self-awareness, women's values and choice. An I Ching reading done this way, using Wilhelm/Baynes or any of the standard texts, is a process of un-layering, of dis-covering women's wisdoms beneath the imposed patriarchal masks. The oracle is powerful and wise and worth delving for. Beneath the patriarchy, women's mysteries and the goddess shine through, and intuitively or consciously women realize the I Ching's female roots. Any philosophy so totally male and yet so relevant must have once been female.

Aware women have re-claimed the I Ching by their use of it, by translating and re-visioning it as they read standard texts, and are beginning to write women's translations. Tina Wright, in *WomanSpirit Magazine,* Spring, 1979, says:

> To understand the I Ching at all, I must translate, if only in my head. Going further means that these words and images floating around in my head cause new fish to jump out. The old ones will not do.[10]

Her version of Hexagram 28, compared to the Wilhelm/Baynes translation is as follows. The section quoted is The Image:

Wilhelm/Baynes:
The lake rises above the trees:
The image of PREPONDERANCE OF THE GREAT.
Thus the superior man, when he stands alone,
Is unconcerned,
And if he has renounce to the world, He is undaunted.[11]

---

[10]Tina Wright, "I Ching Hexagram #28", in *WomanSpirit Magazine,* (2000 K Trail, SV, Wolf Creek, OR, 97497), #19, Spring Equinox, 1979, p. 29.
[11]Richard Wilhelm and Cary F. Baynes, *The I Ching or Book of Changes,* p. 112.

Tina Wright:

the marsh above   the trees,
RISING WATERS.
standing alone   even outcast
she is free.   and joyous seeking higher ground[12]

In *The Kwan Yin Book of Changes,* the first full-text re-visioning of the Chinese I Ching, Hexagram 28 reads differently. The Image is titled here *The Reflection,* and the hexagram itself is retitled from *The Pre-ponderance of the Great* to *Interesting Times* (Wright calls it "Rising Waters").

Diane Stein:

Water over wood:
Interesting times.
The Superior Woman
Withdraws unvanquished.[13]

In all three translations, the Superior person is given a no-win situa-tion and correct action involves knowing when to wait, when to act, when to withdraw. The Wilhelm/Baynes translation images this in a barren marriage. If the man is old and the woman young, there is no blame, but if the woman is a "withered poplar" and bears no fruit, "Everything remains barren."[14] The superior man is directed to withdraw from this marriage situation. While women have rearranged and re-visioned this in using traditional I Chings, ignoring the sexism, agism and misogyny for the book's root wisdoms, both Stein and Wright have removed the negativity, blame and perjorative connotations. All three translations have the same basic message, withdrawal when necessary, but Wright's and Stein's translations are re-volutions that women can relate to.

A written I Ching hexagram has specific structure, and the reading is divided into sections. The passage is headed by the hexagram number and the Chinese and English title of the hexagram. An introductory paragraph follows, a summary of the issue, and a discussion of the lines that compose the hexagram. The next section is titled The Judgment in Wilbelm/Baynes, The Center in *Kwan Yin,* and is in effect the Outcome card of a tarot reading, with perhaps a combination of the Significator, Atmosphere and Obstacle cards of the tarot layout besides. The first few lines of the section are set off as poetry and define the issue or question,

---

[12]Tina Wright, "I Ching Hexagram #28" in *WomanSpirit Magazine,* Spring Equinox, 1979, p. 29.
[13]Diane Stein, *The Kwan Yin Book of Changes,* p. 101
[14] Wilhelm and Cary F. Baynes, *The I Ching or Book of Changes,* p. 111-113.

direct the action and state an outcome. The wording is symbolic and universal, as are the picture images in tarot cards.

The next section of the reading is called The Image in Wilhelm/Baynes and The Reflection in Stein. The section begins with poetry, then discusses in prose the two trigrams that the hexagram is based on. In Hexagram 28, these trigrams are Tui, The Joyous (youngest daughter or The Daughter, water, lake) over Sun, The Gentle (first daughter or the Wisewoman, dark-giving, penetrating, wind/wood). The relationship between the two roles is the basis of the section, and these are applied to the issue or question.

The Lines (Wilhelm/Baynes) or Movement (*The Kwan Yin Book of Changes*) is the final section, and is divided into poetry and prose that analyzes each of the six lines in the reading, the six coin throws, the yin/yang dualities that are the binary basic code of the I Ching. Each line is discussed in turn, its meaning and its place in the hexagram, its relationship to the other lines and the question. These are similar to the interpreting of a tarot reading through the individual cards. The lines can be a series of individual wisdoms or a progression of experiences that build upon each other. They can be six different or complementary possibilities for solution to the question of the reading. In some hexagrams the lines are contradictory and emphasize the need for choice; in some they involve different relationships, different people or situations in each line; and in some there is a continuing narrative.

The woman asking a question of the I Ching obtains her hexagram and reads it, applying its symbolism to her issue or query. What she does with the information is her choice; if she doesn't like the direction things are moving in, she changes them by affirmation and action. If she is given a series of possibilities, she chooses which to employ. If she is given an answer, she chooses when and how to use it, if she chooses its use. Each I Ching hexagram matches a tarot card (leaving some tarot cards out; there are fourteen fewer hexagrams than there are tarot cards in a full deck), and the answer of an I Ching reading can be carried over into tarot or meditation work. The Motherpeace tarot card matching Hexagram 28 in *The Kwan Yin Book of Changes* is The Emperor. Women who perform a tarot reading on their question and then go to the I Ching with the same question discover very similar messages in both readings. An I Ching reading takes less time, about fifteen minutes total, to perform than the more involved tarot does. Both readings are extensive, however, in their information and message.

Mary Lee George, Antiga, is working on a full-text women's I Ching that is not yet completed. Calling her book *Yin I Ching,* two hexagrams of which appeared in the Spring, 1985 *Woman of Power,* she says this about the oracle:

> Though most of the current translations of the I Ching are phrased in patriarchal language and weighed down with examples of daily life in feudal society, I believe that the origins of I Ching are matristic. My own use of I Ching lets me know that the wisdom of the I Ching is worth reclaiming.[15]

In asking the question, "What does it mean to envision life in a feminist world?", she casts a two-hexagram reading (a moving line), with Hexagrams 43 and 45.

> Gathering Together, hexagram 45, makes it clear that our roots need to be firmly planted in the earth of spirituality . . . Spiritual energy can strengthen us personally as well as help us to connect with each other. It also cautions us not to expect a feminist world to be perfect but to remember that we are human . . . It asks us to be as clear as possible about what we want . . .[16]

Hexagram 45, Gathering Together in Wilhelm/Baynes, *The Kwan Yin Book of Changes* and Antiga's *Yin I Ching,* is composed of the trigrams Tui, The Joyous (lake, third daughter, the Daughter) over K'un, The Receptive—in *Kwan Yin* The Pentacle—(earth and the Mother). The hexagram matches the Motherpeace Ten of Discs in the tarot. The Image/Reflection in the three translations follows:

Wilhelm/Baynes:

Over the earth, the lake:
The image of GATHERING TOGETHER.
Thus the superior man renews his weapons
In order to meet the unforeseen.[17]

Diane Stein:

The lake over the earth:
Gathering together.
Women gather and
Matriarchy flows.[18]

---

[15]Antiga (Mary Lee George), "Yin I Ching", in *Woman of Power Magazine,* (POB 827, Cambridge, MA 02238), Issue Two, Spring, 1985, p. 53. Barbara Walker's *I Ching of the Goddess* has also been completed and is available (San Francisco, Harper & Row Publishers, 1986).
[16]*Ibid.,* p. 53-54.
[17]Richard Wilhelm and Cary F. Baynes, *The I Ching or Book of Changes,* p. 175.
[18]Diane Stein, *The Kwan Yin Book of Changes,* p.155

Antiga:

Over the earth, the lake
The image of GATHERING TOGETHER.
Expect the unexpected
 Be prepared for it so that
        unwanted consequences can be
prevented.[19]

Uniting together in community is the subject of all three translations, with leadership, spirituality and who to follow the issue for all three. Wilhelm/Baynes warn of strife and robbery, of human unpreparedness for trouble that does not prevent it or ward it off when people are gathered together in large groups. Position and influence, who the superior man is to align himself with, are major concerns and considerations, hierarchy, competition, rulership and politics—the mindset of patriarchy, its distrust. In Diane Stein's *Kwan Yin Book of Changes,* "Women gather together to live and love, to work and share and heal. In mutual caring and respect is the strength and triumph of matriarchy."[20] The gathering together of women who meet in open sincerity brings blessings and success. They build a coven, an affinity group, a community, a matriarchy; together they learn how to do it and they do it well. Antiga is aware of the problems of building a community, of gathering together, and her hexagram discusses understanding and being prepared as ways to create and nurture unity:

Where people are to be gathered together
        spiritual energy is needed
Only collective moral force can unite
        the world.[21]

Instead of intrigue and maneuvering for position, women's I Ching is founded on trust and understanding, on building for a good that benefits all. The superior man becomes the Superior or Spiritual Woman by goddess and Be-ing based women's values and ideals. No one is in or out of power in women's re-visioning of the world; women work together to create a wholeness, and what is good is good for each and all. Even when the women are not sure how to proceed, their positive intent and common goals lead them to find the way. They reach out to each other, bridge differences, share ideas and work in the circle by consensus.

---

[19]Antiga, "Yin I Ching", in *Woman of Power Magazine,* Spring, 1985, p. 55.
[20]Diane Stein, *The Kwan Yin Book of Changes,* p. 154-155.
[21]Antiga, "Yin I Ching", in *Woman of Power,* Spring, 1985, p. 55.

One grasp from the hand of another
   is enough
To turn away distress . . .

Those who belong together
Will find each other.[22]

The matriarchy, community, circle or affinity group are formed and the women bonded in unity. Women's Gathering Together is matriarchy and sisterhood, and with perseverence, caring, work and women's wisdoms and skills it happens and succeeds.

The full hexagram in Diane Stein's *Kwan Yin Book of Changes* reads:[23]

45. TS'UI—GATHERING TOGETHER

Above: Tui — The Joyous Daughter, Lake

Below: K'un — The Pentacle, Earth

Ts'ui remembers Hexagram 8, *Holding Together*. In the earlier hexagram, the chalice, water is above the pentacle, and in *Ts'ui* the lake is above the earth. Water gathers to fill a lake, and *Gathering Together* is the gathering of many women, as opposed to *Pi's* union of two. Therefore, this hexagram refers to the gathering together of women into matriarchy.

THE CENTER—Women Gather Together. Matriarchy Grows.

   Gathering together
   Into matriarchy.
   Empowerment on the
   Wheel of Life.

Women gathering together is a natural spiral, whether the gathering be of two lovers, of women and their Daughters in a family, or of Sisters in the gathering of matriarchy. Spirituality circles, work sharings, gatherings at night to sing beside a campfire, and gatherings together for the sharing of meals are other types of gatherings in women's lives. Each Sister leads in some type of gathering together; all women are leaders in the matriarchy.

By women's communal spirituality and respect, by caring for each other, matriarchy is made strong and indissolvable. By inner awareness and attunement

---

[22]*Ibid.*
[23]Diane Stein, *The Kwan Yin Book of Changes*, p. 154-157.

to the earth as Goddess, and the Wheel of Life, the women of matriarchy are gathered and united.

REFLECTION

> The lake over earth:
> Gathering together.
> Women gather and
> Matriarchy flows.

Lakewater rises till she flows beyond her banks: the matriarchy flows to become the tides of time. Women gather together to live and love, to work and share and heal. In mutual caring and respect is the strength and triumph of matriarchy. In her nurturing climate, women are prepared for obstacles and dangers; they face them and prevail in peace.

MOVEMENT

> *Six at the beginning:*
> They ask for grounding
> Gathered together.

The women gather together for a first meeting on the new moon. They do not know each other and hesitate to trust. The Sisters are uncentered and unfocused; they are not unified, but know what they wish to build. Gathered into a circle, the women ask for oneness and grounding. They ask for healing, sharing and openness. By their honesty and sincerity the Goddess blesses them. They are not denied her gifts.

> *Six in the second line:*
> They are attracted together.
> Open affirmations.

In gathering together, women are led to correctness. They feel attraction for like-minded Sisters, and a need together to unify the matriarchy. Working as one inside this compelling attraction, yielding to her gladly, the women accept each other quickly and well. The work of building the matriarchy is begun from within, and open affirmations result.

> *Six in the third position:*
> She gathers together late.
> She enters.

A woman wishes to enter the craft, but the circle is closed to newcomers. She joins an outer circle and she studies and waits, participating however she can. In matriarchy, no woman is ignored or excluded; the Superior Woman enters and is welcomed at last.

> *Nine in the fourth place:*
> Gathering together.
> Great good.

The Superior Woman gathers her Sisters together in a common cause. She does not seek self-reward, but acts in the voice of women's unity for the good of all. Women recognize her efforts and they lend her their skills. Together they achieve the strength and triumph of matriarchy.

Nine in the fifth line:
    She gathers her Sisters.
    No error.

While all women are leaders and workers in matriarchy, a Mother rises in purpose among them. By her skills and common sense, by her wisdom and ability to give and receive, the Sisters respect her and love her. The Sisters look to the Superior Woman for guidance, and she gives them her best. With a Mother's honesty and integrity, the Superior Woman facilitates for the good of all.

Six at the top:
    Gathering together.
    She endures.

The Superior Woman wants to work with a Sister, but the Sister does not recognize her skills. The Superior Woman focuses on agreement and understanding, and her Sister grows in awareness. By her persistence and her Sister's acceptance, the matriarchy gains. Each woman has something to offer her circle. In offering what she can, the Superior Woman achieves progress and her matriarchy gathers together.

The possibilities and power of women's re-storing a matriarchal system is evident in the material of this chapter. Re-visioning begins at the roots, with the binary code of the two basic I Ching lines, the dualities of the goddess in the yes (———) and no (—— ——) possibilities of the code. From the line evolves the trigram, and the eight major I Ching trigrams are changed from the patriarchal ranks of the family, from the father at the top and the youngest daughter at the bottom, to a series of equal roles reflecting the three-form aspect of the goddess and female principle. In the re-claimed major trigrams, the re-claimed I Ching major arcana, the re-volution of the world from patriarchy to matriarchy occurs. The re-vising and re-visioning continues in its logical process to the hexagram passages.

In women's I Ching sixty-four principles are expressed in the hexagrams that are similar and matching to tarot cards, and that encompass archetype situations of human/matriarchal life. These passages follow the Wheel of the Year universe of women's spirituality. The transformation effected, the new I Ching becomes a divination tool that re-turns women's Be-ing by reflecting the issues of the woman-within in her own accepted terms. Its transformed use continues the changes of the I Ching reader in her inner Be-ing and labyrinth lunar journey. What was once a female system is a female system again, its power dis-covered and made relevant and real, the ancient power made new.

Women's spirituality is the ancient made new in many ways. In tarot and I Ching are a reflection of the changes in women who experience women's spirituality, Be-ing and the goddess. Their changes from within are brought to light by women's re-claimed divinatory tools. The transformations are re-claiming of the tools themselves, of tarot and I Ching are brought about by the rising awareness in women of the goddess and goddess spirituality, as seen in the material and process of this book. Women learning the concept of divinity as female, and learning that divinity and goddess are in themselves, are women whose inner transformations lead to outward work to change the world. Life on earth can only benefit by their efforts.

> Women can again empower themselves by being aware of the many faces of the moon, remembering that our life cycles are in harmony with the moon and being thankful for those different modes of perception.[24]

The Women's Spirituality Book is an attempt to open up some of these perceptions, to show women the faces of the goddess moon, the faces of the woman in the moon, of Gaia, Yemaya, Spider Woman, Persephone, Demeter and Hecate, Ishtar/Ashtoreth/Inanna—and herself. The book is only a beginning. Many women's tarot decks and I Chings are coming, many breakthroughs in women's healing, in the development of ritual, dis-covery of herstory, and in the sharing of all the knowledge gained. There are many women and many faces of the moon, and the women of women's spirituality are re-claiming and re-turning them all.

10/19/85 Moon in Capricorn

---

[24]Dhyani Ywahoo, "Woman's Role in Planetary Transformation", in *Woman of Power Magazine*, Issue One, Spring, 1984, p. 4.

Related Books from the Crossing Press

Advanced Celtic Shamanism

By D.J. Conway

D.J. Conway tells us how we must each begin our own Great Journey to discover the heart of the Celtic tradition and achieve our true heart's desire.
— Tira Brandon-Evans, Moderator, Society of Celtic Shamans

$18.95 • Paper • ISBN 1-58091-073-4

Apprentice to Power

By Timothy Roderick

Sharing enchanting tales, meditations, rituals, and magical techniques, Roderick gives us a colorful introduction to Wicca, Old Europe's earth centered mystical tradition. He shows us how to access the power of the spirit in everyday life.

$16.95 • Paper • ISBN 1-58091-077-7

Complete Guide to Tarot

By Cassandra Eason

Cassandra Eason makes a popular form of divination accessible and inviting, even for beginners and skeptics. She gradually builds to advanced topics, including cleansing a deck, keeping a tarot journal, analyzing complex spreads, and incorporating tarot into practices like the Kabbalah and numerology.

$18.95 • Paper • ISBN 1-58091-068-8

Crystal Enchantments: A Complete Guide to Stones and Their Magical Properties

By D. J. Conway

D. J. Conway's book will help guide you in your choice of stones from Adularia to Zircon, by listing their physical properties and magical uses. It will also appeal to folks who are not into magic, but simply love stones and want to know more about them.

$16.95 • Paper • ISBN 1-58091-010-6

Essential Wicca

By Paul Tuitéan and Estelle Daniels

Focusing on earth, nature, and fertility, the Wicca religion embraces the values of learning, sexual equality, and divination. While most books on Wicca address either the solitary practitioner or those in covens, Essential Wicca covers all the bases— from core beliefs and practices, basic and group rituals, to festivals and gatherings, holy days, and rites of passage. A glossary with more than 200 entries and over 100 illustrations extends the meaning of the text.

$20.95 • Paper • ISBN 1-58091-099-8

RELATED BOOKS FROM THE CROSSING PRESS

Laying On of Stones

By D. J. Conway

Stones can be used to protect and heal you, your family, and your home, but where to place them is often a source of difficulty. Probably the most important question frequently asked is where to place them on your body. D. J. Conway supplies you with forty detailed diagrams, showing you exactly how to place a variety of stones to help your body heal itself of illness or enrich your life through a magical manifestation of desires.

$10.95 • Paper • ISBN 1-58091-029-7

A Little Book of Candle Magic

By D.J. Conway

D. J. Conway gives a thorough introduction to tapping the reservoirs of magic in candles. She provides chants, meditations, and affirmations to find a mate, achieve enlightenment, or improve life materially and spiritually, and she encourages readers to create their own.

$9.95 • Paper • ISBN 1-58091-043-2

A Little Book of Love Magic

By Patricia Telesco

A cornucopia of lore, magic, and imaginative ritual designed to bring excitement and romance to your life. Patricia Telesco tells us how to use magic to manifest our hopes and dreams for romantic relationships, friendships, family relations, and passions for our work.

$9.95 • Paper • ISBN 0-89594-887-7

A Little Book of Pendulum Magic

By D.J. Conway

Also known as dowsing, pendulum magic is a technique for seeing into the future, whether for information about romance, luck, past lives, or the psychic causes of disease. Conway gives step-by-step instructions for making pendulums and also explains how questions should be asked as well as how answers should be interpreted. She charts the rituals involved in divination and explains how to use pendulums in conjunction with tarot cards, crystals, astrology, and meditation.

$9.95 • ISBN 1-58091-093-9

To receive a current catalog from The Crossing Press
please call toll-free, 800-777-1048.
Visit our Web site: **www.crossingpress.com**

Welcome to Crossing Village

Home of the Crossing Press

Library
Newsstand
Crossing Press
Community Center
Spiritual Center
Visitor's Center
Our Store
Health Center
Pet Shop
Hall of Famous Authors
C.P. Diner
School of Personal Growth

Visit the new and improved Crossing Press Web site for information you can't find anywhere else—interactive author chats, author calendars, reviews, special promotions, press kit materials, and our brand new store!

www.crossingpress.com